Soviet Wages

The MIT Press
Cambridge, Massachusetts, and London, England

Soviet Wages:
Changes in Structure and Administration since 1956

Leonard Joel Kirsch

This book was set in Linotype Baskerville
by Port City Press, Inc.,
printed on Pinnacle Book Offset
by Port City Press, Inc.,
and bound by The Maple Press Company
in the United States of America.

Library of Congress Cataloging in Publication Data

Kirsch, Leonard Joel, 1934–
  Soviet wages.

  Bibliography: p.
  1. Wages—Russia. I. Title.
HD5046.K53   331.2'9'47   71-173924
ISBN 0–262–11045–8

L   E   N   A

A   gratefully,   N
to the women
R   who surround   N
me

A   E

Contents

Tables and Charts

Preface

I have been assured that this monograph is in no sense unique in having a gestation period that far exceeded expectations. However, several persons are responsible for making the preparation of this study a process that was seldom tedious and often stimulating. More than a decade ago, I wrote a term paper for Abram Bergson on Soviet wage determination. He has since encouraged my interest in the subject. Through innumerable conversations and more drafts than I care to admit, his comments have been invaluable. John Dunlop's thoughtful reading and guidance on questions of labor economics and wage theory are also gratefully acknowledged. James Millar and Alexander Erlich, at an early stage in the preparation of this study, helped me to avoid several serious mistakes in my approach to the subject. Marshall Goldman, Leon Smolinski, and Yasushi Toda deserve a special kind of gratitude for years of continual criticism, encouragement, and comradeship. To keep this list from becoming inordinately long, I collectively thank both those Soviet economists who were exceedingly hospitable and helpful during two extended visits to the USSR and those economists who have provided a constant source of intellectual stimulation through their participation in numerous formal and informal seminars at Harvard's Russian Research Center.

I therefore happily share the credit for whatever may be valuable in this book. I alone am responsible for its defects and mistakes.

The Harvard University Russian Research Center has provided an ideal setting for my work. I am unable to imagine how the manuscript could have been completed without the Center's library and other facilities. Drafts were typed by Mary Towle and Rose di Benedetto, in whom the Center is truly blessed with two superb secretaries. The efficiency and accuracy of their work was commendable. The good humor with which they carried it out was astounding. Whatever lapses of acceptable English remain in the book would have been multiplied manyfold without the editorial assistance of Abbott Gleason, Judy Koivumaki, and Jacqueline Hartmann.

As to my system of citations, I identify sources with only the author's name (or shortened title), followed by the date of publication. Since I expect that the majority of readers will not know Russian, and most of my sources are from Soviet publications, my intent is to reduce the clutter of transliteration within footnotes. At the end of the study is a complete bibliography of all cited sources alphabetized according to the shortened citations.

Finally, my wife, my mother, and my daughter deserve a gratitude that I find impossible to express in words. I hope they realize its depth.

Soviet Wages

1
Introduction

The Wage Reform: A Brief History

Arthur Lewis once stated that "socialism is about equality." [1] We might also say that "Marxism is about the industrial proletariat." Few subjects could be more pertinent to socialism and Marxism than the determination of wages for industrial workers in the USSR. However, since the publication of Abram Bergson's *The Structure of Soviet Wages* (1944), Soviet wage policies and practices have continued to evolve, and although not entirely neglected,[2] the recent changes have as yet not been sufficiently explored. Particularly interesting are the developments since the mid-1950s.[3] Previous studies have tended to focus on years prior to World War II,[4] and, in fact, changes in wage policy from that time to about 1958 were relatively limited.[5] More recently, the Soviet government has subjected its wage system to a wholesale reform. One Soviet economist, possibly overstating the case, maintains that the recent changes have been "qualitative" rather than simply "quantitative," and that they "in an essential way changed the very basis of existing differentiation of wages." [6]

In fact, the wage reform of 1958–1960 may legitimately be regarded

1. Lewis, 1952, p. 10. The shortened citations used in the footnotes are explained in the Preface.
2. In addition to Bergson, some Western economists who have been especially interested are Robert F. Fearn, Walter Galenson, G. R. Barker, Emily Clark Brown, Murray Yanowitch, Alec Nove, Gertrude Schroeder, Janet Chapman, and Norman Kaplan, each of whom has written specific studies in Soviet wage determination. The list could easily be expanded.
3. For Western descriptions of these developments, see Fearn, 1963a and 1963b; Galenson, 1960; Yanowitch, 1963; Dewar, 1962; Schroeder, 1966; Chapman, 1970; and Kaplan, 1970.
4. Bergson, 1944, especially pp. 137–154. See also Barker, n.d., pp. 58 ff; Bjork, 1953, pp. 53–58; Yanowitch, 1960.
5. A number of Soviet sources assure us that this is the case: Karinskii, 1963, p. 54; Maier and Markov, 1958, p. 48; Figurnov, 1962, p. 151; Batkaev and Markov, 1964, p. 28; Pasherstnik, 1946, pp. 185–186. Also see Nove, 1961, pp. 115–116. The Soviet economist Bliakhman (1964, p. 282) at least in part justifies this condition as follows: "Our country has already come out of the early period of its development when it was necessary, under the threat of war, within a short period of time to develop the economy at an unprecedented tempo, and therefore wages were determined more by political conceptions and the general economic and military importance of a category of workers than by economic calculation."
6. Maier, 1963, p. 139. Karinskii (1963, p. 58) simply stresses the "radicalness" of these changes as compared to previous Soviet wage reforms.

as a watershed in Soviet wage policy. This study focuses particularly on wage structure and administration under the reforms initiated. As a preliminary, brief reference should be made to the general nature of that reform and the circumstances in which it was introduced. In the course of this study, it will become clear that one need not search for the causes of the wage reform completed in 1960. These are painfully evident. A more interesting question is why this reform did not come sooner.

Much of the rationale behind the wage structure developed during the mid-1930s [7] was lost with the advent of World War II. During the war, numerous specific revisions of basic wage scales were effected by decrees issued by the Council of People's Commissars without reference to branch or geographical administrative organs. Added to this centralized determination of basic scales was a high decree of local autonomy in distribution of actual earnings among workers within a single enterprise, the majority of whom were paid according to piece rate, and output norms were determined at the enterprise level.[8] After the war, there were a number of "one-shot" (*edinovremennyi*) alterations of basic wage rates for specific groups of workers. Each modification was made without reference to its impact upon the general wage structure.[9]

In fact, by the middle of the 1950s the term "wage structure" could appropriately be used only if understood either as summary measures of inequality or as earnings differentials within a specific enterprise. An example of the administrative fragmentation is the fact that, although the Ministry of Machine Tool Production had established basic wage rates for workers employed in that branch, these applied to only 55 of a total of 171 plants engaged primarily in producing machine tools. The other plants were scattered among 19 other ministries,[10] each of which had its own basic wage scale. Moreover, a continuous depreciation in the importance of basic rates as a component of earnings had taken place. In the late 1930s, basic wages constituted 80 to 90 percent of workers' earnings.[11] Because of the growth of payments for the overfulfillment of piece-rate output norms and various

7. See Bergson, 1944, especially chapters 2, 13, and 14.
8. Pasherstnik, 1946, p. 62; Schwarz, 1951, pp. 200–204.
9. Pasherstnik, 1949, pp. 185–186.
10. Hoeffding, 1959, p. 72.
11. Batkaev and Markov, 1964, p. 201.

premiums, by the mid-1950s this percentage had dropped to about 50–60.[12] Even general statistical measures of wage inequality during the more than two decades preceding the wage reform will probably forever remain unknown. Between 1934 and 1956, such data were simply not collected.[13]

For a period, the effects of the "disorganized" wage system were mitigated by massive penal labor as well as a 1940 series of laws that bypassed labor market mechanisms: youths were drafted for industrial training, workers were prohibited from leaving jobs without permission of the enterprise director, and skilled workers could be transferred without their consent.[14] Though these laws were not fully repealed *de jure* until April 1956, their *de facto* demise occurred several years earlier, possibly in 1951.[15] With a labor market that had become both "free" and "tight," [16] the negative effects of the wage system were fully felt. In early 1957, A. P. Volkov, newly appointed Chairman of the Government Labor Committee, reported that

Without exaggeration, it may be said that the existing wage system . . . has not only stopped being a progressive factor but appears to be a serious hindrance on the path of the future growth of the productivity of labor and does not meet the Leninist principle of [providing for] the material self-interest of workers in the result of their labor.[17]

At least in part, the situation described by Volkov can be viewed as a result of Stalinist dogma, which, while affecting all areas of economic analysis, had an especially pernicious impact upon labor economics. In 1951, Stalin stated that

Problems concerning the rational organization of productive forces, the planning of the national economy, and so on, are not the subject

12. See chapter 2.
13. Rabkina and Rimashevskaia, 1966b, p. 88; Loznevaia, 1968, pp. 128–129.
14. See Schwarz, 1951, pp. 106–129 for a detailed discussion of these laws.
15. *Labor Law*, 1964, p. 22; Brown, 1966, p. 16.
16. With some exceptions, the Soviet worker is now free to change his place of work if two weeks' notice is given. There are two important exceptions. Some major urban centers are "closed," with migration into the city being most difficult. As discussed in chapter 5, there is also the "obligation" to work in an assigned place after completion of a vocational-technical school.

Emily Clark Brown's (1957 and 1970) description of the Soviet labor market indicates a general "tightness." However, recently there have been reports concerning difficulties encountered by young persons in finding employment. For Western appraisals of the significance of this phenomenon, see "Transition from School to Work," 1963, and *Unemployment in the Soviet Union*, 1966. For hitherto unavailable data on labor turnover in the Soviet economy, see Bliakhman et al., 1965, pp. 15–16.
17. Volkov, 1957, p. 4.

for political economy but rather the subject of the economic policy of directing (*rukovodiashchikh*) organs. These are two separate spheres that must not be mixed. To foist upon political economy questions of economic policy would nullify it as a science.[18]

Thus cut off from policy questions, what remained of the specialty of labor economics passed out of existence. E. I. Kapustin, probably the leading Soviet authority on wage determination, described the situation as follows:

Not only central government organs that were directly involved with these questions [of labor and wages] were liquidated, but also those scientific-investigative organizations which studied these problems. To a significant degree the cadres of scientific and practical personnel in the field of labor and wages were dissipated. No sort of scientific discussions took place. . . . In the whole country there was not one special organ where questions of labor and wages could be raised and discussed.[19]

The desirability of a major overhaul of the system of wage determination was evident to numerous Soviet commentators. However, to carry out general restructuring of the wage system there was a need for pertinent data on existing wage patterns, an organization or organizations with the administrative competence to implement changes in wage determination, and personnel having some expertise in wage problems. In 1955, none of these needs was met. In retrospect, the formation in that year of a new administrative organ that was to fulfill just such tasks appears to have been a prerequisite for the industrial wage reform completed only in 1960.

In fact, the first hint that major changes were to take place in Soviet wage policy came on May 24, 1955, with a decree entitled "Concerning the Formation of a Government Committee of the Council of Ministries of the USSR on Questions of Labor and Wages." The avowed goal of the decree was the "strengthening of government control in the field of labor and wages." In July of the same year, the administrative role of the Government Labor Committee, as we shall henceforth call it, was clarified to some extent by a decree of the Central Committee of the Communist Party, which stated that the new organization's function was "to carry out inspection and control over the work of ministries, departments, and enterprises on questions of labor and

18. Stalin, 1952, p. 171.
19. Kapustin, 1964, p. 4.

wages." [20] The following January, it was announced that Lazar
Kaganovich had been appointed head of the Committee.[21]

However, the exact meaning of "inspection and control" was not yet
clear. More than a decade earlier Bergson had said that "the precise
role of the various agencies which since 1931 have become participants
in wage-scale construction is by no means easy to delineate." [22] By the
mid-1950s this had become an understatement of the degree of confusion. It seems that the ministries organized by branches of industry were responsible for setting the wages of personnel who fell within
their jurisdiction. Two Soviet commentators, however, maintain that
even among enterprises of a single ministry, there was no coordination of wage-setting policies.[23] The situation was not clarified by
Premier Bulganin, who, while stressing the "important" role of the
Government Labor Committee, went on to note, "The formation of
this agency, however, does not absolve Ministries and heads of enterprises . . . from their duties in the matter of fixing labor norms, introducing order in wages and improving the organization of labor at
enterprises." [24]

Only in January 1956 was it made clear that the Government Labor
Committee had the power not only to develop proposals, but also to
stop the enforcement of orders and instructions from other economic
agencies if, in the Committee's view, such instructions were in viola-
tion of existing wage regulations.[25] At approximately the same time,
the draft of the Sixth Five-Year Plan (1956–1960) was published.
Included in the draft were general proposals for extensive reforms
in wage setting.[26]

For approximately the next eighteen months, however, neither the

---

20. *Vedomosti*, no. 8 (826) , June 8, 1955, article 196, p. 240. Also see "Directive
of the Central Committee of the Communist Party, the Council of Ministries of
the USSR, and the All-Union Central Council of Trade Unions on the Corrections
of Deficiencies in Norming of Labor and Wages," Direktivy, 1957–1958, vol. 4, p. 435.
21. *Vedomosti*, no. 1 (843) , January 14, 1956, article 11, p. 16.
22. Bergson, 1944, p. 173.
23. Maier and Markov, 1958, p. 48. According to Nove (1961, pp. 115–116) , from
1945 until 1956, no body below the Council of Ministers existed that could decide
national wage questions, and there simply was no systematic consideration of these
problems.
24. Bulganin, 1955, pp. 11–12.
25. *Sots. Trud*, no. 1, 1956, pp. 5–6, as cited in Karinskii, 1963, p. 55.
26. *Pravda*, January 15, 1956.

activities of the Government Labor Committee nor the progress of the wage reform was particularly impressive. Through the first half of 1957, the reform consisted of little more than a series of inconclusive experiments.[27] Conflicts concerning the respective roles of the Committee and the ministries apparently continued, and the complaint was voiced that "departmental barriers" were holding the Committee back from solving the basic problems of wage regulation.[28] Partly because Kaganovich was, in June 1957, identified as a member of the "anti-Party group," the activities of the Committee under his chairmanship will probably long remain unclear.[29] In any event, the accusation was made that Kaganovich consciously "deflected" the Committee from its important work and that under him it "pursued the harmful line of separating technology from economics." He was also charged with attempting to liquidate the Committee, which "moved from a standstill" only after he left it.[30]

Both the Committee and the wage reform rapidly "moved from a standstill" in mid–1957. Any existing ambiguities concerning the competence of the ministries in wage setting were eliminated by N. S. Khrushchev's announcement in May 1957 that the ministries for the various branches of industries were to be replaced by regional administrative units.[31] Working through the newly established *sovnarkhozy* (regional economic councils), the Committee in early 1958 began in earnest to reform wages, and by the end of that year new wage schedules had been imposed in the metallurgical, coal, chemical, and cement industries.

In September 1959 a new pattern was established. Instead of continuing on a branch-by-branch basis, the wage system underwent reform for all industrial workers in each of several large geographical areas. Moreover, wage reform was now accompanied by a reduction in the standard work week from 46 hours to 41 hours.[32] By the end

27. For a detailed description of these experiments, as well as a more extended history of the wage reform, see Fearn, 1963b, pp. 13–20, and Galenson, 1960.
28. Gromov, 1957, p. 19.
29. It might be noted that Volkov replaced Kaganovich as Chairman of the Government Labor Committee several months before the attack on the "anti-Party group."
30. "Nastoichivo," 1957, pp. 5–8.
31. See Hoeffding, 1959.
32. The customary structure of the 41-hour work week was seven hours each weekday and six hours on Saturday. More recently, the 41 hours generally has come

of 1960, all industrial workers had been transferred onto the new pay schedules.[33]

Thus, despite the fact that the phrase "the wage reform" indicates a process that occurred simultaneously for all industrial workers, it in fact refers to the piecemeal process that took place during the period between 1958 and the end of 1960 when the essential changes were introduced.

The scope of the Government Labor Committee's activities increased in pace with the progress of the wage reform. In 1957, several economists on the pages of the Committee's journal, *Socialist Labor* (*Sotsialisticheskii Trud*), called for the creation of a centralized organization, possibly an "All-Union Ministry of Labor," which would have authority "right up to the publication of obligatory decrees on questions of labor and wages." [34] By the beginning of the 1960s, the Committee essentially had become such an organization.[35] Its responsibilities came to include participation in decisions concerning the size and structure of the total wage fund; [36] construction and/or authorization of all wage handbooks,[37] or changes in existing wage handbooks; promulgation of decrees concerning virtually every aspect of the wage system; and numerous lesser matters, down to decrees concerning wage payments in single enterprises.[38]

The reform of wages was accompanied by a rebirth of Soviet labor

---

to be distributed over a five-day work week. This reduction of the statutory work week was accompanied by a reduction in the actual average work week which stood at 45.3 hours in 1957, 42.1 in 1960, and 40.4 in 1967. Data on the statutory work week in various branches of industry can be found in *Trud v SSSR*, 1968, p. 239, and those for the actual average in *Vest. Stat.*, no. 9, 1968, p. 85.

33. Fearn, 1963b, pp. 18–20.

34. Shishkov and Kmets, 1957, p. 20; Gromov, 1957, p. 19.

35. According to an organizational chart for June 1963, the Committee was directly subordinate to the Council of Ministries, along with several other committees, including Foreign Economic Relations and State Security. The great majority of other government committees are shown as indirectly subordinate to the Council of Ministries. "Organization," 1963, pp. 2–3.

36. At least a mission from the International Labor Office was so informed. ILO. 1960, p. 99.

37. Discussed in chapter 4.

38. The scope of the Committee's activities was indicated by a listing of 184 different decrees (*postanovlenii*) issued between March 1957 and April 1959. The listing includes only those decrees concerning machine construction that are no longer in force. *Biulleten'*, no. 9, 1964, pp. 42–58. As it has turned out, the more important of these decrees have been issued jointly by the Committee and the All-Union Central Committee of Trade Unions. See Karinskii, 1963, pp. 54–56.

economics. This discipline has been revived in large part through the activities and publications [39] of the Government Labor Committee and its subordinate organization, the Scientific Research Institute of Labor. The Labor Institute, as it will henceforth be called, is charged with conducting research and developing proposals in the general sphere of labor and wage administration.

Elements of Soviet Wage Determination

As is generally understood by Western economists, wage structures depend upon conceptually distinct "pure" differentials, each of which ideally should be treated separately. For example, if the economist seeks to test the hypothesis that there is an interindustry wage differential in favor of industry A over industry B, a simple demonstration of higher average wages in A is not sufficient. The difference might be caused by factors such as a higher average level of skills among workers in A or location of the plants in A in high-wage areas. The goal is to measure the size of some differential net of the effects of other differentials. Following our example, the economist would seek to adjust the data so as to eliminate geographical and skill differentials before attempting to determine the size or existence of a pure interindustry differential. In Western wage data, statistics usually "blend and confuse two or more types of pure differentials." [40] Although the raw data may be ingeniously restructured by a number of devices to isolate the effect of some single pure differential, the results are seldom satisfactory.[41]

---

39. The journals published by the Government Labor Committee include *Sotsialisticheskii Trud*, a large journal comparable in size to *Voprosy Ekonomiki;* the *Biulleten'* of the Committee, specifically devoted to decrees and decisions in the field of labor and wages; and the *Biulleten' Trud i Zarabotnaia Plata* of the Scientific Research Institute of Labor, which ended its five years of publication in 1962. These journals have a remarkably wide distribution. Their circulation as of January 1965 was respectively, 33,555, 38,100, and 29,500 (December 1962) . This may be compared to a circulation as of January 1965 of 11,950 for *Vestnik Statistiki* and 31,450 for *Voprosy Ekonomiki.*
40. Reynolds and Taft, 1956, p. 9.
41. For example, the answer to the seemingly straightforward question "Do trade unions increase the relative wages of their membership?" depends upon which differentials are to be measured. In spite of massive raw data, our analytical tools are not fine enough to isolate, or even to establish the existence of, a "bargaining" element in wage differentiation. An excellent discussion of the conceptual and empirical problems can be found in a collection of papers edited by Richard Perlman (1964) entitled *Wage Determination; Market or Power Forces.*

Table 1.1
Western Basic Elements of Wage Differentiation and Soviet "Pure" Differentials

Western	Soviet
I. Interpersonal ————————————→	I. On-the-job incentive
	II. Quality of labor (skill)
II. Occupational	
	III. Quantity of labor (working conditions)
III. Interfirm — — — — — — — — — — — →	None[a]
IV. Geographical ——————————————→	IV. Geographical
V. Interindustry ——————————————→	V. Interindustry

Note: These Western elements are as presented in Kerr, 1957, p. 80, and in Reynolds and Taft, 1956, p. 9. The Soviet elements are based upon Soviet practice in wage administration and generally correspond to those presented in Soviet wage theory. The shortened citations used throughout this study are explained in the Preface.
[a] The Soviet economist recognizes the statistical fact of interfirm differentials, but he views it as the result of different combinations of the five pure differentials.

For the Soviet economist, not only are the pure wage differentials conceptually distinct, but recently there has also been an attempt to make these differentials administratively and quantitatively distinct in the system of wage determination. The matter may be clarified by reference to table 1.1, in which the pure differentials of Soviet wage administration are compared to what the Western economist might call the "basic elements" of wage differentiation. Unanimity among Western or Soviet economists as to the proper listing of basic elements or pure differentials is not to be expected. The basic elements are simply those that are most often used in Western literature and that generally correspond to the Soviet pure differentials. The enumeration of the five pure Soviet differentials rests upon firmer ground. Virtually all current Soviet wage theory,[42] a considerable body of published statistics, and specific aspects of Soviet wage policy reflect attempts to set or measure one or more of these differentials.

It is important to stress that the Soviet pure differentials are con-

42. Even when a Soviet economist uses a somewhat different classification, his analysis can easily be fitted into the scheme used in Table 1.1. For example, Kapustin (1964, pp. 56–58) used the phrase "quality of labor" to include skill level and working conditions, rather than (as used here and usually in the Soviet literature) to designate skill differentials. However, later in his study he separately discusses skill differentials (pp. 116–157) and differentials for working conditions (pp. 252–285). The latter correspond to our "quantity of labor."

ceptually distinct from statistical differentials. For example, if skill level, or "quality," of labor expended is determined according to a methodology standard throughout industry, statistical measures of interindustry wage differentials will be affected. If the average skill level of workers in industry A is higher than that of workers in industry B, basic wage rates will tend to be greater in A. According to Soviet wage administration, this is not to be viewed as an interindustrial differential, but rather as a reflection of skill differentiation.

In both Soviet and Western literature, the differentials in table 1.1 are used *ex post*, as a "basis for classifying and summarizing new data. . . ." [43] The five Soviet pure differentials have an additional *ex ante* function as elements in the administrative determination of the wage structure. Ideally, each differential is statistically quantifiable and administratively determined. As will become clear in the course of this study, since they are often out of phase with differentials demanded by labor market scarcity conditions, the administratively determined pure differentials in practice tend to lose their purity.

In a very general sense, the five pure differentials in Soviet wage administration are akin to a job evaluation plan for the determination of all money wages. However, the term "job evaluation" can be applied most accurately to one aspect of Soviet wage setting—the determination of relative intraindustry basic wage rates.

The existence of job evaluation in Soviet industrial enterprises hardly will be surprising to the labor economist. This technique is generally accepted in the West as a useful tool in wage setting for an industrial organization. Job evaluation in some form exists in most branches of American industry. Although such systems range from simple rules of thumb to highly sophisticated techniques,[44] they are all based on the "assumption that each job has a certain number of common factors which vary between jobs, and that these factors can

43. Reynolds and Taft, 1956, p. 9.
44. Job evaluation systems may range from a simple ranking of jobs according to what management might consider their relative difficulty to a system that Daniel Bell (1956, p. 13) describes as follows: "Perhaps the Ultima Thule in rationalization is the mathematical formula to determine the fine shadings of skill between jobs recently worked out by the Aluminum Corporation of America in order to set wage differentials scientifically. The program, which covered 56,000 jobs, took three and a half years to complete, at a cost of $500,000. The final equation, three pages long, juggles fifty-nine separate variables; it took thirty-five hours of Univac time, at a cost of $10,000 to compute."

be isolated and measured." [45] The fundamental characteristic of the process is that it "makes no attempt to determine the absolute value of a job but establishes only relative base rates for jobs," which are grouped into classes "for ease of wage administration." [46] The base, or basic, wage rate is the "money rate paid for a job performed at a standard pace," exclusive of shift differentials, overtime, premiums, and payments to piece-rate workers for overfulfillment of output norms.[47]

The surprising aspect of job evaluation in the USSR [48] is that the technique recently has been called upon to perform functions far more ambitious than that of setting wages within a single enterprise. The system of basic wage rates established according to job evaluation techniques has become the most important component of Soviet central wage policy. Statements such as the following are common throughout the literature:

In essence, government regulation of [differentiation of] wages now exists only in the sphere of basic wage rates.[49]
. . . The degree of effectiveness of wage regulation emanating from a single planning center is to a large extent dependent upon the position occupied by the basic wage in the earnings received by the employed person.[50]

Soviet job evaluation procedure, unlike that used in Western economies, supposedly ensures an equitable structure of basic wage rates throughout industry, a structure determined by an "essential law of socialism." Virtually all Soviet wage literature informs the reader that under socialism the "law of distribution according to labor" [51] determines relative wages in accord with the quality and quantity [52] of the labor expended by the individual worker. Most frequently, such phrases are simply empty rhetoric based upon the following reason-

45. I.A.M., 1954, p. 11.
46. Brennan, 1963, p. 443.
47. Ibid., p. 63.
48. The Soviet term that most closely corresponds to "job evaluation" is *tarifikatsiia rabot.*
49. I. A. Orlovskii, 1961b, p. 187.
50. Karinskii, 1963, p. 188.
51. This is possibly the only Soviet economic "law" that has a corresponding judicial law. According to the Soviet labor code, a worker must be paid wages in accord with the quality and quantity of labor expended, as determined by previously established norms and standards independent of the income of the enterprise in which the worker is employed. Karinskii, 1963, p. 22.
52. These terms should not be confused with those used in Marxist philosophy. As used by the Soviet labor economists, quantitative changes are never "dialectically transformed" into changes of quality.

ing: capitalist exploitation is absent in the Soviet economy, all incomes are earned, earnings can only be dependent upon the quality and quantity of labor expended, and therefore any Soviet wage structure is, and must be, in accord with the "law." [53]

A different and more meaningful approach to the "law" is fortunately also presented in the Soviet literature. For, let us say, an hour's work, quality and quantity are taken as two distinct and quantifiable aspects of the work process. "Quality" refers to a worker's skill level. "Quantity" is dependent upon the conditions under which the work is performed; that is, working conditions determine the "intensity" of work, hence, its quantity. Determination of relative basic wage rates in terms of these two variables is the goal of Soviet job evaluation techniques. Through utilization of a consistent methodology for determination of the magnitude of these variable, an equitable system of basic wage rates is supposedly constructed. Not only is the rule of equal pay for equal work [54] implemented in such a system, but any inequality in work performed is determined exclusively by job content analysis, rather than by some measure of productivity. [55] Thus quality and quantity may be viewed as two of the pure differentials in Soviet wage policy and ideally are the sole determinants of intraindustry differentiation of basic wage rates.

The example presented in table 1.2 provides an illustration of the role of these differentials as established during the wage reform and introduces several terms that will be used throughout this study. Here we see the system of basic wage rates for workers employed in that all-important branch [56] of industry, machine construction and metal working, henceforth to be called "machine construction."

53. This is the position taken by Kuzminov (1961a and 1961b) in a collection of papers entitled *Questions of the Political Economy of Socialism*. In the same volume, Figurnov (1961, especially pp. 315–316) demolishes this species of cant.
54. The theoretical possibility of "perfecting" the labor market, that is, increasing potential labor mobility so that the market itself might provide for equal pay for equal work, is simply not considered in the Soviet literature. As discussed in our concluding chapter, in wage negotiation, American and other Western trade unions also attempt, with some success, to impose this consideration, "which is deeply ingrained in the thinking and tradition of trade unions." Goldfinger, 1957, pp. 52–56; Douty, 1963, pp. 225–241.
55. For a relatively complete statement of the Soviet position, distinguishing differences in job content from differences in productivity, see Aganbegian and Maier, 1959, pp. 72–86. This matter is discussed in chapter 8.
56. See note to Table 1.2. Throughout this study, because of the way the data are presented, we follow the often inconsistent Soviet use of the term "branch." Usually

Table 1.2
"Quality" and "Quantity" of Labor as Determinants of Relative Basic Rates of Pay and Rates in Kopeks per Hour: Machine Construction

	Relative basic rates for working conditions	Skill Group (Razriad)					
		I	II	III	IV	V	VI
		Skill Scale (Setka)					
		1.0	1.13	1.29	1.48	1.72	2.0
1. Time-rate workers, normal working conditions	.86	(26.3k.) .86	(29.7k.) .97	(33.9k.) 1.09	(38.9k.) 1.27	(45.2k.) 1.48	(52.6k.) 1.72
2. Piece-rate workers, normal conditions, and time workers, hot, heavy, or unhealthy conditions	1.0	(30.5k.) 1.0	(34.5k.) 1.13	(39.4k.) 1.29	(45.2k.) 1.48	(52.6k.) 1.72	(61.0k.) 2.0
3. Piece-rate workers, hot, heavy, or unhealthy conditions, and time-rate workers, especially heavy or unhealthy conditions	1.15	(35.0k.) 1.15	(39.4k.) 1.30	(45.2k.) 1.48	(51.8k.) 1.70	(60.2k.) 1.98	(70.0k.) 2.30
4. Piece-rate workers, especially heavy and unhealthy conditions	1.24	(37.8k.) 1.24	(42.9k.) 1.40	(48.9k.) 1.60	(56.0k.) 1.84	(65.2k.) 2.13	(75.7k.) 2.48

Notes: Table 1.2 is constructed according to the skill scale in Maier, 1963, p. 143. The actual rates in kopeks are from Dorokhov, 1962 p. 236. The data refer to the rates introduced with the wage reform in 1959 and apply to the seven-hour work day. Lack of perfect correspondence between the rates and coefficients is due to rounding.

The kopek rates in the table were the most widespread of three sets of rates existing in machine construction. These rates were increased by about 5 percent for those machine construction workers engaged in production for heavy industry, radiotechnology, and several other subbranches. A third and unimportant set of rates for machine construction workers employed in enterprises administered by local councils were 10 percent lower than those presented in the table. Aganbegian and Maier, 1959, p. 170; Dorokhov 1962, p. 236.

This differentiation of basic rates according to subbranch is usual in current Soviet wage administration. Such differentiation in machine construction was in part due to the heterogeneous output of the branch. Possibly more important, prior to the reform there were significant differentials between subbranches, and to establish one set of rates without major wage reductions would have meant too large an increase in wage expenditures. The lower rates for enterprises administered by local councils were supposedly temporary and based on the poor quality of norming (that is, easy-to-overfulfill norms) in those enterprises. Kapustin, 1964, p. 292. In fact, the lower rates for enterprises administered by local councils were abolished in 1968. Kunel'skii, 1968b.

The skill scale is the same for each of these subbranches.

Near the top of the table is the *setka*, which will from now on be referred to as the "skill scale." The term *setka* has a specialized meaning in Soviet wage administration, which might be fully translated as "the structure of relative intraindustry basic rates under given working conditions." Thus, skill scale appears the least clumsy English rendition of the term. The skill scale in the table is the row of six coefficients ranging from 1.0 to 2.0. Each coefficient relates to one of the six *razriady*, henceforth designated as "skill group(s)." This skill scale expresses the pure quality, or skill, differential in Soviet wage administration. In the first column of the table, the four coefficients, ranging from .86 to 1.24, set the relative basic rate differentials for the quantity of labor expended, or the pure differential for working conditions. Ideally, any job should be independently classified according to skill group and according to working conditions. Together, these two sets of differentials generate the system of twenty-four relative levels of basic wage rates presented in the body of the table. The coefficient in each cell expresses the basic rate for any job in terms of the rate for the work of an unskilled (first skill group) pieceworker performing a job under "normal" working conditions. This rate, italicized in the table, will be referred to as the "initial" basic rate (*iskhodnaia raschetnaia stavka*). While we will later discuss the key role played by this rate in interindustry differentiation of basic wages,[57] here we simply note that once the absolute value of the initial basic rate is given (30.5 kopeks an hour), the entire system of basic money wage rates, as presented in parentheses, is determined.

The six skill groups of the skill scale are not to be identified with the wage grades encountered in Western job evaluation. In the United States, the usual practice is to divide workers in a given plant [58] into

---

"branch" corresponds to the "two-digit" industry classification groups used in the Standard International Industrial Classification, that is, "machine construction" is analogous to the British two-digit branch called "engineering." See OECD, 1965, pp. 24–25. In 1960, the first year for which the figures include members of former industrial cooperatives, 30.4 percent of all industrial workers were employed in that branch, a higher percentage than that of light and food industries combined. *Nar. Khoz.*, 1962, p. 130.

57. See appendix A, especially on interindustry differences in the definition of "normal" working conditions.

58. More rigorously speaking, in both the West and the Soviet Union, jobs rather

seven to sixteen wage grades, the average being about eleven.[59] Since
such groupings take working conditions as well as skill level as variables, they are most closely akin to the twenty-four separate coefficients
presented in the body of the table.

In the early 1960s, basic wages constituted about three-fourths of
workers' earnings. The remaining portion was accounted for by various
incentive payments.[60] Virtually all wage differentiation involves incentives: a regional differential provides the incentive for workers' inter-
area migration; a skill differential supposedly induces a worker to
increase his level of qualifications, and so on. In much Western analysis
of wage determination,[61] however, the term has taken on a specialized
meaning—incentive wages, or incentive wage plans, refer to that portion of wages that is directly tied to short-run measures of output.[62]
Throughout the period under discussion, more than 90 percent of
Soviet workers were receiving, in addition to basic wages, some sort of
incentive wage.[63]

There are six basic systems of wage payments for workers in Soviet
industry: [64] straight time rate, straight piece rate, piece plus premium,
time plus premium, progressive piece rate, and collective piece rate.

Only the straight time rate system involves no incentive additions
to earnings.[65] Here, the worker's basic hourly wage rate is multiplied
by the number of hours he has worked during a specified period of

---

than workers are divided into wage groups. However, in both types of economies,
the distinction between a personal rate and a job rate is by no means clear, because
of limitations of management's right to downgrade workers. Galenson (1963, p. 302)
discusses this distinction in Soviet industry. For legal regulations concerning this
issue, see *Trud*, January 11, 1966, p. 3.
59. Brennan, 1963, pp. 189–120.
60. See chapter 2.
61. For example, see Morgan, 1962, pp. 140 ff.; Brennan, 1963, p. 224; *Wages*, 1964,
pp. 28–37.
62. "Output" is to be taken as physical units and should be clearly distinguished
from concepts such as "value of marginal product."
63. See chart 2.2.
64. There is no standard classification of wage systems in the Soviet literature. For
one of the more detailed attempts to establish such a classification, see Shkurko's
discussion (1965, pp. 32–50) of "determination and classification of forms and
systems of wages."
65. As discussed in chapter 7, bonuses from the enterprise's material incentive fund
have been possible since 1965.

time. With a few minor exceptions,[66] monthly earnings vary with the actual number of work days in any calendar month.[67]

Straight piece rate is the system in which a worker's wage is dependent upon the number of units of output he processes. Each unit processed means a specified wage payment, and earnings are determined by multiplying the number of units processed by the rate per unit, or piece rate. The actual establishment of piece rate, however, is closely connected to basic wages through the establishing of an output norm. The pay per unit of output may be established according to the following formula: [68]

$$P = \frac{B_I S_i}{N}$$

where P is the pay per piece; B_I is the basic rate for a worker of the first skill group; S_i is the coefficient relating the rate of pay for a worker of the first skill group to that of the skill group of the worker whose piece rate is being established; and N is the output norm.

Thus we can establish the output norm for a task to be performed by a machine operator of the sixth skill group in machine construction under "normal" conditions. His basic rate, as given in Table 1.2, is 61 kopeks an hour. If it is calculated that the piece that he is to fabricate demands 35.4 seconds of work time at a normal work pace in accord with the above formula, the output norm is 102 pieces an hour and each piece is worth 0.6 kopeks in earnings:

$$\frac{(30.5k)(2.0)}{102} = 0.6k.$$

If, during a given period, the worker has averaged 102 pieces an hour, he receives his basic rate. If he has fulfilled his norm by 150 percent,

66. A small number of time-rate workers are not classified according to skill groups and are paid monthly "salaries" independent of the actual number of work days in a given month. Judging from a list of eleven occupations in machine construction that are paid according to such salaries, these workers generally perform unskilled service tasks such as cleaning and repairing work clothes, sweeping workshops, and operating storerooms. Karinskii, 1963, pp. 78–79; *Raschety,* 1963, pp. 20–21.
67. "Zarabotnaia Plata," 1964, p. 7. See footnote 2, chapter 4, on the relationship between hourly and monthly wage rates.
68. *Trudovoe Pravo,* 1959, p. 384. This appears to be the basic formula. For variations of the formula as well as examples of how it is applied, see Kukulevich, 1964, pp. 53–56.

an average of 153 pieces an hour, his earnings are 91.5 kopeks an hour.
However, in the case of such overfulfillment of output norm, the
worker's basic wage remains at 61 kopeks, or about two-thirds of earnings, while payment for norm overfulfillment constitutes the other
third of earnings. As will be discussed in the following chapters, one
of the more dramatic results of the 1958–1960 wage reform was the
sharp decline in the share of earnings attributed to overfulfillment of
output norms.

In the case of norm underfulfillment, earnings are influenced by
establishing the responsibility for the poor performance. If the norm
is fulfilled, let us say, by only 50 percent (51 pieces) and the blame
falls on the individual worker, his hourly earnings are 30.5 kopeks,
determined by piece rates without reference to any established minimum wage rates.[69] However, if underfulfillment is due to, let us say,
an insufficiency of raw materials,[70] the worker is guaranteed two-thirds
of his basic rate, or, in our example, 40.6 kopeks an hour. With norm
overfulfillment, there is no ceiling on earnings.[71]

Thus, piece rates are established according to basic wages and measures of normal, or normed, output. A slight variation of the system is
indirect piece rate (kosvennaia sdel'naia). If an auxiliary worker is
charged with providing work materials to ten operators and the latter
had an average norm fulfillment of 120 percent, this auxiliary worker
would receive 120 percent of his basic wages.[72]

Progressive piece rate (sdel'no-progressivnaia) differs from straight
piece rate in that the rate paid per unit of output increases with the
level of norm fulfillment.[73] Under one variant of this system, the
straight rate is paid for output up to 100 percent of norm fulfillment,
from 100 to 110 percent the rate is doubled, and for output over

69. Maier (1963, pp. 106–115) objects to this and maintains that the minimum wage
should be an absolute floor under wage rates. Also see Chapman, 1964, pp. 7–8, and
appendix B.
70. Other such factors would be the breakdown or improper functioning of the
machine with which the job is to be performed, substandard raw materials or
tools, and unexpected unsanitary or unhealthy conditions in the work space.
Kukulevich, 1964, pp. 57–58.
71. Batkaev and Markov, 1964, p. 211.
72. Kostin, 1960, p. 40.
73. This system is simply a variation of the "differential piece-rate plan" developed
by Frederick W. Taylor in 1885. See Brennan, 1963, p. 266.

110 percent the rate is tripled.[74] Thus, if we assume that our machine operator was paid according to this progressive system, norm fulfillment would still indicate earnings of 61 kopeks an hour. If, however, his level of norm fulfillment was 150 percent, his wages would be 147 kopeks per hour [75] rather than the 91.5 that he would have received with straight piece rate. In Soviet statistics this difference, here 55.5 kopeks, is identified as "additional wages due to progressive evaluation."

Two additional wage systems are generated by addition of premium or bonus payments for performing some specified task or tasks. These are called the piece-premium (sdel'no-premialnaia) and the time-premium (povremenno-premial'naia) systems. The magnitude of premium payments is always expressed in percentage terms: for time-rate workers as a percentage of basic wage rates, and for piece-rate workers as a percentage of piece-rate earnings.

Premium systems (henceforth the term will be used to include both time premium and piece premium), with their corresponding additions to earnings, must be distinguished from various prizes and "one-time" premiums.[76] The latter include payments for economizing on fuel,[77] being employed at a winning enterprise in a "socialist competition," [78] development of some technological improvement or rationalization of the productive process,[79] and so on.

74. Aleksandrov, 1958, p. 91; Gurin, 1960, p. 30. The system can become very complex. For example, Bliakhman (1960, p. 18) reported that in 1956 in the chemical industry there existed ten different values for the piece, dependent upon norm fulfillment level. The difference between the highest and lowest value was five to one.
75. The first 102 at 0.6 per piece, the next ten units at 1.2 kopeks each, and from 113 to 153 at 1.8 kopeks each comes to 147 kopeks per hour (61 + 12 + 74).
76. Such payment can be distinguished from regular premiums in two ways. First, according to instructions issued by the Central Statistical Administration, prizes and one-time premiums are not to be included in the enterprise's wage fund, but rather stand as a separate account. (Biulleten', no. 3, 1964, pp. 7–8). Second, these payments are recorded in a worker's labor book to indicate special success in work. Regular premiums are not so recorded. Karinskii, 1963, pp. 123–125.
77. See Sots. Trud, no. 4, pp. 135–138.
78. "O Sostave," 1964.
79. The regulations concerning these premiums, as well as examples of how remuneration is to be determined, can be found in Raschety, 1965, pp. 116–142. A special sort of payment for technological innovation exists (or did in 1959) for piece-rate workers. If the innovation makes possible greater output and increased work norms, the innovator can continue to be paid according to the old work norm for a period of six months. Aganbegian and Maier, 1959, p. 77. It is impossible to

Under premium systems, additions to wages are a legally established and regular part of earnings determination. The worker is guaranteed a premium payment, usually calculated on a monthly basis,[80] if some specific task is fulfilled, in the same way that the piece-rate worker is guaranteed certain payments with norm overfulfillment. Unlike similar payments to administrative personnel, or bonuses from the material incentive fund established in 1965, the premiums under discussion are not affected by the economic performance of the enterprise or "shop," as measured by indices such as cost reduction or wage fund expenditures.[81]

Several of the major types of premiums that existed for Soviet workers in the early 1960s are presented in table 1.3. A worker may receive more than one of these premiums, with a monthly maximum established according to industrial branch. The ceiling on premium payments established during the wage reform ranged from 20 to 30 percent of basic rates for time-rate workers, and 20 to 30 percent of the piece-rate worker's piece earnings.[82]

Thus, the Soviet worker's earnings are comprised of two elements: the basic wage and various incentive additions to this basic wage. During the recent past, both components have undergone considerable change, and the nature of these changes constitutes the focus of our study.

Structure of This Study
While this study will settle little concerning questions of socialism and equality in the USSR, it will provide the reader with information about, and hopefully some insights into, recent developments in Soviet wage determination. The period under consideration is the past decade

---

gauge the importance of this provision. Apparently all such additional earnings are simply included as part of the payments for overfulfillment of work norms.
80. *Raschety*, 1965, p. 23.
81. Kukulevich, 1964, p. 90; Tsederbaum, 1963, p. 139. It might be noted that premiums can be taken away from workers for infractions of labor discipline. Some complaints have appeared that managerial personnel are sometimes overzealous in denying workers' premiums because of minor infractions such as being a few minutes late to work. Karinskii, 1963, pp. 116, 121. The material incentive fund is discussed in chapter 7 of this work.
82. Mutsinov, 1962–1965, p. 609. Under special conditions, this maximum may be raised to 40 percent. The maximums do not apply to the "one-time" premium payments, which are independent of other premiums. *Raschety*, 1963, p. 216. As noted in chapter 4, in 1968 some regulations were changed.

Table 1.3
Illustrations of Major Types of Premium Payments for Soviet Industrial Workers

Type of Premium	Branch of Industry	Possible Premium Recipients	Possible Size of Premium Percentage Addition to Basic Rate for Time-rate or Piece-rate Earnings
Filling and over-filling of output plan for a group of workers or work crew [a]	Major branches of industry except food products and textiles	All workers, time-rate, piece-rate, basic, and auxiliary	From 10-20 percent for fulfillment and 1-2 percent for each percentage overfulfillment, differentiated by branch. Maximum increase for piece-workers 20 percent [b]
Improvement of quality of output	Natural gas, oil refining, ferrous and nonferrous metals, chemicals, cement, textiles, knitting, furs, food products, and printing	Usually basic workers, time-rate and piece-rate	By branch, up to 30 percent
Fulfilling tasks competently and on time	In all branches	Usually auxiliary time-rate workers	By branch, up to 30 percent
Completion of repair and maintenance work in allotted or less than allotted time	In all branches	Time-rate and piece-rate workers engaged in such tasks	By branch from 10 to 20 percent [c]
Fulfilling and overfulfilling technically based [b] output norms	Machine construction, textiles, woodworking, and fishing	Basic piece-rate workers	By branch up to 20 percent for fulfillment and 1-2 percent for each percentage over-fulfillment

Note: Constructed according to information given in Maier, 1963, p. 163; Bliakhman, 1964, p. 169; Kapustin, 1961a, pp. 35–36; Mitin, 1962, pp. 362–363; Gurin, 1960, p. 29.
[a] Usually a "bridge" or work crew that may be composed of from four to forty workers. See Bakrakh, 1962a.
[b] A 30 percent maximum possible, under special conditions, for workers on a moving assembly line.
[c] These percentages are for time-rate workers.
[d] Technically based norms are discussed on pp. 49–55.

and a half. During these years, a unique wage structure that stresses consistency and equity has been developing. The period of the wage reform, 1958–1960, will receive most attention. However, prereform conditions provide necessary background, and Soviet wage policy continues to evolve during the more recent period. The goals as well as actual accomplishments of Soviet wage policy are considered.

Attention is directed toward the wages of workers in industry, the group most closely corresponding to Marx's industrial proletariat. Throughout the study, "worker" should be taken as synonomous with the Russian *rabochii*. Excluded from this category are "managerial-technical personnel (through foremen) (*inzhenerno-tekhnicheskie rabotniki*); office workers (*sluzhashchie*) who are clerical and sales personnel; "junior service personnel"; [83] and students. According to Soviet statistical practice, workers are distinguished from other categories of personnel in that their wages generally are calculated on a daily or hourly basis.[84] "Industry," following Soviet usage, includes all manufacturing and mining, but excludes construction and transportation. Thus, we are concerned with approximately twenty million persons, about 83 percent of industrial employment in 1962.[85] Finally, wages and earnings are used synonymously and taken to mean gross money earnings.[86] "Real wages" and "fringe benefits" are alluded to only when necessary to elucidate the discussion of money wages.

The book is in large part organized around the concept of pure wage differentials. Our concern is centered upon the three pure differentials that determine intraindustrial wage differences: on-the-job incentives, skill differentials, and differentials for working conditions. Interindustrial and geographical differentials are discussed when tangential to these considerations. Chapters 2 and 3 concentrate on the scope and structure of various incentive systems of wage payment.

83. Often referred to as M.O.P. (*mladshii obsluzhiaiushchii personal*), personnel who are engaged in nonproductive services—doormen, coatroom attendants, and those who do janitorial tasks not associated with the productive process. Labok, 1962–1965, p. 369.
84. However, see footnote 72.
85. *Nar. Khoz.*, 1962, p. 130.
86. Compared to Western countries, Soviet income taxes are relatively insignificant. Monthly earnings above 100 rubles a month are subject to the maximum marginal rate of 13 percent. No income taxes are paid on earnings under 61 rubles. In January 1968 a reduction in rates for those earning between 61 and 80 rubles a month was announced. See "O Podokhodnom," 1968, p. 140; Kunel'skii, 1968a, p. 85.

Differentiation of earnings according to skill provides the focus for chapters 4 and 5. Chapter 6 discusses differentials for working conditions. A tentative evaluation of the impact upon the wage system of recent reforms in economic administration is developed in chapter 7. The concluding chapter, for the most part, is an evaluation of Soviet wage setting within the general framework of Western labor economics. Two issues have been relegated to appendixes: measurement of interindustry differentials and aggregate measures of earnings inequality. During 1970 Janet Chapman and Norman Kaplan [87] have each published work dealing with these matters in great depth and detail. Thus, these two appendixes are provided as little more than a convenience for the reader.

87. Kaplan, 1970, and Chapman, 1970.

2

Wage Systems and the Composition of Earnings

Systems of Wage Payment

The most dramatic changes brought by the 1958–1960 reform were in the sphere of wage payment systems. On the eve of the wage reform, in 1957, about two-thirds of all Soviet industrial workers were paid according to straight or progressive piece rate. By the completion of the reform in 1961, the number had dropped to one-third. During the same period, the share of average earnings represented by basic wages rose from approximately 67 to 87 percent.[1] These developments should be viewed as an attempt to reconstruct an incentive wage structure that by the mid-1950s had become, to use a term prevalent in Western labor economics, grossly "demoralized."[2]

Among the characteristics of a demoralized incentive system are substantial unjustified inequalities in earnings, caused by a mixture of tight and loose standards, and a growing average incentive yield, or gap between basic wages and total earnings.[3] Within the Soviet context, the growing incentive yield prior to the reform had the additional meaning of a reduction in the degree of central control over intraindustry earnings differentiation, for "the degree of effectiveness of wage regulation emanating from a single planning center is to a large extent dependent upon the position of basic wage in earnings received."[4]

As discussed in our subsequent chapter, norm setting and corresponding payments for norm overfulfillment were, and continue to be, matters settled essentially on an enterprise level. In attempting to reassert central control, the Soviet revision of incentive earnings accomplished during the reform was not unlike that often adopted by a Western firm when it reduces the gap between total and base wages by signifi-

---

1. See charts 2.1 and 2.2.
2. For example, see Slichter et al., 1960, pp. 497–519, and Mangum, 1962, pp. 252–256.
3. Two other characteristics of demoralized incentives presented by Sumner H. Slichter et al. (1960, p. 497) are "a high proportion of 'off-standard' payment and time" and "a declining average level of effort." The Soviet data do not permit us to measure the importance of the former, nor is there any way to quantify the latter. The fact, however, that the wage reform was accompanied by a five-hour reduction of the standard work week (from 46 to 41 hours) without a corresponding decrease in output per worker indicates that the prereform "average level of effort" probably left much to be desired.
4. I. A. Orlovskii, 1961b, p. 187.

cantly raising basic wages (while not generally reducing earnings levels). At the same time, the percentage of workers paid according to "high yield" incentive systems is reduced.

To facilitate our discussion, a distinction should be made between an incentive wage system and an incentive wage payment. The former indicates how earnings are determined, and the latter refers to an amount, or share, of earnings that the worker receives because he has fulfilled some specific task(s). If the worker receives a specific remuneration for each unit of output that he processes, he is paid according to a piece-rate system. His total earnings, however, may be viewed as composed of two types of wage payments: his basic wage for fulfilling the output norm, and an incentive payment for overfulfilling the norm. Similarly, the worker paid according to some premium system receives his basic wage, and if certain conditions are met, he also receives an incentive payment in the form of a premium. Thus, two indexes may be used to gauge the significance of incentive wages: the number of workers paid according to each system and the share of earnings ascribed to one or another incentive wage payment. We turn first to the former.

Chart 2.1 presents the percentage of workers paid according to the five systems of wage payment recognized in Soviet statistics. The data refer to four periods: prereform; March 31, 1961; August 1, 1962; and August 2, 1965. Despite certain ambiguities later discussed concerning the classification of workers paid according to collective piece rate, several substantial changes in the scope of the various systems are clear.

If one divides incentive wage systems into two groups, those that provide incentive payments according to piece rate and those that utilize premium payments, it is apparent that the wage reform brought about a considerable growth of the latter type. In the prereform period, more than 65 percent of the workers were paid according to either straight or progressive piece rate, while premium systems, both piece plus and time plus, encompassed somewhat more than 27 percent of industrial workers. By March 1961 the relationship had been virtually reversed. More than 60 percent were paid according to one of the two premium systems, and only a little more than 33 percent according to straight or progressive piece rate.

If, on the other hand, all wage systems are divided into the two general groups of essentially time rate (straight and plus-premium)

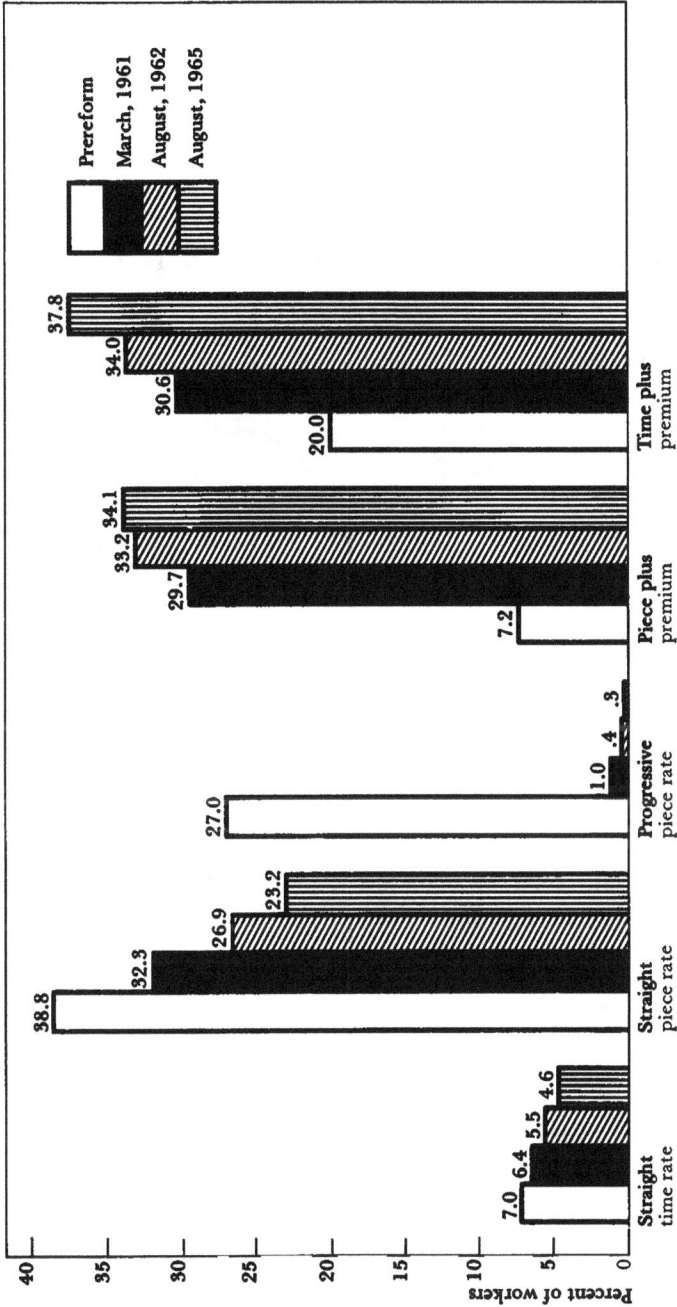

Chart 2.1
Percentage of Workers Covered by Five Systems of Wage Payment: Prereform; March 31, 1961; August 1, 1962; and August 2, 1965
Note: The prereform data, probably for 1956 or 1957, are from "Zarabotnaia Plata," 1964, p. 5. For the three latter dates, data are from *Vest. Stat.*, no. 6, 1962, p. 94; no. 6, 1964, p. 94; and no. 3, 1966, p. 95.

and piece rate (straight, progressive, and plus-premium), the reform brought a notable expansion of the former. In the prereform period, 27 percent of the workers were paid according to some form of time rate; by March 1961 the percentage had increased to 37. Data for twelve major branches of industry show that in each industry the percentage of workers paid according to time rate increased with the wage reform.[5]

The most striking changes concern progressive piece rate. In the prereform period, approximately every fourth worker was paid according to this system.[6] By 1961 the earnings of only one percent of all Soviet workers were determined by progressive piece rate, and by 1965, this system of wage payment had all but disappeared.

A consistent pattern of change in the scope of the various wage systems is apparent. At least through August 1965 there was an intensification of the changes initiated during the wage reform. The causes and general significance of these shifts will be discussed subsequently, but we first should present the alterations in the composition of earnings that accompanied these shifts.

Incentive Payments and the Composition of Earnings

Table 2.1 shows the composition of the wage fund [7] for Soviet industrial workers in seven selected years for which data are available. According to Soviet statistical practice, average wages are determined by dividing the total amount of wages paid by the average number of equivalent full-time workers [8] during a given year. Excluded from the fund are the "one-time" premiums and bonuses [9] and any payments associated with social insurance funds.

5. Maier, 1963, p. 161. The smallest reported increase occurred in ferrous metals, where the share of workers paid according to time rate grew from a prereform 30 percent to 34 percent. The largest increase was in oil extraction, from 49 percent to 79 percent.
6. Shkurko (1956, pp. 24–25) maintains that in 1956 approximately 35 percent of industrial workers were paid according to the progressive piece rate system.
7. A general check on the accuracy of the data was provided with the publication of the statistical compendium *Trud v SSSR* (1968, p. 146), which gave similar information for the years 1940, 1950, 1955, 1960, 1965, and 1966. A detailed explanation of the composition of the wage fund can be found in the instructions issued by the Central Statistical Administration in "O Sostave," 1964, pp. 3–8.
8. Apparently the average wage figures for 1964 were calculated in this way. See *Nar. Khoz.*, 1964, pp. 554–556, 824.
9. See footnote 76, chapter 1.

Table 2.1
Structure of Wages for Workers in Soviet Industry as Percentage of Wage Fund: Selected Years and Adjusted for Vacation Pay

Components	Percent of Wage Fund						
	1950	1955	1957	1958	1959	1961	1963
1. Straight piece-rate earnings, of which	63.1	63.5	63.4	62.6	59.4	50.6	50.6
a. basic wages	(46.4)	(44.1)	(39.6)	(—)	(—)	(42.6)	(—)
b. norm overfulfillment	(16.7)	(19.4)	(23.9)	(—)	(—)	(8.0)	(—)
2. Basic wages of time-rate workers	17.3	16.6	16.7	18.4	21.2	30.4	30.1
3. Additions for progressive piece rate	5.5	5.9	5.0	4.3	3.0	0.2	0.1
4. Premiums for time-rate workers	6.5	2.6	3.1	3.5	4.0	3.9	4.1
5. Premiums for piece-rate workers		1.8	2.7	2.8	3.1	3.5	3.7
6. Seniority bonus for years of service	3.3	4.0	3.3	2.8	2.4		1.3
7. Bonus for overtime work	0.3	0.2	0.2	0.2	0.2		0.3
8. Payments to piece-rate workers due to changes in working conditions	0.3	0.4	0.4	0.3	0.3	11.4	0.3
9. Payments for time lost on job	0.2	0.2	0.2	0.2	0.2		0.1
10. Free communal services, and payments in kind	0.3	0.2	0.2	0.2	0.2		0.2
11. Other wage payments included in the wage fund	3.2	4.6	4.7	4.7	6.0		9.1
Total[a]	100.0	100.0	100.0	100.0	100.0	100.0	99.9

Notes to table are in appendix C.
(—) Not available.
[a]May not equal 100 because of rounding in distributing vacation pay.

These data must be approached with some caution. They should not be taken to represent the structure of wages for all Soviet industrial workers. For the year 1955 and 1957, the information applies only to workers in enterprises subordinate to All-Union and Union Republic Ministries. The post-1957 data cover workers in "industry of the *sovnarkhoz*." In both cases, some workers in small-scale local industry are excluded, and some change in scope may well have occurred. Moreover, we have adjusted the data, since Soviet practice presents "vacation pay" as a separate element in the wage fund.[10] We have distributed this among the other elements of the wage fund, for two reasons. First, the amount of vacation pay received by a worker is essentially determined by his average monthly wage during the preceding twelve-month period.[11] Thus, the practice followed by some Soviet economists in eliminating vacation pay as a separate component of the wage fund appears legitimate. Second, one important set of data can be made compatible with other sources only by treating vacation pay in this manner.[12]

Those aspects of the data presented in table 2.1 that are not directly pertinent to our discussion appear in appendix C. The meanings of the first five entries, as well as subtotals 1a and 1b are unambiguous. Note, however, that entry 3, "additions for progressive piece rate," refers only to the difference between what a worker's earnings would have been under straight piece rate, including norm overfulfillment, and actual earnings resulting from the placement of a progressively higher value on the piece as the percentage of norm fulfillment increases.[13]

"Seniority bonuses," entry 6, are payments to workers for remaining employed in a given industry and/or geographical region for a certain number of years and are not necessarily associated with uninterrupted employment in a given enterprise. Since the 1930s these payments have

10. Vacation pay constituted the following percentages of the wage fund: 1950, 5.8 percent; 1955, 6.3 percent; 1957, 6.6 percent; 1958, 6.5 percent; 1959, 6.7 percent; 1961, not available; 1963, 7.0 percent.
11. If a worker has been employed in a specific enterprise for less than twelve months, his vacation pay is determined according to the average wages received since taking employment at the given enterprise. For laws governing the calculation of vacation pay, see *Raschety*, 1965, pp. 65–70.
12. See appendix C for explanation of data taken from Batkaev and Markov, 1964.
13. See pp. 94–98.

developed in a most haphazard way in various branches and regions.[14] In March 1957 a decree was issued that eliminated, decreased, or froze the size of these bonuses at existing levels. All such bonuses were subsequently established only through specific decrees issued by the Government Labor Committee.[15]

Entry 11, "other wage payments," covers about thirty sundry forms of wage payments, including such items as expenses borne by the enterprise in supporting workers temporarily in educational institutions, wages paid to workers while they are helping in harvesting operations at collective farms, and pay to nursing mothers.[16] The enormous growth of this category of wage payments, as shown in Table 2.1, is largely a matter of definition. Prior to the wage reform, geographical wage differentials usually took the form of establishing higher basic wage rates for workers in given areas. These differentials are now calculated as percentage additions to earnings and, in wage fund calculations, fall into the "other" category.[17] Thus, in 1959, geographical differentials probably constituted about one-third of the "other" category, and approximately one-half in the 1960s.[18]

In short, had earlier practice in classifying regional differentials been maintained, the percentage of the wage fund accounted for by basic wages would have shown an even greater increase in the postreform period.

In part because of the confusion caused by the growing share of "other" payments and the interindustry or regional character of seniority bonuses, the changing structure of the forms of wage payments can better be seen in summary form as presented in chart 2.2. In constructing the chart, we have taken entries 1a, 1b, 2, 3, 4, and 5 of table 2.1 as constituting 100 percent of the wage fund. These are the only forms of wage payment that can be directly associated with one or more of the five wage systems previously discussed. These entries have been en-

14. This process is described in Gintsburg, 1958, pp. 93–100 and 156–157.
15. See Kostin, 1960, p. 48; Karinskii, 1963, pp. 82–83; and Gintsburg, 1958, p. 102.
16. See "O Sostave," 1964, pp. 4–7.
17. Maier, 1963, p. 160; Batkaev and Markov, 1964, p. 226; Kapustin, 1964, p. 311.
18. Karpukhin (1963, p. 66) states that in March 1959 this was about 2.1 percent of the wage fund—about 2.2 with our adjustment for vacation pay. According to Batkaev and Markov (1964, p. 221) the adjusted figure had grown to 4.9 percent of the wage fund by 1961, and this appears to be consistent with data presented in *Trud v SSSR*, 1968, p. 146.

Percentage of Share of Total Wage Fund Ascribed to Key Elements[a]

| 0 | 10 | 20 | 30 | 40 | 50 | 60 | 70 | 80 | 90 |

1955
Earnings of
piece-rate workers   78.8

of which
a. basic wages   (48.8)
b. norm overfulfillment   (21.5)
c. progressive additions   (6.5)
d. premiums   (2.0)

Earnings for
time-rate workers   21.3

of which
a. basic wages   (18.4)
b. premiums   (2.9)

1957
Earnings of
piece-rate workers   78.3

of which
a. basic wages   (43.5)
b. norm overfulfillment   (26.3)
c. progressive additions   (5.5)
d. premiums   (3.0)

Earnings of
time-rate workers   21.8

of which
a. basic wages   (18.4)
b. premiums   (3.4)

1961
Earnings of
piece-rate workers   61.3

of which
a. basic wages   (48.1)
b. norm overfulfillment   (9.0)
c. progressive additions   (0.2)
d. premiums   (4.0)

Earnings of
time-rate workers   38.7

of which
a. basic wages   (34.3)
b. premiums   (4.4)

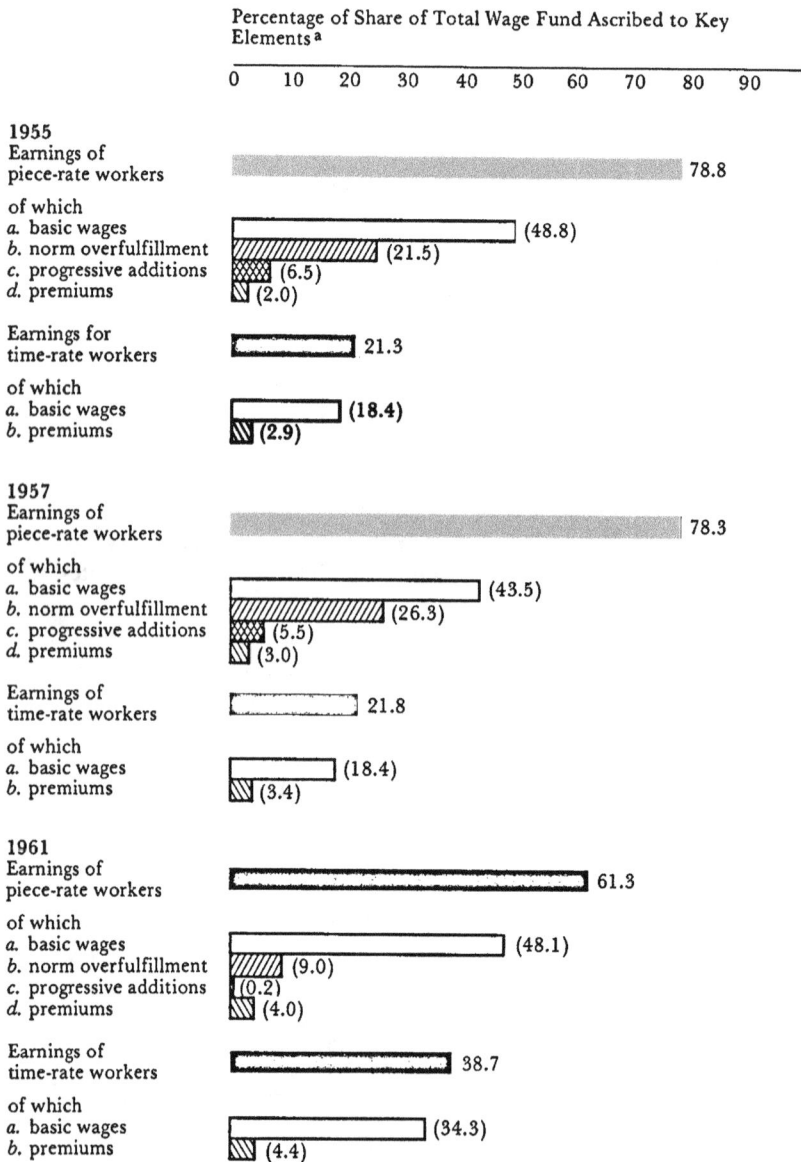

[a] Total may not equal sum of components because of rounding.

Chart 2.2
Relative Roles of Key Elements in Intraindustry Wage Determination: 1955, 1957, and 1961

Notes: Derived from the data presented in table 2.1. The sum of the "key elements" for 1955, 1957, and 1961 were, respectively, 90.4 percent, 91.0 percent, and 88.6 percent. Each entry in the chart is expressed as a percentage of the sum of the key elements for the given year. Thus, if "K_x" represents a single entry, it is calculated from the data of table 2.1 as follows:

$$K_x = \frac{Y_x}{\sum\limits_{t=1}^{5} Y_t}$$

where "Y_x" is the entry in table 2.1 corresponding to K_x and the denominator is the sum of the first five elements of the table.

titled "key elements." Data for 1955, 1957, and 1961 are presented in chart 2.2.

Chart 2.2 provides some information about various wage systems that cannot be obtained from chart 2.1. Between 1957 and 1961, the percentage of workers paid according to some sort of premium payment, either time plus or piece plus, increased from 27.2 to 60.3. In the same period, the percentage of the wage fund ascribed to premium payments increased from 6.4 to merely 8.4. The percentage of workers paid according to piece plus premium increased from 7.2 to 29.7, and the percentage of the wage fund ascribed to premiums for these workers from 3 to 4 percent. Thus, in terms of the number of workers covered, the growth of premium systems appears impressive. However, in terms of the role of premiums as a component of earnings, the growth is considerably less impressive.

The most vivid feature of chart 2.2 is the share of basic wage rates as a component of earnings. Largely as a result of the extension of time-rate systems and a reduction in payments to piece-rate workers for overfulfillment of output norms, basic wages for time-rate and piece-rate workers taken together increased from 67.2 percent in 1957 to 82.4 percent in 1961. We now turn to the possible economic rationale behind such changes.

Time-Rate and Piece-Rate Systems

From 1936 until the eve of the wage reform, about three-fourths of Soviet industrial workers were paid according to some form of piece rate.[19] No complaint has appeared in the Soviet literature that the 1936 figure was too high. However, since the beginning of the reform

19. See chart 2.1, and Aganbegian and Maier, 1959, p. 134. According to this source, the maximum expansion of piece rate occurred in 1953 when 77 percent of workers in industry had their earnings determined according to this system.

there has been virtual agreement that by the mid-1950s the scope of piece rate was uneconomically overextended. The overextension is easily documented.

For a significant percentage of Soviet workers, the piece-rate system had no rationale. Workers on automated or semiautomated assembly lines, having no control over the work pace, were nevertheless paid by the piece. If a worker's job could not be normed directly, he was paid according to indirect piece rate, with his wages dependent upon the normed output of other workers.[20] Setting wages according to indirect piece rates demanded such complex calculations that a worker simply did not understand how his wage was determined.[21]

Some reported instances of overapplication of the piece-rate system seem incredible. The effect of the introduction of piece rate should at least cover the cost of establishing an output norm.[22] However, at the Nevskii Machine Construction Plant, "the expenditure of work on the calculation of norms for several parts increased the cost of these parts by three times." [23] As late as 1958, it was necessary to reprimand enterprise administrators who placed repair personnel on a piece-rate system, thus making the "material self-interest" of the repairmen correspond to high levels of broken or damaged equipment.[24]

Soviet economists have had little to say about the virtual elimination of progressive piece rate. Possibly its complexity violated the principle that a worker should understand how his wages are determined, but a financial consideration was apparently also important. A basic dictum in Soviet wage policy is that wage increases should lag behind increases in productivity. Under the progressive piece-rate system, earnings increase more rapidly than the increase in physical output, once the output norm is fulfilled. An overexpenditure of the enterprise's planned wage fund often results.[25] Allegedly, and the contention is supported by the data of chart 2.1, this system of wage payment is currently used only for liquidating temporary bottlenecks in production.[26]

Explanation, if not rationale, can be found for the extensive use

20. B. V. Vlasov, 1962, pp. 164–171.
21. Sonin and Mechkovskii, 1958, p. 130.
22. Aganbegian and Maier, 1959, p. 155.
23. Morozov, 1955, pp. 13–14.
24. Petrochenko and Shkurko, 1958, p. 52.
25. Aganbegian and Maier, 1959, p. 152.
26. Kukulevich, 1964, p. 50.

of piece rate during the 1930s. In part, its use was tied to Stalin's attack on "egalitarianism" [27] (*uravnilovka*) in wage setting. Moreover, during the first two five-year plans, a large percentage of the industrial labor force was comprised of unskilled recent arrivals from rural areas. John Dunlop's analysis indicates that under such conditions, especially if there is a shortage of supervisory line personnel, piece rate has considerable economic advantages.[28] By the 1950s these reasons no longer existed, and the continuation of piece rate for three out of four workers during that decade can be ascribed to two basic factors.

First, the established basic wage rates constituted too low a percentage of earnings to permit any massive transfer of workers from piece rate to time rate. Reportedly, in the years immediately preceding World War II, basic wages comprised 80 to 90 percent of earnings.[29] By 1958, this share had dropped to about 50 to 60 percent.[30] Most of this gap between earnings and basic rates was accounted for by payments for norm overfulfillment, payments that were not available to time-rate workers. According to one study of wages in the machine construction industry in 1956, average earnings for piece-rate workers were 33 percent higher than those for time-rate workers; in fact, average wage figures actually understate the discrepancy that then existed. Earnings for piece-rate workers in the three most frequently assigned skill groups stood at about 160 percent of the earnings for time-rate workers in comparable skill groups.[31] Apparently such a relationship was representative of the prereform conditions in Soviet industry as a whole.[32]

Thus, without a general and significant increase in basic wage rates such as that which took place with the wage reform, any transfer of workers from piece rate to time rate would have brought a reduction of earnings for workers so transferred.[33] Enterprises were virtually forced to use piece rate if only to keep actual earnings in line with planned wages.[34]

27. See Bergson, 1944, pp. 177–206.
28. Dunlop, 1958, pp. 366–367; Robertson, 1960, p. 128.
29. Batkaev and Markov, 1964, p. 201.
30. See table 2.1, and discussion in Aganbegian and Maier, 1959, p. 95.
31. Batkaev, 1958, pp. 71–72.
32. Aganbegian and Maier (1959, p. 232) reported that for a given skill group, average piece-rate earnings stood at 150 percent of time-rate earnings.
33. An excellent discussion of this problem is presented in Batkaev, 1958.
34. Aganbegian and Maier, 1959, p. 134.

Although it is apparent that any change in the system of wage payment must be related to changes in levels of basic wage rates, we are left
with a different question. Why did Soviet authorities wait until the
late 1950s to increase basic wages, thus permitting a reduction in both
norm fulfillment levels and the percentage of workers paid according
to piece rate? Part of the answer is provided by our previous discussion
of inadequacies within the Soviet economic administration.[35] The remainder of the answer may be found in Stalinist economic dogma,
which maintained that "the basic form of wages in industry is the
piece-rate system, because it better corresponds to the socialist principle
of payment according to work." [36]

In 1956, one Soviet economist found the gap in earnings between
time-rate and piece-rate workers to be desirable because it provided a
stimulus for the timeworker to "strive" to become a pieceworker.[37]
The piece-rate system was considered superior in all cases except "in
the type of work in which a piece-rate system cannot be applied,"
that is, the jobs of plant watchmen, inspectors, quality control personnel, workers fabricating unique products, and so on. Not only was
it stressed that piece rate was to be used "whenever possible," [38] but
discussions concerning conditions under which time rate might be
effectively used "virtually disappeared from the economic literature." [39]

During the first stages of the wage reform, it became clear that the
percentage of time-rate workers was to be expanded. Soviet wage theory
may not have fostered this development, but it quickly acquiesced to
it. For example, a 1958 article on systems of wage payments, instead
of taking a "whenever possible" position, attempted to specify the
conditions under which the piece-rate system should be employed,[40]
describing them as

1. The availability of indicators of work done that correctly express
the amount of work performed by the worker

35. See above, pp. 2–6.
36. Manevich, 1948, p. 30. With slightly different terminology this same position
was repeated as late as 1956 by Kuznetsova, 1956, p. 25.
37. Kuznetsova, 1956, p. 22.
38. This is the position taken in the textbook *Politicheskaia Ekonomiia*, 1955, pp.
476–477. The textbook *Politicheskaia Ekonomiia Sotsializma* (1960, pp. 325–326)
published five years later, discusses the "conditions under which the piece-rate system
is effective."
39. Shkurko, 1961, p. 103.
40. Petrochenko and Shkurko, 1958, p. 53.

2. The necessity and possibility of increasing workers' output under the given technological conditions

3. The economic effectiveness of increasing the expenditure of labor upon the calculation of norms and the measurement of work performed

4. The assurance that piece-rate remuneration will not decrease the quality of goods produced, nor increase the waste of materials.

Since 1958, almost every Soviet study dealing with wage systems has been devoted to elaborating these conditions and adding new considerations for determining when piece-rate payment is to be considered the desirable system of wage payment. Current discussions are similar to those that appear in standard Western texts on labor economics or wage administration.[41]

The wage reform reduced but did not eliminate the differential between time-rate and piece-rate workers. For a given skill group, post-reform basic rates for the piece-rate worker are seldom more, and often less, than 15 percent greater than those of time-rate workers.[42] A study of the early 1960s showed that the earnings differential between these two groups was about 115–135 percent, a significant reduction as compared to prereform conditions. This narrowing of the gap was accomplished through a reduction in payments for overfulfilling output norms and an expansion of premium payments.[43] We now turn to the latter.

Premiums and Collective Piece Rate

The striking expansion in the percentage of workers covered by some form of premium systems (from 27.2 percent in the prereform period to 69.9 percent in 1965[44]) is viewed by the Soviet economist as an

41. A most lucid discussion of incentive wages "in principle" is found in Robertson, 1960, pp. 92–114.

42. In plants where the pace of the time-rate worker is sharply regulated by the productive process, for example, in some assembly line work, his basic rate may be raised to that of a piece-rate worker. Certain other conditions under which the rate may be raised are presented in Kapustin, 1961a, p. 29, and Kapustin, 1964, pp. 276–285. The latter source (p. 281) presents the basic rate for piece-rate workers as a percentage of that for time-rate workers in 27 branches of industry. In only two of these branches was the differential more than 15 percent, and in 19 the differential was either nonexistent or under 10 percent.

43. Note that according to table 2.1, the respective percentage of earnings from premium payments for time-rate and piece-rate workers was about 11.4 and 6.5 percent.

44. See chart 2.1.

initial step in a long-term trend. Supposedly, as jobs become more regulated by machine processes with the work pace essentially independent of the individual worker, the effectiveness of piece-rate payments as an incentive is reduced.[45] Premium payments for time-rate workers supposedly foster "material self-interest," which would be lacking under straight time rate. Moreover, because of the growth of automated processes, it is more difficult than it once was to regard a single worker as responsible for a single piece. The responsibility rests more directly on the group, and premium payments are suitable for rewarding groups of workers.[46] Even in productive processes that are not sharply regulated by the pace of machine operations, the premium system is supposedly desirable when workers have a "broad occupational profile," that is, when a single worker performs tasks that might be performed by workers of different occupations.[47]

The current literature repeatedly emphasizes the "necessity of strengthening collective forms of material incentives," [48] and, in the colorful language of Academician S. Strumilin: [49]

Individual piecework will evidently continue to retain its influence in many industries for quite a while. The center of gravity, however, is inexorably shifting, if it has not already shifted, toward collective stimulus, as being better suited to our aims and to the new content of our life. The old clothes are becoming tight.

Given the decision to reduce the percentage of piece-rate workers, premium systems have one desirable quality not often stressed in the Soviet literature. The importance of a centrally determined and standardized system of basic wage rates within and among the various branches of industry was markedly increased with the wage reform. However, the types of incentives needed in different branches vary, and premium systems may be adapted to meet these specific requirements. As indicated earlier in table 1.2, fulfilling technically based output norms [50] is supposedly important in machine construction, whereas

45. Shkurko (1961, pp. 96 ff.) presents an analysis of these factors.
46. For example, see the discussion in Shkurko, 1961, pp. 146–148, and Kapustin, 1961a, pp. 34–36.
47. Shkurko, 1961, pp. 130, 119, and 120–121, "Oplata po Konechnym," 1965, pp. 2–3.
48. This is a quotation from A. Volkov (1964) who is Chairman of the Government Labor Committee. Seven years earlier Volkov (1957, p. 6) maintained that "the basic form of payment for work . . . must be piece-rate payments."
49. Strumilin, 1965, p. 23.
50. Technically based output norms are fully defined and discussed in chapter 3.

the quality of output is considered to be of special import in textiles. Thus, a premium system can be structured to be "dependent upon the concrete conditions of production and the role of different workers in successfully meeting one or another index for premium payment." [51]

One type of premium payment has in the postreform period received widespread application and attention. Collective piece rate is a hybrid system of wage payment that Soviet statistical practice classifies as a variation of piece plus premium. Here, the individual worker's earnings are dependent upon his basic wage rate and the success of his work crew in fulfilling the collective output norm. The crew's norm and the value of each piece is established in essentially the same way as with straight piece-rate payment. Total earnings received by the crew are determined by the number of pieces produced multiplied by the rate per piece. These total earnings are distributed among the members of the crew in proportion to the share of each worker's basic pay in the total basic pay of the crew. For illustrative purposes, we might construct a "crew" of two workers, one in the first skill group and the other in the sixth. Basic hourly wage rates are respectively 30.5 and 61 kopeks.[52] If the "crew" fulfills its norm by, let us say, 150 percent, earnings will be 45.75 kopeks an hour for the unskilled worker (30.5×1.5) and 91.5 kopeks an hour for the skilled worker (61×1.5).

Several variations of this system exist in Soviet industry. Work crews, usually groups of workers on the same shift, may be of various sizes. However, the work crew may include workers employed in the same work place over a twenty-four-hour period—a variation that has been reported to be successful in reducing intershift loss of work time.[53] Though distribution of the crew's piece earnings is usually simply proportional to basic rates,[54] the pattern may be varied according to the relative performance of individual workers, as determined either by the leader of the crew or by a meeting of the members of the crew.[55] In one reported case, the procedure is to distribute earn-

51. Batkaev and Markov, 1964, pp. 212, 213–218; Shkurko, 1961, pp. 138–139.
52. The rates continue to be taken from table 1.2 and refer to piece-rate workers under "normal" conditions.
53. "Oplata po Konechnym," 1965, p. 2.
54. Chirkov, 1965; Shkurko, 1961, p. 130; Maitsen, 1964; Maslova, 1966b, pp. 18–20.
55. "Oplata po Konechnym," 1965, pp. 2 and 7; Shkurko, 1964.

ings for norm overfulfillment in a way that is advantageous to the more skilled workers.[56]

Whatever the system's variation, it could easily be argued that Soviet statistical practice errs in classifying collective piece rate as piece premium rather than as time premium. Within the work crew, differentiation of basic wage rates generally determines differentiation of earnings. This system differs from straight piece rate in that payments for overfulfillment cannot exceed a certain percentage of the basic wage rates.[57] Possibly most important, there are few of the social and psychological consequences often associated with individual piece rate. Most Western trade unions [58] as well as Karl Marx [59] have expressed opposition to piece rate because it tends to weaken feelings of solidarity among workers.

Since collective piece rate is subsumed as a variation of the piece-plus-premium system of wage payment, specific data on its scope are scarce. The literature maintains that the importance of collective piece rate has grown enormously in the postreform period, but we have little more data [60] than those that are presented in table 2.2.

The proponents of collective piece rate, finding it to be both economically and morally most desirable, advocate the rapid continuation of its expansion. Their general position is that individual piece rate was the most desirable system in earlier stages of Soviet industrializa-

56. Chirkov, 1965, reports that the "model rules" (tipovoe polozhenie) for small-scale enterprises in the food industry specify that payments for overfulfillment of group norms be differentiated by more than the differentiation of basic rates to the advantage of workers in skill groups four through six. Thus, the relationship of basic rates for skill group one to skill group six is 1:1.8, but distribution of payments for overfulfillment of group norm is made at a ratio of 1:2.
57. See table 1.3.
58. Although sample studies presented by Woytinsky, (1953, pp. 423–424) clearly show this to be the case, there is considerable variety in trade union reaction. It seems that both workers and their trade unions readily accept virtually any system of incentive wages if incentive payments are a means of increasing earnings when basic wages are "frozen." For example, during World War II, American trade union opposition to incentive wages significantly lessened because incentives appeared to be a way of circumventing the "hold-in-line" restrictions on basic rates. See Mangum, 1962, p. 243; Slichter et al., 1960, pp. 492–497.
59. Marx, 1906, vol. 1, pp. 602–611. Deutscher (1950, pp. 107–114) lucidly presents a Marxist view of the relationship between systems of wage payment and trade union ideology.
60. As early as 1961, Shkurko (pp. 116–119) stated that collective piece rate encompassed 70 percent of all coal miners in the Donbas region, 65 percent of those employed in a subbranch of the forestry industry (lesogatovka), and a "significant number" of those in machine construction.

tion, but that now, because of changes in technology, collective piece rate is the most effective way to determine wages. The argument is much like that used to advocate collective types of premiums, although it does not rest exclusively upon the need to create "material self-interest." The transfer of workers from piece-rate payments, which took place with the reform, is taken to be characteristic of the period of the "extensive building of communism." Collective piece rate is the "transitional form" and creates a feeling of collective responsibility somehow associated with the communist goal of "distribution according to need."[61]

On a more practical level, proponents stress that collective piece rate partially overcomes inadequacies in norm setting at the enterprise level, a subject that will receive extensive discussion in chapter 3. There appear to be at least two approaches to improving the work of the normer: first, to increase the number and/or qualifications of personnel engaged in this work; second, to reduce the amount of work to be performed. It is maintained that transferring workers from straight and progressive piece rate to collective piece rate has reduced the normer's work load. For example, if twenty men work together in one brigade and are paid according to collective piece rate, only one norm need be calculated, and the normer's burden is considerably lightened. In one furniture enterprise, shifting a group of workers from individual piece rates to collective piece rates meant that "in place of 150 documents a month concerning wages, now only six need be filled out." Under wage systems based upon "collective" indicators of performance, the worker does not shun the jobs with "harsh" norms, nor seek those with "easy" norms, as is the case with individual piece rate.[62]

Some economists are far less sanguine about the rapid expansion of collective piece rate. They hold that the application of this system of wage payment is strictly limited by technological considerations and, perhaps even more important, it may contain elements of an old enemy

---

61. For example, see M. A. Vlasov's (1961, pp. 125–141) chapter entitled "The Formation of a Communist Attitude Toward Labor." The book is virtually a paean to the superiority of collective piece rate. Also see Maier, 1963, pp. 209–213; Shkurko, 1961, p. 122; Ermakov, 1962; Palkin, 1962; and Maslova, 1966b, pp. 16–17. A. Volkov (1962), the Chairman of the Government Labor Committee, selected Vlasov's book for specific criticism.
62. "Oplata po Konechnym," 1965, pp. 5, 8.

Table 2.2
Approximate Percentages of Workers Paid According to Some Form of Piece Rate and Collective Piece Rate, 1964–1965

Branch of Industry	Percentage of Workers	
	Paid according to some form of piece rate	Paid according to collective piece rate
Coal mining	48.4	30.4
Ferrous metals	58.0	28.5
Oil extraction	13.0	4.8
Machine construction	54.4	11.6
Chemical	33.0	10.3
Light industry (excluding textiles)	81.4	14.8
Textiles	64.1	7.3
Food	55.6	30.6

Note: Data in the first column refer to August 1965 and are from *Trud v SSSR,* 1968, pp. 148–149. Column two is derived from Maslova's (1966a, p. 34; 1966b, pp. 16–17) information on the percentages of piece-rate workers according to collective piece rate.

of Soviet wage policy—egalitarianism.[63] The charge has been made that "some" Soviet economists are repeating an earlier mistake in associating changes in wage systems with changes in society, and that such a position is as incorrect as the earlier theory that piece rates were the basic form of wages under socialism.[64]

As early as 1962, in an article that appeared in *Pravda,* the Chairman of the Government Labor Committee, A. Volkov, indicated that the application of collective piece rates had been overextended and he stressed that individual piece rate was to be regarded as the most effective wage system in a number of branches of industry, including machine construction and textiles. Thus he strongly opposed the position taken in an article in the *Ekonomicheskaia Gazeta* that maintained that continued use of individual piece rate was in opposition to the socialist development of society. Granting that collective piece rate helps to create a "communist attitude toward work," he still found elements of egalitarianism in some of the popular literature concerning this system of wage payment.[65]

63. See Bergson, 1944, especially pp. 177–206, and Yanowitch, pp. 683–684.
64. Karpukhin, 1963, p. 32.
65. Volkov, 1962. The egalitarianism took the form of holding that equal distribution of brigade earnings, without reference to workers' skill groups, might be desirable.

Although the statement that collective piece rate "has nothing in common with egalitarianism" [66] continually reappears in the Soviet literature, it is clear that, under this form of wage payment, variation of the earnings of workers within a brigade will not be generally greater than the variation of basic wage rates. Since collective piece rate is to be used when calculation of individual performance is not considered feasible, Chairman Volkov's proposal that "it is necessary to calculate the personal contribution of each member [of the brigade]" when determining earnings seems most impractical.[67]

The Scope of Soviet Incentive Wages
Whatever their specific form, the broad scope of Soviet incentive wage payments is striking. American data on incentive wages are notoriously poor,[68] but clearly "payment by results" is much more narrowly applied. As of 1960, less than 30 percent of American factory workers were covered by some sort of incentive wage ranging from piece-rate payments to a yearly bonus.[69] For the Soviet industrial

---

One discussion of the question appeared in *Molodoi Kommunist*, the monthly organ of the Young Communist League, during 1962. In the January issue, an engineer held the idea to be rather attractive. In the September issue, two commentaries appeared. In the first a mechanic viewed such proposals for "introducing unconditional egalitarianism" as unacceptable, and in the second an economist seemed to support the position taken by the engineer. Volkov also attacked an article that appeared in the pictorial weekly *Ogonek*. The caption under a photo of a skilled workman states that "his brigade . . . has been transferred onto a new wage system. The total brigade earnings are divided equally among the members." All of these articles concerned groups of workers who had received the designation of "brigades of communist labor." See Palkin, 1962; Golubia, 1962; Ermakov, 1962; and Knorring, 1962.

66. For example, this phrase is used in Shkurko, 1964; Volkov, 1962; and "Oplata po Konechnym," 1965.

67. Volkov, 1962. Shkurko (1962) and Maslova (1966b, pp. 18–20) support the idea of assignment of "conditional" skill groups among brigade members dependent upon the effectiveness of a worker's contribution to the group's output. Shkurko, however, recognizes that this "could clearly lead to conflicts" among members of a brigade.

68. For example, J. E. Maher (1956, p. 130) in his study on "Union, Nonunion Wage Differentials" was forced to exclude from consideration workers who were paid according to incentive wages. Also see Woytinsky, 1953, pp. 495–496.

Possibly the most detailed western analysis of the effects of incentive wages upon earnings can be found in D. J. Robertson's (1960) study of wage setting in the British engineering industry. His data show that various incentive payments and overtime work constitute about one-half of workers' gross earnings (pp. 19, 33–35).

69. According to Mangum (1962, pp. 238–239), in May 1958 about 27 percent of workers in manufacturing industries were paid on an incentive basis, and this figure shows no significant change from the percentages reported in 1945 and 1946.

worker, this figure was between 90 and 95 percent, with better than
60 percent paid according to some form of piece rate.[70] Some insight
into the nature of Soviet incentive wages might be gained through an
attempt to explain this difference.

In the first place, the overwhelming majority of Western economists
would agree with the Soviet contention that technological progress in
the form of increased mechanization or automation tends to lower the
effectiveness of incentive payments based upon the performance of an
individual worker.[71] Thus, taking into account a relatively lower level
of mechanization than in the United States, one might expect that
in Soviet industry a larger percentage of workers would be paid by
the piece or by some other incentive system. By the same token, recent
Soviet reductions in the scope of piece rates seem to be a belated and
possibly only partial recognition of the relationship between more
advanced technological processes and the effectiveness of this form of
wage payment.

Some Soviet economists offer an interesting explanation for the
greater scope of incentive wages in the planned economy. They explain that an incentive wage system is less needed under capitalism
because the worker, knowing that he will join the ranks of the unem-
ployed if fired, will work at a highly intensive pace even if he is paid
according to time rate.[72] Given the job security that the Soviet economy provides, incentive wages are needed to induce the worker to
perform at a level close to his potential. However, limitation of the
scope of incentive wages in America can in part be explained by
trade union opposition to systems of "payments by results." [73] Furthermore, not only may job security in the USSR be less than the Soviet
economist assumes,[74] but in a capitalist economy the fear of dismissal

70. See chart 2.1.
71. Shultz and Weber, 1960, p. 195; Belcher, 1960, p. 101. J. M. Clark (1923, p. 78)
noted that when working with a large amount of complex capital equipment, labor
"takes the form of supervising the harnessed forces of nature and becomes an 'overhead cost,' virtually without control over output."
72. For example, see Aganbegian and Maier, 1959, pp. 158–162.
73. See footnote 58 of this chapter. For example, incentive payments are not used
in U.S. government-operated industrial establishments. In shipyards they have
been banned by a federal law prohibiting the use of stopwatches for determination of
output norms. Woytinsky, 1953, p. 421.
74. At least it was less than anticipated by the group of economists and sociologists
who conducted the Leningrad Survey (see footnote 32, chapter 5). In their questionnaire, the worker was to check which one of the 23 specified "causes for leaving last

is often considerably reduced through collective bargaining agreements about seniority in determining patterns of layoffs and dismissals.[75] Still, judging from recent Western studies, the Russian worker currently has much more job security than his American counterpart,[76] and the Soviet economist's explanation has at least partial validity.

A further plausible hypothesis for explaining the relatively wider use of incentive wages in the Soviet Union might be that in an older industrialized society, pride in workmanship, reliability, and discipline are more firmly established worker attitudes.[77] Therefore, the need for systems of payments by results to assure adequate performance would be less in U.S. industry.

None of these explanations can be summarily dismissed, but the basic reason for and rationale of the greater scope of incentive wages in Soviet industry revolve around labor market conditions. Relatively "free" local labor markets exist in both economies. In the United States, the individual firm is generally able to adjust wage rates in accordance with local scarcity conditions. A theme that runs throughout this study is that for the Soviet enterprise, such adjustment must be accomplished mainly through the distribution of incentive payments.[78] Thus, the wide application of various incentive systems adds flexibility to an otherwise relatively rigid system of wage administration. The most important source of such flexibility is in the sphere of norm setting.

---

place of work" applied in his case. After viewing the results of the survey, the authors made the following evaluation of the questionnaire: "Too large a group of answers were concentrated on the 'other reasons' category (14.5%); this was for the most part due to the fact that reduction in employment (*sokrashchenie shatov*) was not included as a cause [for leaving the previous place of employment]." Bliakhman et al., 1965, p. 36.

75. See Dunlop and Healy, 1955, pp. 229–292.

76. See McAuley, 1969, pp. 210–225; Brown, 1966 and 1970.

77. The importance of such attitudes is stressed in Gerschenkron, 1962, p. 9.

78. Robertson (1960, p. 128) stresses that within the context of a capitalist economy inventive payments may provide flexibility for the manager faced with national wage agreements determining basic wage rates. This issue receives detailed discussion in chapter 8.

3

Norm Setting

Prereform Conditions

Numerous types of norms exist for workers whose earnings are determined by any of the previously mentioned systems of wage payments. For example, service norms are established for determining the number of time-rate workers to be employed in the production of some given quantity of output.[1] In this chapter, however, we are concerned with a specific type of norm, the output norm for workers paid according to individual piece rate. For approximately one-half of all Soviet industrial workers,[2] the level of fulfillment of an individual worker's output norm is the essential determinant of income.

Prior to the wage reform, the 1950s saw a considerable increase in average levels of norm fulfillment. In 1950, this level was reported to be 139 percent,[3] but on the eve of the reform, average fulfillment had risen to 169 percent,[4] with the most rapid growth occurring between 1954 and 1958.[5] A corresponding increase in the share of earnings ascribed to payments for norm overfulfillment was seen in table 2.1.[6] Norm overfulfillment accounted for 16.7 percent of the wage fund in 1950 and 23.9 percent in 1957. From 1951 through 1955, 40.8 percent of the total increase in the wage fund was accounted for by increased payments for norm overfulfillment, and for the year 1956, this percentage was 78.6.[7]

---

1. These norms are essentially a tool for planning labor inputs rather than a determinant of workers' earnings, and they seem to be of questionable value even for planning purposes. See Shkurko, 1961, pp. 111–112.
2. Not having a breakdown of the piece-plus-premium system into individual piece plus premium and collective piece rate, we cannot be more specific about the number of workers paid according to individual piece rate.
3. Kapustin (1957, p. 30) also presents yearly average levels of norm fulfillment in nine ministries engaged in heavy machine construction for the years 1950 through 1956. In 1950 these levels ranged from a low of 146 to a high of 174. Corresponding percentages for 1956 were 175 and 218.
4. See table 3.1.
5. Batkaev and Markov (1964, p. 169) report that between July 1954 and December 1958 the average level of norm fulfillment grew from 146 percent to 160 percent
6. Also see chart 2.2.
7. Batkaev and Markov, 1964, p. 199. According to Aganbegian and Maier (1959, p. 66), between 1950 and 1955 average money wages increased by 10 percent, of which 4.3 percent was accounted for by increased norm fulfillment. A 10 percent increase in money wages appears to be consistent with the figures for all workers and employees given in *Nar. Khoz.*, 1964, p. 555.

Growth in average fulfillment levels should not be interpreted as indicating that norms remained at some given level while piece-rate workers' abilities to fulfill such norms improved. Norms were increased each year, but apparently workers' output increased even more rapidly. Until 1957, a "massive review" of all output norms took place once a year in all Soviet enterprises, usually during a two-week period in February.[8] "Review" seems to have been a euphemism for "increase."

While workers' attitude to changes in output norms will later be discussed, it should be mentioned here that Aganbegian and Maier present a fascinating analysis of the disruption of wage and productivity patterns caused by the yearly norm reviews. They also provide considerable insight into reactions at the enterprise level to norm changes during the prereform period.[9] In reporting the results of a study in the machine construction industry, these authors describe how enterprise managers held back the introduction of "organizational-technical" changes in the months before the norm review. This was done in order to introduce these changes at the time of the review, thus lessening the decrease in wages for piece-rate workers resulting from the increase in output norms. During these same months, workers tended to hold back output, anticipating that high output levels would result in the institution of considerably higher output norms. When these new norms were introduced, piece-rate workers' wages fell by about 5 percent, usually between January and March. During this latter period, workers increased their work pace to maintain previous wage levels, and enterprise management engaged in various subterfuges to lessen the significance of the higher norms.[10] A few months after the review, wages tended to increase up to and even beyond their previous levels. Hence, the total increase in yearly labor productivity took place essentially in the first two or three months of the year, while average wages tended to fall during those months.

As the percentage of earnings from payments for norm overfulfill-

8. Kapustin, 1961a, p. 33.
9. See Aganbegian and Maier, 1959, pp. 106–123.
10. These included the introduction of fictitious "new products" that had lower output norms, premium payments that had nothing to do with actual performance, and the temporary extension of progressive piece rates. All this was done within the framework of the wage fund assigned to the enterprise, because when the size of the wage fund was determined a reduction of wages during February and March was not anticipated. Aganbegian and Maier, 1959, p. 110.

ment increased, intraenterprise wage differentiation [11] among those paid according to piece rate—about 65 percent of industrial workers—increasingly became an issue settled at the enterprise level.[12] Although there are few reliable data concerning the scope and effectiveness of the centralized norms established by the ministries, it appears that by the mid-1950s such norms had little influence in wage determination. Furthermore, no authority existed to establish interindustry work norms. In view of the lack of correspondence between the administrative unit of ministry and a functional definition of "branch," the significance of centrally determined intraindustry output norms must be questioned.[13]

The prereform conditions were summed up by Premier Bulganin when he maintained that "for a number of years" enterprises adjusted norms so that available increased wage funds would be absorbed by overfulfillment. Norms thus no longer determined earnings, but rather were set at levels that would provide proper levels of earnings.[14]

Norm Fulfillment Levels

Table 3.1 presents average all-industry and branch norm fulfillment levels in four periods. The most vivid aspect of these data is the general reduction in fulfillment levels accomplished during the 1958–1960 wage reform. Despite a corresponding decrease in payments for overfulfillment, prereform earning levels were either maintained or enlarged because of increases in basic wage rates.[15] There was no report of workers' resistance to the new norms; and since increased

11. Interenterprise differentiation could be controlled through the central establishment of the enterprise's wage fund and average wage rate. The role of the wage fund is further discussed later in this chapter and in chapter 7.
12. Batkaev and Markov (1964, p. 197) maintain that while the system of basic wage rates can be centrally determined, the establishment of output norms is "by its very essence (po svoemu sushchestvu) decentralized."
13. See the discussion of prereform conditions in chapter 1, and Hoeffding, 1959, p. 72.
14. Bulganin, 1955, p. 12.
15. The change in the composition of earnings for piece-rate workers can be seen in table 2.1 and chart 2.2. Although Soviet sources consistently maintain that average earnings increased during the wage reform, data concerning wage increases immediately accompanying the reform in the various branches are not available. Postreform data for 1959 in industries where the reform had been completed showed, as compared to the prereform year of 1956, the following increases in workers' average monthly earnings: 26 percent in coal; 13 percent in ferrous metals and chemicals; and 10 percent in nonferrous metals. Poletaev et al., 1969, p. 222.

Table 3.1
Average Percentages of Norm Fulfillment by Piece-Rate Workers: All Industry and
Selected Branches, Prereform, Postreform, October 1963, and April 1967

	Average Percentage of Norm Fulfillment			
	Prereform	Postreform	October 1963	April 1967
All industry,	169	118	120	125 [a]
of which				
Ferrous metals	137	113	115	117.4
Nonferrous metals	142	116	115	121.2
Coal	123	106	106	108.8
Petroleum refining	134	129	127	133.2
Machine construction	209	126 [b]	133	139.4
Chemical industry	158	115	120	125.0
Woodworking	170	118	120	(—)
Building materials	114	116	113	(—)
Textiles	146	110	111	(—)
Sewing	155	113	113	(—)
Fish	171	117	118	(—)
Meat and milk	157	107	(—)	117.9
Bread baking	134	111	(—)	(—)
Printing	184	112	(—)	(—)

Note: The prereform and postreform data are from Batkaev and Markov, 1964,
p. 198. These authors state that data from both periods were gathered in a special
study associated with the wage reform. The above averages are apparently arithmetic
means rather than medians. Median averages would tend to be several percentage
points lower than the above figures as distribution of workers by norms fulfillment
is usually skewed to the right. See Maier, 1963, p. 201. The branch figures for April
1967 are from Dubovi, 1967, pp. 59–60, and the all-industry figure in that column is
from *Trud v SSSR* 1968, p. 171.
(—) Not available.
[a] For 1966.
[b] Because of a typographical error in the source, this percentage is there given as 186.
The error is corrected in other data given on the same page concerning norm fulfillment by branch as a percentage of the all-industry figure; and our 126 is based upon
those data. Independent information in Maier (1963, p. 198) clearly indicates that
126 is the correct percentage.

earnings accompanied the changes, opposition may in fact have been
minimal. As shown by the branch data, the postreform norms were
not equally "tight" (*zhestkii*) in the various branches. For the Soviet
economist, the general measure of the tightness of norms is inversely
related to the average level of norm fulfillment.[16] We will discuss the

16. Prigarin et al., 1968, p. 45.

Table 3.2
Distribution of Piece-Rate Workers According to Levels of Norm Fulfillment:
Postreform Machine Construction; All Industry and Selected Branches, October 1962,
and All Industry, 1966.

	Levels of Norm Fulfillment (%)					
	Under 90	91–100	101–110	111–120	121–150	Over 150
	Postreform					
Machine construction	6	5	21	20	32	16
	October 1962					
All industry	5.2	6.2	30.0	20.4	27.0	11.2
Ferrous metals	1.5	3.6	46.6	23.1	21.9	3.3
Chemical	1.7	3.2	33.5	24.9	29.7	7.0
Woodworking	4.4	6.6	26.6	23.0	30.6	8.8
Light	4.3	7.9	43.7	21.9	18.9	3.3
Food	8.5	9.5	36.0	22.2	19.1	4.7
Coal	14.7	16.7	28.8	20.3	16.7	2.8
	1966					
All industry	4.3	4.2	24.9	18.7	30.0	17.9

Note: The data for machine construction are from Maier, 1963, pp. 202–203. Because
the level of average norm fulfillment is the same as that in table 3.1, it seems that
those figures were also gathered during the special study associated with the reform.
The all-industry 1966 data are from *Trud v SSSR*, 1968, p. 171. All other information
in the table is from Batkaev and Markov, 1964, p. 208. These authors also present
fulfillment data for the machine construction industry for October 1962, but a typographical error (total percentage of piece-rate workers according to levels of norm
fulfillment is 90 instead of 100 percent) makes these figures useless. Had we the
October 1962 figures for this branch, there would be a larger percentage of workers
at the upper end of the distribution, due to the relatively rapid growth of average
fulfillment levels between the reform and October 1963. See table 3.1.

reasons for such interindustry differences shortly. However, average
fulfillment levels are but one aspect of variations in norm-setting
practice among branches. The distribution of piece-rate workers according to levels of norm fulfillment is presented in table 3.2. In spite
of their grossness, these data indicate that interindustry measures of
skewness or concentration of fulfillment levels differ significantly.[17]
Compared to the rapid increase of average fulfillment levels during
the 1950s, table 3.1 shows only a small upward drift. Soviet sources
maintain that this relative stability is associated with a change in norm
review policy.

17. Maier (1963, pp. 199–205) presents in diagrammatic form the fulfillment levels
in the prereform and postreform periods for coal and machine construction. The
data in table 3.2, because of differences in the ranges of the intervals—three ranges
of 10 percent, "under 90," "over 150," and the range of 30 percent between 121 and
150—do not lend themselves to diagrammatic presentation.

On August 15, 1956, the Council of Ministers issued a decree that ended the practice of massive yearly norm review. Yearly directives specifying percentage reductions in average norm fulfillment levels were abolished; from the beginning of 1957, norm review allegedly became a year-round and decentralized process. Management, with the agreement of local trade union committees, was given the right to change norms at any time during the year by introducing "technical, organizational and economic measures providing for an increase in labor productivity." [18] Introduction of new norms, however, was not strictly a local affair. Enterprise administration was "required to construct a yearly plan for replacing existing norms with new norms, based upon planned tasks concerning increasing labor productivity, average wages, and cost reduction." [19] One study in the machine construction industry credited the new approach with significantly reducing both the proportion of norms reviewed each year and the percentage by which the norms reviewed were increased.[20] Scattered data indicated that after 1961 the percentage of norms reviewed each year tended to drop.[21]

Thus the wage reform lowered average norm fulfillment levels, and these levels were generally maintained through the policy of continual norm reviewing. Moreover, by Soviet standards, the output norms established during the reform were considerably superior to those that they replaced.

Centralized Standards and the Quality of Output Norms

According to Soviet sources, the quality of output norms was improved during the reform by a large-scale substitution of "scientific,

18. Kudriavtsev, 1965, pp. 243, 244. Also see Kapustin, 1961a, p. 15; Aganbegian and Maier, 1959, p. 113.
19. Dorokhov, 1962, p. 53; Kapustin, 1961a, p. 33.
20. The study was limited to enterprises in the Leningrad region. In 1955 and 1956, 70 to 75 percent of norms were reviewed annually, and on the average, their levels were increased by 30 to 35 percent. Correspondingly yearly figures for the period 1959–61 were 30 to 35 percent undergoing review and an average increase of from 5 to 8 percent. Bliakhman, 1964, p. 342. These figures are puzzling. Since under previous procedure more norms were reviewed and they were increased by a greater percentage, one would not expect the new year-round procedure to result in greater stability of fulfillment levels. Possibly enterprise management was very efficient in diluting the significance of the higher norms under the yearly norm review. For a discussion of the early results of the year-round norm review, see Aganbegian and Maier, 1959, pp. 113–123.
21. Kotelkin, 1966, p. 83.

technically based" norms for "empirical-statistical" norms. The first type of norm is based upon an analysis of the work process and ideally reflects what the worker could produce if his work place and movements were organized in an optimal fashion.[22] Such norms are akin to those that might be established by a time-study expert in a Western enterprise. The empirical-statistical norm, on the other hand, is based upon statistical records of previous output and levels of norm fulfillment, without any analysis of the nature of the work process. Since Soviet classification is bifurcated, norms being either technically based or empirical-statistical, one must assume that a considerable share are determined by a combination of these two approaches and do not neatly fit into either category. The most important characteristic of technically based norms is a relatively low average level of overfulfillment, usually not exceeding 110 percent.[23] The general assumption made in the literature is that a large percentage of technically based norms is associated with low average overfulfillment levels.[24]

Whatever the problems in classifying norms, all Soviet commentators agree that the wage reform brought an increase in the share of piece-rate workers whose earnings were determined according to technically based norms. Prior to the reform, 31 percent of piece-rate workers in light industry and 44 percent in heavy industry were reportedly covered by technically based norms.[25] As a result of the reform these figures increased to 44 percent and 70 percent respectively. How much

22. For a Soviet textbook description of the nature of such norms, see Kudriavtsev, 1965, pp. 177–223. Technically based norms were not always considered desirable. In 1935, at the height of the Stakhanovite movement, a deputy commissar for heavy industry stated: "The essence of the Stakhanov movement lies in the fact that the Stakhanovite—actually with his own hands, not just in theory, but in practice—overthrows all so-called technical work norms. . . . Technically based norms represent a phantom that served to intimidate us, a brake that held us back." Schwartz, 1951, pp. 191–199.
23. Orlovskii (1961b, pp. 133–184) held that such norms have average levels of fulfillment of 105 percent. Kapustin (1957, p. 31) maintained that the range was between 100 and 110 percent.
24. Data presented by Prigarin et al. (1968, p. 60) indicated that in fact the relationship was very weak. If, using the information that he presents, one were first to rank industries by the percentage of norms considered technically based and then rank them according to average fulfillment levels, little relationship between the two rankings would be apparent. This same problem in the prereform period is mentioned by Gliksman (1960, p. 112).
25. Bugrov and Chubarov, 1964, p. 3. According to Kostin (1963, pp. 8–9), the share of technically based norms was 38 percent in 1959, and Bugrov and Chubarov give a figure of 48 percent in 1960.

of this increase was caused by transferring workers from piece rate to time rate during the reform has not been discussed in the literature.[26] Although it was anticipated that the year-round norm review would gradually eliminate empirical-statistical norms,[27] progress in increasing the share of technically based norms actually came to a halt with the completion of the reform. According to one source, for industry of the *sovnarkhoz*,[28] 48 percent of piece-rate workers were covered by technically based norms in 1960, 49 percent in 1961, and 48.4 percent in 1962.[29] By 1968, it was reported that "in the past few years the quality of existing norms not only has not shown improvement, but it has become worse." [30] Poor norm-setting practices at the enterprise level, a subject to which we shall shortly turn, are usually blamed for the decline in the share of technically based norms. Moreover, the Soviet economists maintain that the situation would be considerably worse were it not for recent attempts to establish and implement norms constructed by agencies superior to the enterprise.

In 1957, the Central Bureau of Industrial Labor Norms [31] (henceforth Central Norming Bureau) was established under the Labor Institute of the Government Labor Committee.[32] This bureau was to be responsible for the construction of standard output norms, the establishment of general methodological guideposts in norm setting, and the coordination of norming work among enterprises as well as among the more than 1,000 "norming research" organizations.[33] By

26. It appears likely that the overwhelming majority of workers so transferred had been normed on an empirical-statistical basis.
27. Gliksman, 1960, p. 116.
28. These percentages would be lower for all industry. Bugrov and Chubarov (1964, pp. 26–27) reported that out of about 11 million piece-rate workers, 4.4 million, about 40 percent, were normed according to technically based norms.
29. Bugrov and Chubarov, 1964, pp. 3–4. Karpenko (1965, p. 13) reported that at one machine construction enterprise that he visited in 1965 the percentage of technically based norms was the same as in 1960, when the reform was completed in that plant. He also stated that this was true for most enterprises in that and other branches of industry.
30. Prigarin et al., 1968, p. 42.
31. The decision to establish this Bureau (Tsentral'noe Biuro Promyshlennykh Normativov po Trudu) was announced in 1957, and it began operations in the following year. Petrochenko, 1962, p. 64, and 1963, pp. 224–225.
32. The origin and nature of this organization were discussed in chapter 1.
33. Kozlovskii, 1962, pp. 88–89. Although this is not entirely clear, the norming research organizations are probably independent of any single enterprise and therefore exclude those persons engaged in norm setting at the enterprise level. In 1962, it was reported that there were "more than 900 such organizations," and two years

the end of 1964, the bureau had published numerous methodological instructions and more than 400 separate norm handbooks.[34] At least two sources report that these handbooks could be used to establish technically based norms for more than one-half of all Soviet industrial workers.[35]

The percentage of piece-rate workers normed according to standards set by the Central Norming Bureau is difficult to determine. Among the first tasks entrusted to the bureau, in anticipation of the coming wage reform, was the establishment of output norms for workers in heavy industry. The charge was to establish actual norms rather than the more general "standards" or "methodological guidelines." However, because enterprises were able to adjust and correct these norms, a sharp line should not be drawn between centrally established norms and standards. Norms for the most widespread jobs were established first,[36] a job being defined as a task in which identical work movements and equipment are used.[37] The bureau later established such norms in light industry as well.

These norms are developed according to a three-stage process. The norm is constructed by an "expert commission" and is then imposed on a group of enterprises, where detailed reports are made concerning the results. If the results are considered satisfactory, that norm becomes standard for all such work performed in the industry.[38] These norms are always considered technically based.[39]

---

later, 1,050. The reported number of personnel employed by these organizations ranged from 6,000 to 9,000 in 1962. Bugrov and Semenkevich, 1964, p. 86; Kozlovskii, 1962, p. 87; and Petrochenko, 1962, p. 65.

34. Kozlovskii, 1962, p. 87; Bugrov and Semenkevich, 1964, p. 81; Karpenko, 1965, p. 81.

35. These handbooks apparently also include various service norms for time-rate workers. Bugrov and Semenkevich (1964, p. 82) maintain that between 1962 and 1964 the percentage of industrial workers whose norms were determined "according to materials emanating from the Central Norming Bureau" increased from 48.5 percent to 60.9 percent. Karpenko (1965, p. 13) holds that the figure for 1964 simply represents the potential application of such norms, and that they are actually applied to considerably fewer workers, because enterprise authorities often disregard the existence of centrally established norms.

36. Petrochenko, 1963, pp. 224–225.

37. Aganbegian and Maier, 1959, pp. 119–120.

38. For a detailed description of this process, including examples of the various documents that must be processed by the enterprises as well as a discussion of the proper percentages of enterprises to be included in the sample, see Bugrov and Chubarov, 1964, pp. 219–247.

39. Karpenko, 1965, p. 13, Bugrov and Chubarov, 1964, p. 27.

In 1962–1963, one investigation attempted to determine the percent-age of piece-rate workers who were covered by centralized norms. The results of the study are reproduced in table 3.3 and should be ap-proached with considerable caution. Apparently, the standard used was not the number of work norms set in accordance with centralized norms, but rather the percentage of workers who fulfilled tasks for which centralized norms existed. P. F. Petrochenko, in reporting these data, recognized that such a methodology produces "some error" but held that "the degree of error is not very great, and can therefore be disregarded." [40] Other Soviet sources are more skeptical.[41]

A serious problem in interpreting these figures is posed by the ambiguity of these centralized norms for actual wage setting at the enterprise level. One authority points out that these norms should not be interpreted as unchanging and obligatory standards to be adopted in all enterprises having such jobs.[42] Other sources maintain that the centralized norm is to be regarded as a general guideline [43] or a minimum standard [44] for the enterprise in its norming work. Finally, it should be noted that in some enterprises the existence of applicable centralized norms is simply disregarded.[45]

The matter is somewhat elucidated by the Soviet book *Otraslevye Normy Truda* (Branch Labor Norms), published in 1964.[46] The authors of this apparently authoritative study state that there are four types of centralized norms, which may be distinguished according to their administrative origin. These four types are (1) typical norms fixed by administrative unit (*vedomstvennye tipovye normy*), (2) single (*edinye*) norms fixed by administrative unit, (3) typical branch norms, and (4) single branch norms.

The typical norms, (1) and (3), are simply recommended, and can be adjusted at the enterprise. Single norms (2) and (4) are mandatory for all enterprises covered but may be adjusted upward by the enter-prise. Branch norms (3) and (4) are set by the Government Labor

40. Petrochenko, 1964, p. 111.
41. For example, see Melnikov (1962, p. 153), who questions the meaning of such figures and maintains that the 62.3 percent for machine construction "clearly embellishes reality."
42. Petrochenko, 1962, p. 65.
43. Melnikov, 1962, p. 153.
44. Karinskii, 1963, p. 156.
45. Karpenko, 1965, p. 13.
46. Bugrov and Chubarov, 1964, pp. 18–19.

Table 3.3
Percentage of Piece-Rate Workers Employed at Jobs for Which Centralized Norms Exist: Selected Industries, January 1962

Branch of Industry	Percentage of Piece-Rate Workers
Ferrous metals	27.9
Nonferrous metals	15.4
Ore mining	89.5
Chemical	21.6
Machine construction	63.2
Building materials	41.7
Forestry	77.1
Woodworking	1.3
Light	57.0
Food	32.0

Note: From Petrochenko, 1964, p. 112. Not included in the table is the figure of 73.8 percent for the branch identified as "loading and unloading work," which is apparently not a branch figure but refers to the percentage of those engaged in such operations. Petrochenko entitled these data the percentage of workers "normed according to all-industry or branch norming material."

Committee, and if they are single, they must also be affirmed by the central trade union organization, the All-Union Central Council of Trade Unions (V.Ts.S.P.S.). As of 1964, norms set by administrative unit could be determined by a ministry, *sovnarkhoz,* or territorial government authority.[47] If such norms are single, agreement of the corresponding trade union organization is necessary.[48]

According to *Otraslevye Normy Truda,* in 1963 only 1.4 million out of approximately 11 million piece-rate workers were normed according to one of these four types of norms, and of these, only 400,000 according to either branch or administrative single norms.[49] Thus, it seems clear that Petrochenko's data, reproduced in table 3.3, considerably overstate the scope of the centralized norms. Nevertheless, the data are interesting insofar as they suggest that the scope of centrally deter-

47. Executive Committee (*ispolkom*) of territorial or regional soviets.
48. In 1968, there was a change in procedures. Two types of centralized norms were identified: "branch norms" for work performed within one all-union ministry, and "interbranch norms," which are to be applied to work performed in more than one ministry. Furthermore, the authority of ministries seems to have been increased at the cost of the Government Labor Committee. See Lifshits and Sofinskii, 1968, pp. 109–110, 116; and below, chapter 7.
49. Bugrov and Chubarov, 1964, pp. 26–27. Also see Bliakhman et al., 1965, pp. 122–123.

mined output norms in the various branches has little relationship to either the average fulfillment levels presented in table 3.1 or the distribution of workers according to fulfillment levels in table 3.2.[50]

Taken alone, data on the relatively small scope of centralized norms overstate the freedom enjoyed by the enterprise in this sphere of wage administration. In addition to directly setting output norms or norming guidelines, superior agencies have certain indirect controls over norm setting.

At least until 1965, a consistent element in wage setting was centralized determination of the total wages that the enterprise could pay to its workers (that is, the workers' wage fund) and the average level of earnings received.[51] Without some reference to possible bargaining between the enterprise and a superior authority about the size of the wage fund, enterprise autonomy in determining wage differentiation among piece-rate workers is exaggerated.

The enterprise submits a wage plan to a superior authority [52] for approval, and included in the enterprise's projection are figures for average skill group, average basic wage rates, percentage of average wage accounted for by premium payments, and the percentage of average wages represented by basic rates.[53]

It is likely that in deciding the size of the enterprise's wage fund the superior agency might refuse to increase the fund because payments for norm overfulfillment are considered excessive, or might issue instructions to economize on wages by instituting new norms.[54] According to one source, for a given branch of industry within a single *sovnarkhoz,*

50. Tables 3.1, 3.2, and 3.3 appear on pp. 43, 48, and 54, respectively.
51. The term "wage fund" refers to total wages paid to all those employed by the enterprise. Workers' wages are calculated separately as a component of this fund. As discussed in chapter 7, with the reforms initiated in 1965, only the enterprise's wage fund, and not the average level of earnings, is to be set centrally.
52. Prior to 1958, this authority was the Ministry; from then through 1965, the *sovnarkhoz.* Kunel'skii, 1962, p. 52. Podolskii (1962, p. 99), on the other hand, maintains that the *sovnarkhoz* has little actual influence in setting these indices. For a description of at least the formal roles of the various administrative levels in determining the wage fund, see Maier, 1963, pp. 240–242. After 1965, the authority was once again the Ministry.
53. I. A. Orlovskii, 1964, pp. 114–117; "Zarabotnaia Plata" 1964, pp. 14–15.
54. I. A. Orlovskii (1961b, pp. 182–185) clearly implies that such policies are general. Plans are established in the sphere of norm setting and levels of norm fulfillment for different groups or workers within the enterprise must at some point be reviewed by superior authorities. It seems that Nove (1961, pp. 116–121, 231–234) overstated the role of the enterprise in wage determination by neglecting these considerations.

differences among enterprises in average levels of norm fulfillment "had basically been eliminated" by 1965. But for a given branch, average fulfillment levels differ considerably among these various economic regions, and such differences are "basically explained by different demands made concerning norming among the *sovnarkhozy*." [55] The means for enforcing such demands were not specified.

Moreover, at least in one important case, high average levels of norm fulfillment cannot be associated with weakened central control over norm setting. In the machine construction industry, centrally determined output norms were consciously set at "loose" levels as a part of interindustry wage regulation. As later discussed,[56] an unanticipated result of the wage reform was that relatively more precise and detailed skill-group standards were applied in machine construction. A worker of a given qualification in this branch tended to be classified in a lower skill group than was the case in other industries. As a result, from the vantage point of interindustry wage differentiation, relative average basic wages in machine construction were too low. The situation was "corrected" by ensuring relatively large premiums and payments for norm overfulfillment as a component of earnings.[57]

However, even after recognizing both direct and indirect constraints over enterprise autonomy in norm setting, the Soviet economists' position that "in essence" norm setting is an enterprise affair appears valid. Thus, in 1963, for approximately 9.6 million piece-rate workers the value of the piece was determined according to standards that had essentially been developed at the enterprise level. In light of the literature documenting the "disorganized" [58] condition of norming in the

55. Bliakhman et al., 1965, pp. 119–120. Not mentioned is the possibility of a high degree of interenterprise labor mobility for a given branch within a single economic region. If this were the case, enterprises would be forced to set norms and corresponding piece-rate earnings at similar levels.

56. See table 4.7 and accompanying discussion.

57. Prigarin et al. (1968, p. 81), taking an existing situation for two plants in the Moscow region as representative, presented the following illustration. Average basic wages in the machine construction plant are 61.2 R a month and in the textile plant, 74.7. However, average norm fulfillment levels are 142.5 percent in the former plant and 112.2 in the latter. Because of premiums and payments for norm overfulfillment, average wages in the machine construction plant exceeded those in the textile plant, 108.8 R a month compared to 104.0.

58. "Disorganization" is usually taken to mean that output norms may differ for "identical" work. See Petrochenko, 1962, p. 62; Bliakhman, 1964, p. 128.

enterprise, it is little wonder that many Soviet economists have seen the extension of centralized norms as highly desirable.

Within the enterprise, the task of norm setting is performed by personnel designated as "normers" (normirovshchiki). It is impossible to imagine that these undereducated, overworked, and underpaid normers could "scientifically" evaluate or implement the tens of millions of output norms that exist in Soviet industry.[59]

One Soviet economist maintains that the quality of norming work is dependent "in the first place" on the theoretical and technical training of the normer.[60] Most normers have apparently not received any such training. Though the normer's job is considered as demanding as that of the engineer or economist, his educational level is significantly lower. In 1963, it was reported that in the chemical industry 48.9 percent of the "engineers of all specialties" and 37.8 percent of the "economists" had received higher education. The corresponding figure for normers was 13 percent.[61] The large Gorkovskii automotive factory employed 325 normers; of these, only 21 had completed their higher education, and about 150 had received seven years of schooling or less.[62]

Another problem is that those managerial-technical [63] personnel who are designated as "normers" in fact spend little time setting output norms. A survey of metallurgical plants in the Moscow region showed that in addition to setting output norms, the normer was called upon to calculate the premiums for all personnel in the enterprise, control and document the education received by workers, construct work and vacation schedules, and "periodically" engage in actual production work. In the basic shops such activities consumed from 75 to 90 percent of the normer's work time; in auxiliary shops the percentage was even higher.[64]

59. Petrochenko (1962, p. 68) maintained that 90 million output norms existed in 1962. Karpukhin (1963, pp. 158–159) gave the same figure for the number of norms existing in 1957. While the quantity of norms probably remains enormous, it is difficult to believe that their number was not reduced with the decrease in piece-rate work that took place during the reform.
60. Morozov, 1955, pp. 13–14.
61. Pogostin, 1963, p. 75.
62. Gliantsev, 1962, p. 86. Savich and Maksuri (1963, p. 41) reported that the "middle and higher specialized institutes" simply do not prepare people to become normers.
63. In Russian, inzhenerno-teknicheskie rabotniki.
64. Amel'chenko, 1962, pp. 79–80. Also see Voronikov, 1957, p. 16.

The specific administrative department (*otdel*) within the enterprise out of which the normer should work is not as clear as "model" Soviet administrative structures indicate.[65] According to one source, administrative patterns are here "more disorganized than in any other sphere of economic activity within the enterprise." [66]

For some reason, enterprise administrators tend to set salaries among the engineering-technical personnel so as to discriminate against the normers. Ranges for salary scales are set centrally, with that of the normer equivalent to the scale of the economist or engineer with similar work experience, without reference to educational level.[67] The difference between the high and low level of a specific range for such personnel is about 10 or 20 percent.[68] According to one reported survey, the actual salary level of the normer was usually at the bottom of the range, and that of other engineering-technical personnel close to the top.[69]

Finally, possibly because of these factors, but surely in part because of the nature of the work, the profession of normer is simply considered to be unattractive, a "specialty of the second or third rank" (*ranga*).[70] Such work is often regarded by the young specialists as something temporary, to be given up the moment a "proper" job for an engineer is open.[71] The job necessitates continual and often acrimonious conflict with the piece-rate workers. To quote the head of the Kirov *sovnarkhoz*'s labor department, "It is not a secret that [this job] is not to everyone's taste" (*ne prikhoditsia po dushe*).[72]

65. See Feshbach, 1960, p. 31.

66. Gliantsev, 1962, p. 85; Podolskii, 1962, p. 98.

67. Gliantsev, 1962, p. 83.

68. The actual range is dependent upon the branch of industry, size of plant, type of product, and several other factors. The range of 10 to 20 percent refers to machine construction. See Dorokhov, 1962, pp. 256–257.

69. Gliantsev, 1962, p. 83. Amel'chenko (1962, p. 80) also expresses concern with the relatively low wages received by the normer.

70. *Trud*, September 9, 1965, p. 1.

71. Savich and Maksuri, 1963, p. 41.

72. Podolskii, 1962, p. 95. Gliantsev (1962, p. 84) states that workers often take a disrespectful attitude toward normers. He relates an occurrence—naming the enterprise and the persons involved—that demonstrates how difficult a normer's life can be. In accordance with newly established centralized norms, some new output norms were established in a shop within the enterprise. The foreman of the shop demanded that the old norms be reestablished, and called a meeting of the workers. On his initiative the assembled workers adopted a resolution that the normer be fired. Only the intervention of the enterprise's department of labor prevented the resolution

Certainly these conditions help to explain why the normer might prefer to use the simple expedient of the empirical-statistical norm rather than the technically based norm, which demands "scientific analysis of the productive process." The general impression that the disorganized condition of norm setting results at least in part from the inadequacy of personnel at the enterprise level is reinforced by the Soviet estimates of the percentage of norms considered technically based. These estimates show a sharp increase with the wage reform and then a tendency for this percentage to remain constant or to decrease slightly.[73] Only during the reform did the "whole staff of engineering-technical personnel" in the various enterprises take part in the establishment of output norms. Since then, the normer alone has carried the burden.[74]

In short, conditions surrounding this aspect of wage administration appear to preclude the construction of "scientific," technically based norms at the enterprise level. However, as will be argued [75] immediately after a brief discussion of Soviet theory on norm setting, even if the enterprise were able to develop such norms, there is reason to believe that it would shun their application.

Soviet Theory and Proposed Reforms

Two general groups of problems are identifiable in Soviet discussions about norming. One may be called "static" considerations dealing with optimal fulfillment levels of established norms, and the other may be called "dynamic" factors indicating when output norms should be altered.

In the realm of static considerations, one opinion of "proper" norm fulfillment levels is that "the indication of the quality of a norm is the average percentage of its fulfillment: the closer it is to 100 percent, the better the norm." [76] This proposition is often associated with the idea that "norm should equal plan." At present, the average level of norm

---

from being put into effect. For a superb on-the-spot discussion about norm setting in several Leningrad factories, see McAuley, 1969, pp. 89–102.
73. Karpenko, 1965, and above, pp. 50–51.
74. Podolskii, 1962, p. 95.
75. This argument is again developed in chapter 8.
76. Maier, 1963, p. 202. He also finds the norm-plan proposal useful in that it tends to reduce the earnings differential between time-rate and piece-rate workers of the same skill group, thus "easing the transition" of workers from piece-rate to time-rate systems of payment (pp. 207–208).

fulfilment by piece-rate workers in a given enterprise in no way indicates the success of that enterprise in meeting its output plans. Under the proposed system, if the enterprise meets its yearly output plan, norms will be fulfilled by an average of 100 percent, and any higher fulfillment level would indicate that the enterprise had overfulfilled its planned tasks.[77] Athough held universally desirable by some economists, this system seems to be most applicable to enterprises where a large percentage of workers are on a collective piece-rate system. In 1960, at a conference called by the Government Labor Committe, the "norm-plan" proposal was favorably discussed, and the conference recommended that the system be applied in ferrous metals. The fact that average fulfillment levels in that branch increased from 113 percent in 1960 to 117 percent in 1966 indicates that the recommendation was not followed.[78]

According to the proponents of the norm-plan system, not only should the arithmetic mean and the median level of fulfillment be 100 percent, but the distribution of workers according to levels of norm fulfillment should correspond to the normal bell-shaped curve. Statistical measures of variance are expected to be higher for workers engaged in hand labor, and lower for mechanized work.[79] From data already presented,[80] it is clear that implementation of this proposal would mean a major restructuring of Soviet norming practices.

One critic of the norm-plan proposal maintains that average levels of norm fulfillment reflect the intensity of the work performed. The "good norm" for intense work should permit an average level of fulfillment higher than that for less intense work.[81] Another criticism is that no generally optimum level of norm fulfillment can be found; rather, average levels should reflect one of three technological levels of production. With a highly automated and uninterrupted technological process, the norm-plan proposal is desirable. If a high degree of mechanization exists, norms should be set so that average fulfillment is about 105 percent. If a large share of the labor performed is hand labor and

77. Aganbegian and Maier, 1959, pp. 89–94; Maier, 1963, pp. 199–205.
78. Maier, 1963, p. 211; *Trud v SSSR*, 1968, p. 171.
79. Aganbegian and Maier, 1959, p. 231; Maier, 1963, p. 199–203. In the latter appear several diagrams of actual distribution of workers according to levels of norm fulfillment, as well as a discussion of the methodology for measuring such variance.
80. See tables 3.1 and 3.2.
81. Bliakhman, 1964, p. 132.

amount of mechanization is no more than average, statistical records should be used for establishing proper average levels of fulfillment.[82]

Despite such arguments, certain indices for evaluating output norms enjoy almost universal acceptance among Soviet economists. The quality of output norms for piece-rate workers is taken to be directly associated with the percentage classified as technically based; the degree to which average fulfillment approximates some given level, usually 100 to 110 percent; and, finally, how close the distribution of workers according to fulfillment levels approximates a normal distribution.[83]

More interesting than the attempts to determine a proper level of norm fulfillment is the literature concerned with the theoretical basis for establishing criteria for the dynamics of norm setting, that is, when the output norms of piece-rate workers should be changed. Much of the Soviet discussion is based upon a general approach to wage setting involving the concepts of "subjective" and "objective" causes of changes in labor productivity. Derived from Marx,[84] this approach was incorporated in some Soviet writings on wages during the 1920s. It later passed out of the literature, being criticized as "inappropriate" to conditions of Soviet socialism,[85] but it again began to appear in Soviet theory in the late 1950s.

The attempt to explain increases in labor productivity according to either objective or subjective factors involves the broad general question of the relationships between money wages and productivity, as well as the more narrow question that is our immediate concern— norm setting. Thus, we must first summarize the general approach.[86]

Most Soviet economists consider any increase in labor productivity to be due to a number of causes or "factors," all of which may be classified under one of two headings. First there are the objective factors, those that may be considered independent of the activity of individual workers, such as improvements or increases in the capital equip-

82. I. A. Orlovskii, 1961b, pp. 183–184.
83. For example, see Prigarin et al., 1968, pp., 44–45, for a direct statement of these indices.
84. Karpukhin (1963, pp. 58–59) traces this derivation. The meaning of the term "objective factors" in the Soviet literature is not to be confused with its meaning in Western time-study analysis, where it refers to the measurement of the "most efficient" way of performing some given operation. See Woytinsky, 1953, p. 422.
85. See Barker, n.d., p. 7.
86. The most complete discussions of this approach appear in Bliakhman, 1964, pp. 213–348 and in Aganbegian and Maier, 1959, pp. 28–87.

ment the worker uses.[87] The subjective factors are those related to the activity of individual workers, for example, increases in the skill level or intensity of the work process.[88] The basic assumption in this approach is that a relative increase in labor productivity due to subjective factors should be accompanied by the same relative increase in money wages. On the other hand, increases in productivity due to objective factors should not involve any corresponding increase in money wages: rather, the total additional product should revert to "society as a whole" in the form of lower prices on consumer goods, increased social services, and so on.

Professor E. L. Manevich, among others,[89] has criticized this analysis, holding it to be theoretically unacceptable in that it has much in common with the "bourgeois" theory of the "three factors of production." [90] He also maintains that for purposes of economic analysis and planning, it is simply impossible to determine the ratio of objective to subjective factors in planned or actual increases in productivity.

Judging by more recent literature, Manevich seems to have lost the argument on both counts. The factor approach is fast becoming an established part of Soviet wage theory, even appearing in at least one standard text on planning.[91] It was reported that this approach had been successfully used for planning productivity and wages in the Leningrad economic region in 1963.[92] Possibly the most interesting applications of the factor approach are in the area of wage policy that is our immediate focus of attention—norm setting.

The factor approach hypothesizes the following relationship between norm setting and output: any increases in productivity due to subjective factors should involve no changes in output norms, while increases caused by objective factors necessitate new output norms.

87. That is, if the new capital equipment does not necessitate any increase in the quality or quantity of the work of the operators of such equipment.
88. Increased productivity due to subjective factors does not change the "rate of exploitation," but if such an increase is caused by objective factors, this ratio increases. See footnote 66, chapter 5.
89. This includes all those Soviet economists who hold that Marxist categories cannot be applied to socialist wage problems. For example, see Kuzminov, 1961a and 1961b.
90. Manevich, 1961, pp. 82–83. Karpukhin (1963, p. 59) correctly points out that these theories have nothing in common except that they both use the word "factor."
91. *Planirovanie*, 1963, pp. 470, 477–478; also see *Metodicheskie Ukazaniia*, 1969, pp. 294–295.
92. Bliakhman, 1964, p. 27.

Attempting to quantify this approach, Aganbegian and Maier were the first to propose that enterprises make a yearly calculation of the causes of increased productivity. They suggested that the total increase in labor productivity be divided among three categories: [93] (1) monetary considerations, (2) factors that increase labor productivity and necessitate changes in output norms, and (3) factors that increase productivity and do not call for the establishment of new output norms.

The first category accounts for differences between "real" and monetary measures of labor productivity such as changes in output assortment and variations in the amount of "double counting" of raw material inputs. The second category defines the increase in labor productivity due to technological changes, such as modernization of the capital stock, and some specific organizational measures. The third category, changes in labor productivity not calling for new output norms, includes renovation of capital equipment; changes in the occupational structure of workers; reduction of intershift lost time; and, possibly most important, the residual entitled "increase in the level of output," or increases in the average level of fulfillment of existing output norms.

Thus, according to this approach, despite an increased level of fulfillment, some existing output norms ought not to be changed. The corresponding increase in piece-rate earnings is considered desirable because the higher fulfillment level results from subjective factors; that is, because there has been an increase in the intensity of the work performed or because the worker has become more competent and better acclimated to his task.[94]

Were this approach consistently followed, however, it would probably conflict with attempts to keep average norm fulfillment at some "optimum" level. According to Aganbegian and Maier:

If output norms are reviewed not in accordance with the total increase in labor productivity of piece-rate workers, but only in accordance with the growth of labor productivity due to technical and organizational improvements in production, then from year to year the percentage fulfillment of output norms will grow, and with it the earnings of piece-rate workers.[95]

Several other implications of this "subjective-objective" approach are

93. Aganbegian and Maier, 1959, pp. 118–123.
94. "Povysheniia umelosti i intensivnosti," Aganbegian and Maier, 1959, p. 118.
95. Aganbegian and Maier, 1959, p. 123.

better discussed within the context of a general evaluation of Soviet norm setting.

Evaluation

Although most of the Soviet discussions of norm reviews, technically based norms, the norm-plan proposal, and the existence of an optimum fulfillment level are best understood from the vantage point of the adequacy of basic wage rates, the change in norm review policies deserves special attention. The idea of year-round reviews and of norms that are altered only because of changes in "objective" factors was, within the context of Soviet wage administration, clearly an innovation. For the Western economist, however, what is surprising is not the new policy, but rather the pre-1957 practice of massive yearly norm reviews.

Insofar as the Soviet worker's attitude toward the value of the piece can be identified with that of workers in other industrialized countries, the yearly norm review reveals the strength of the planning authorities and enterprise management. The massive review appears to have been simply an institutionalization of "rate cutting," or a reduction of the value of the piece. In no small part because of past experience with rate cutting, the majority of Western trade unions have opposed piece-rate wages.[96] At least in the contemporary American economy, it is usually stipulated that when earnings are to be determined by the piece, piece rates will not be changed unless there is some change in the job content of the work performed.[97] However, it should be noted that this rule is often subject to diverse interpretations.[98]

96. As stated by Dobb (1959, p. 59), "The worker naturally regards such cases [of rate cutting] as evidence that the chief intention of the system is to encourage the worker to increase his pace, and when this has been achieved to cheat him of increased earnings by scaling down the rate at which he is paid."

It may not be without significance that the mission from the International Labor Office reported that the change in Soviet norming policy was brought about "on the initiative of the All-Union Central Council of Trade Unions." ILO., 1960, p. 102.

97. It is usually stated that if there is no change in job content the rates will not be changed during the life of the agreement. However, even when the agreement comes to an end, the union will attempt to maintain the established rates for the next contract period. See Douty, 1963, p. 247; Brennan, 1963, pp. 54–56; *Wages,* 1964, p. 31; Rees, 1962, p. 141.

98. For several examples of the complexities involved in determining when a change in "job content" or a "change in operation" actually occurs, see Dunlop and Healy, 1955, pp. 417–432.

The contention that the yearly review engendered a considerable loss of output appears to be correct. Most, if not all, incentive systems involve some restrictions of output by workers.[99] Such restrictions must have been especially pronounced for piece-rate workers who knew that their norms were to be raised each February.

Initially, reports indicated that the year-round norm review was very successful. However, within a few years, it became clear that the "theoretical" foundation of norm reviews was being violated and that a general escalation of fulfillment levels was taking place despite the new policy. Several economists even expressed support for a return to the system of single massive yearly reviews. The hypothesis that norms should not be altered except in the event of changes in objective conditions seems to be universally accepted only in the realm of Soviet theory. As stated by a group of authors in 1968, while this principle is "completely valid, its unreserved application is far from always possible." [100] According to one carefully constructed estimate, of all norms reviewed, twenty percent undergo review only because they show a high fulfillment level; in other words, the norm is increased because subjective factors have improved the worker's ability to overfulfill the norm.[101]

The disruption of patterns of worker productivity that was so apparent with the single massive review [102] has continued since 1957 in a somewhat different form under the policy of continual review. The results of an impressively detailed study of workers' reactions to norm reviews were reported in 1968. Comparing piece-rate workers' output in the three months prior to the review with output during the succeeding months, the study found the following pattern. For workers whose fulfillment levels were under 120 percent, the establishment of a higher norm generally meant that output or pieces processed increased by an amount equal to or greater than the increase of the norm. For workers who had fulfillment levels in excess of 120 percent, the institution of a higher norm usually entailed a decrease in the

---

99. This is apparently in no way connected with the strength of, or even the existence of, a trade union. Mathewson (1931), whose study was limited to nonunion factories, clearly demonstrates the ingenuity of workers in "beating" the normer.
100. Prigarin et al., 1968, p. 97.
101. Ibid.
102. Aganbegian and Maier, 1959, pp. 106–123.

number of pieces processed, meaning that these workers were demoralized by the higher output norms.[103] Thus, in terms of worker productivity, the looser the norm, the more costly is the attempt to raise it.

The policy of continual norm review has not been able to solve what is usually regarded as the most important problem in this sphere of wage policy—the low and virtually stagnating percentage of output norms that can be considered technically based. Soviet economists urge that this percentage be increased, both for reasons of efficiency (because technically based norms uncover "hidden" sources of increased productivity) and to increase the role of basic wage rates in determining earnings. Aside from finding descriptions of inadequacies in norming work on the enterprise level, one seldom finds explanations as to why this problem has defied solution since the wage reform. Its resolution may have to await another general reform of basic wage structure, for under present administrative procedures there are no direct inducements for enterprise management to impose technically based norms. Concern is centered upon "more or less intelligently dividing the wage fund . . . and not permitting its overexpenditure." [104] While targets for the imposition of technically based norms and average levels of fulfillment continue to exist,[105] failure to meet them entails no penalties. On the other hand, there are excellent reasons for enterprise management to avoid any increase in technically based norms.

If for the moment we disregard premium payments,[106] it is clear that, for the enterprise, the higher the percentage of the wage fund that represents payments for norm overfulfillment, the greater the freedom it enjoys in wage determination. Basic wage rates are set by higher authorities, but output norms and corresponding piece-rate earnings may be manipulated. The control [107] over intraplant earnings differentiation that rests with the individual enterprise is largely dependent

103. Prigarin et al., 1968, pp. 103–107.
104. Gliantsev, 1962, pp. 84–85.
105. See chapter 7.
106. These payments are discussed below, pp. 69–71.
107. As used here, "control" is far from absolute; that is, the enterprise may be forced by labor market conditions to set easy norms and correspondingly high wages for some jobs. See chapter 6 for a discussion of jobs performed under difficult working conditions.
    Evidenced by the unanticipated differences in distribution of workers according to skill groups, the enterprise was, at least during the reform, not powerless in influencing basic wages.

upon the enterprise's ability to establish tight or loose output norms for different jobs. In light of some of the inadequacies of the structure of basic wages, such flexibility is supremely desirable for management. For example, were an enterprise to have all piece-rate workers paid according to technically based norms, it might find that no workers were willing to undertake "hot and heavy" jobs, because basic wages are not sufficiently differentiated according to working conditions.[108] Thus in this case there is no ground for the charge that the refusal to impose technically based norms shows that enterprise management and the local trade union committee "do not utilize their right to rationally organize labor." [109] For the enterprise, maintenance of high levels of norm fulfillment on some jobs may be the essence of rationality.

A further brake on the imposition of technically based norms may be an inadequate differentiation of basic rates between time-rate and piece-rate workers. Both Soviet and Western economists agree that, *ceteris paribus,* piece-rate payment results in a more intensive work pace, and that some earnings differential for workers paid according to this system is necessary. Virtually by definition, technically based norms mean piece-rate earnings that are close to basic wage rates. For a given skill group, the piece-rate worker's basic rate is not more than 15 percent above that received by a time-rate worker. Though it seems clear that the earnings differential between these two groups of workers was excessive prior to the reform,[110] some gap appears necessary. At no point in the Soviet literature has there been a discussion as to whether the differentiation incorporated into the structure of basic rates alone would be sufficient.[111] If not, it is possible that only through

108. This point is more fully developed in chapter 6. Karpenko (1965) notes that technically based norms are often opposed by enterprise administration because they "soon become a fixed element in the enterprise's wage fund." Also see Podolskii, 1962, pp. 93, 99.
109. *Trud,* August 31, 1965, p. 2.
110. See footnote 42, chapter 2.
111. Livernash (1957, p. 169), in discussing American age differentials, states that in spite of existing variations in the figure, a "simple but debatable assumption is that normal incentive effort is 30 percent [and] there has been some tendency, perhaps, to concentrate at about 30 percent." Brennan (1963, p. 368) finds the percentage to be "commonly" 20 to 25 percent. Dobb (1959, p. 79) reports that national wage agreements in the English boot and shoe industry do not directly set piece rates. The agreement merely stipulates "that piece-rates shall be fixed in each locality so as to give the average operative an earning capacity of 25 percent" over the basic rates established by the agreement. Finally, the International Labor Office's publication, *Wages* (1964, p. 30) holds the differential to be generally between 20 and 30 percent.

high fulfillment levels are enterprises able to induce workers to remain at jobs that are paid by the piece.

However, not all patterns of variation in levels of norm fulfillment are due to the enterprise's attempt to "correct" the centrally determined structure of basic wage rates. The ease with which "scientific" norms can be established on some jobs has, at least in one important case, aggravated rather than mitigated an inadequacy in the structure of basic wages. As will be discussed later in detail, at least until 1968 the basic wage of a machine operator was too low relative to that of a mechanic.[112] The situation was made worse by the higher levels of norm fulfillment enjoyed by the mechanic. This difference in average fulfillment levels was not due to any reaction on the part of the enterprise to labor market conditions that indicated the desirability of "loose" norms for the mechanic. It was merely that the operator, because of his steady work pace and relatively homogeneous tasks, could be easily normed according to centrally established and technically based norms. The diverse tasks of the mechanic were usually normed on an empirical-statistical basis with the resultant high level of fulfillment.[113]

A similar situation exists in establishing output norms for workers in "basic" and "auxiliary" shops within an enterprise. Those in the latter group have higher fulfillment levels and earnings, largely as a result of the difficulty of establishing technically based norms for their work.[114]

112. See chapter 8. It is possible that the relatively high preform norm fulfillment levels for skilled workers (chapter 5) were not unrelated to inadequacies in the technique of norm setting. It is far simpler to establish a "scientific" norm for the unskilled worker. The skilled worker, perfoming a more intricate task, has more opportunity to pace his work so that a loose norm is established. See *Wages*, 1964, p. 30.
113. "Kadry," 1965, p. 19; "Puti," 1962, pp. 40–41; Andreev and Belikanov, 1965. Aganbegian and Maier (1959, p. 119) note that the more "fractionalized" (*drobnost*) the work, the greater the difficulty in establishing central norms. Kotelkin (1966 p. 59) maintains that sociological studies have shown that the high percentage of technically based norms is responsible for the shortage of operators as well as for the fact that their turnover rate is 15 to 20 percent higher than the average.
114. Bugrov and Chubarov, 1964 (p. 15) reported that in the ferrous metals industry, average norm fulfillment (probably 1962 or 1963) in basic shops was 109.3 percent and in auxiliary shops, 112.3 percent. The corresponding percentages in light industry were 109.8 and 125.4. Also see Kapustin, 1964, pp. 44, 296; Bliakhman et al., 1965, pp. 120–122. According to the latter, "A major step forward in solving this

Bearing in mind the recent growth in the percentage of workers covered by the various premium systems,[115] it might seem that these payments could solve many of the problems caused by norm setting. Technically based norms might replace existing empirical-statistical norms without a corresponding decrease in earnings if the change were accompanied by premium payments for "fulfilling technically based output norms." [116] One study of the relationship between norm fulfillment levels and premium payments showed that in the nine branches investigated, workers paid according to piece plus premium had average fulfillment levels 10 to 15 percent lower than those workers paid straight piece rate.[117] Even under the norm-plan proposal, adequate differentials between time-rate and piece-rate workers could be maintained by premium payments for the latter group. However, such flexibility is not as great as it might appear.

It is reported that by the early 1960s, there was little room to maneuver within the existing premium system. The recipients of such payments had come to regard them as a regular and stable part of earnings. In the Leningrad economic region in 1964, 90 percent of all time-rate workers and 70 percent of the piece-rate workers "systematically received the maximum amounts of premiums established for them." [118] Furthermore, a certain percentage of existing premium payments was established not to create any specific incentives, but to help correct the unanticipated interindustry earnings differentials created by differences in standards for classification of workers by skill groups during the 1958–1960 wage reform.[119] This consideration seems to be the origin of some premium payments in the machine construction industry, where a mechanic-repairman receives a premium payment if he "strives" for "liquidation of idle machine time due to poor

---

problem was taken" during the reform by transferring a number of categories of auxiliary workers onto a time-rate system of wage payments. However, as noted by the authors, the Leningrad survey clearly indicated that a given worker was more likely to receive higher wages if he were employed in an auxiliary shop. On the problem of classification of workers as "basic" or "auxiliary," see Victorova, 1967, pp. 26-29.
115. See chart 2.1.
116. See table 1.3.
117. Prigarin et al., 1968, p. 87.
118. Bliakhman, 1964, p. 223; also see "I Vse-taki Tarif," 1965, p. 11. It is striking to note that writing four years earlier, Bliakhman (1960, p. 19) voiced exactly the same criticism of the prereform system of premium payments in the Leningrad area.
119. Petrochenko, 1962, p. 63.

quality of repair work" and does not "hold equipment for repairs longer than a given period of time." [120]

Furthermore, the amount of total premiums paid may not be sufficient to maintain earnings levels if technically based norms are imposed. For workers paid according to either of three piece-rate systems in 1961, payments for overfulfillment constituted about twice what they received in the form of premiums.[121]

In short, the Soviet economist desires and expects an expansion of time-rate systems of wage payments and an increase in the percentage of technically based norms for those workers paid according to piece rate. Given the structure and levels of basic wages established during the reform, these changes will probably entail a significant expansion of the percentage of the wage fund earmarked for premium payments.[122] In fact, in 1965, a decree was issued that permits enterprise management to utilize a portion of wages "economized" through norm review for premium payments to workers whose norms were tightened. These premiums can be paid during a three- to six-month period subsequent to the norm review. It is reported that because of the temporary nature of the premiums thus created, the measure has had little impact.[123] As will be later discussed,[124] the material incentive fund established under the "new system" of economic administration during the latter half of the 1960s could provide premium payments in a magnitude sufficient to maintain piece-rate workers' earnings despite the establishment of technically based norms. There is, however, an alternative solution.

In 1965, a discussion of the necessity of an adjustment in basic wage rates took place in the weekly *Ekonomicheskaia Gazeta*.[125] Letters to the editor indicated that the basic obstacle to imposing technically based norms was the gap between basic wages and earnings. The majority of letter writers joined several economists in maintaining that it would be desirable to return to the previous policy of a yearly norm

120. B. V. Vlasov, 1962, pp. 74–75.
121. For workers paid according to straight, progressive, or plus-premium rates, see chart 2.2. We do not have these data for later dates.
122. As shown in table 2.1, the expansion of this percentage has been a tendency since the reform.
123. Prigarin et al., 1968, p. 111.
124. See chapter 7.
125. "I Vse-Taki Tarif," 1965.

review, if such reviews were accompanied by the possibilty of an increase in basic wage rates.[126] Other sources have complained that the continual norm review creates constant tensions for both workers and management. A once-yearly massive norm review would, in their view, simplify norming work as well as create "much calmer" conditions within the enterprise during the remainder of the year.[127] All participants in the discussion agree that the quality of norming, measured by the percentage of technically based norms, improved only during the wage reform, when basic wages were changed. Since then, basic rates have not been systematically changed,[128] and the percentage of technically based norms has tended to remain constant or decline.

In 1959, A. G. Aganbegian and V. F. Maier published the first thoroughgoing analysis of the nature of the wage reform. Although they wrote in the midst of the reform, these economists noted that general reviews of basic wage rates, possibly once each five years, would be necessary if basic wage rates were not to lose their role as determinants of earnings.[129] Subsequent chapters will demonstrate that such a review is long overdue.

126. This is the position taken by Karpenko, 1965, and Kishkin, 1965.
127. Prigarin et al., 1968, p. 108.
128. Although the reduction of skill differentials caused by the 1968 increase in minimum wages (see chapter 5) must be considered significant, it cannot be regarded as a systematic reform of basic rates. Minor adjustments of basic wages have been frequent and are regularly reported in the Government Labor Committee's *Biulleten'*.
129. Aganbegian and Maier, 1959, p. 123. Brennan (1963, p. 363) states that in the West general reviews of job evaluation plans are usually conducted at regular intervals, ranging from once each year to every five years.

4

Skill Differentials I: Impact of the Reform

Standardization and Simplification

It is difficult to delineate or even discuss the "system" of skill differentials that existed during the decade or so preceding the 1958–1960 wage reform. It is clear that skilled workers received higher earnings than the unskilled, but this differentiation appears to have been neither planned nor controlled. Each of the various ministries had established skill scales [1] that directly related a worker's basic wage to his skill level. The relationship between skill and earnings, however, had become seriously weakened by fragmentation of administrative jurisdiction,[2] and, more important, by the erosion of basic wages as a determinant of earnings. These matters, as well as the increased role of basic wage rates brought by the reform, have been discussed.[3] We here turn to the success of the wage reform in standardizing, simplifying, and systematizing skill differentials.

Table 4.1 presents a summary comparison of the prereform and postreform skill scales *(setki)*. Though there is no reason to question the standardization brought about by the reform (as shown in the first two columns of the table), one must be extremely cautious about the data given in columns (3) and (5) concerning the prereform skill scales.

The actual significance of the prereform skill scales is unclear. For piece-rate workers, payments for norm overfulfillment rather than basic wages appear to have been the important determinant of skill differentials.[4] Moreover, actual differentiation of basic rates was not as great as the data presented in column (5) would indicate. The lower

---

1. As discussed in chapter 1, "skill scale" corresponds to the Russian *setka,* which might be defined as "the structure of relative intraindustry basic rates under given working conditions."
2. See chapter 1. Early in the reform, the Government Labor Committee dealt with the problem of administrative jurisdiction by adopting the principle that wages were to be set according to branch, being defined in terms of the nature of work performed. Thus, "machine construction workers, in whatever industry they work, are paid according to the basic rates and skill scales established for the machine construction industry, seamstresses according to the basic rates and skill scales established for the sewing industry, and so forth." This quotation is from an English translation of a book by Kostin (1960, p. 47) and is slightly altered to correspond to the terminology used throughout this study.
3. See chapter 2.
4. See chapter 2.

Table 4.1
Skill Differentiation of Basic Wages According to Prereform and Postreform Skill Scales in Selected Industries

Branch of Industry	Number of Skill Scales		Number of Skill Groups in Skill Scale(s)		Ratio of Basic Wage of Highest Skill Group to That of Lowest	
	Prereform	Postreform	Prereform	Postreform	Prereform (range)	Postreform
	(1)	(2)	(3)	(4)	(5)	(6)
Ferrous metals [a]	7	1	12	10	3.34–4.06	3.2
Nonferrous metals [a]	25	1	8	7	2.47–3.62	2.6
Mining iron ore	11	1	10	8	2.52–3.14	3.2
Mining nonferrous ores	54	1	10	7	2.53–3.68	2.85
Petroleum industry	65	1	8	6	2.46–3.09	2.0
Chemical industry [b]	4	2	7, 8, 10	7	2.01–3.24	2.3, 2.6
Machine construction	900 [c]	1	7,8	6	1.86–3.56	2.0
Cement	15	1	8	7	2.38–3.05	2.4
Glass	28	1	7, 8, 15	6	1.79–3.26	2.0
Building materials	18	1	7	6	1.79–3.26	2.0
Woodworking	12	1	7	6	2.07–2.72	2.0
Cellulose and paper	15	1	8	6	2.11–2.59	2.0
Food products	31	1	7	6	1.85–2.17	1.8
Fish (processing)	28	1	7	6	1.38–2.63	1.8
Meat and milk	192	1	7,8	6	1.25–2.20	1.8

Note: From Batkaev and Markov, 1964, p. 67.
[a] Basic production.
[b] Including mining of materials for chemical industry.
[c] Approximate.

skill groups of the skill scales were simple fictitious classifications in most cases. For example, in some subbranches of the machine construction industry, there was a formal eight-group skill scale with a ratio of extreme groups of 1:2.47. Since almost no workers were classified in the lowest two skill groups, the actual ratio was 1:1.96 (third to eighth skill group).[5]

Actually, the wage reform brought an even greater degree of standardization than indicated in table 4.1. A single skill scale, being an expression of only relative intraindustry basic rates according to skill levels, can be used in any number of industries that have different absolute levels of basic rates. One authority maintains that with the completion of the reform, there remained only six "typical" or "basic" skill scales in industry. The structure of these six, which replaced 1900 to 2000 prereform skill scales,[6] is presented in table 4.2.

Methodology of Skill Measurement

The nature and adequacy of the skill scales introduced during the reform are discussed in our next chapter. Here we shall concentrate upon the more narrow matter of the methodology of skill measurement, that is, the determination of a worker's skill-group classification within a given skill scale.

In implementing the wage reform, new wage handbooks [7] were drawn up for each branch of industry by the Government Labor Committee. These handbooks consisted of compilations of detailed job descriptions and skill-group classifications for all work performed in a given industry.[8] An interindustry wage handbook, based on the same methodology,[9] was also constructed.

Although this methodology attempts to determine skill level per se,

5. Batkaev and Markov, 1964, pp. 54–55; Kapustin, 1961a, p. 28. In the latter source, prereform and postreform distribution of workers according to skill group are compared for four branches of industry (pp. 42–44). See Galenson's (1960, p. 6) discussion of the importance of empty lower skill groups to the differentiation of basic wages. The continued existence of empty lower skill groups in the postreform period is discussed later in this chapter.
6. Volkov, 1957, p. 5; Kapustin, 1961a, p. 26; Maier, 1963, p. 149.
7. The existing ministerial handbooks were largely disregarded in wage administration. Had they been adhered to, far more workers would have been classified in the often empty lower skill groups.
8. The general structure of these handbooks is similar to that of the Unified Handbook discussed later in this chapter.
9. Kapustin and Mysev, 1961, p. 23; Batkaev and Markov, 1964, p. 76.

Table 4.2
Six Basic Skill Scales Introduced during the Wage Reform

When Instituted	Branch	Skill Group									
		I	II	III	IV	V	VI	VII	VIII	IX	X
1956–1958	Underground work in coal mine	1.0	1.13	1.50	1.67	2.5	3.13	3.33	3.75	—	—
1957	Basic ferrous metals production	1.0	1.13	1.28	1.45	1.65	1.87	2.13	2.43	2.78	3.20
1958	Underground and surface work in nonferrous ore mines	1.0	1.19	1.41	1.68	2.0	2.38	2.86	—	—	—
1958	Basic nonferrous metals production	1.0	1.17	1.37	1.61	1.88	2.21	2.60	—	—	—
1959	Machine construction and metal working	1.0	1.13	1.29	1.48	1.72	2.0	—	—	—	—
1959	Light and food industries	1.0	1.11	1.25	1.41	1.59	1.8	—	—	—	—

Note: Data are from Maier, 1963, pp. 147, 150. Maier maintained (p. 149) that these six scales are basic in the sense that all others, aside from minor and formal differences, correspond to one of the above. Kapustin (1961a, p. 26), possibly setting more store by these minor differences, stated that the total number of postreform skill scales was twelve.

explicitly excluding any consideration of working conditions, it is not unlike the "weighted point rating plans" widely used in the West.[10] Five "functions" (*funktsii*) are taken as the determinants of a worker's skill group. Each function varies over four levels of difficulty, and a range of points is assigned for each level. The total number of points determines the skill group in which a job is classified. The system as it was used for determining the skill groups in machine construction is presented in table 4.3.

Different point spreads are used in classifying workers according to scales other than that used in machine construction. Apparently, the skill scale is first established,[11] and the general principle followed is that the maximum number of points necessary for classifying a worker in a skill group higher than the first is equal to the relationship between the basic wage of that skill group and the basic wage of the first skill group.[12] Thus, in machine construction, the relationship of basic wages between the first and third skill groups is 1:1.29, and maximum number of points for classification in the third skill group is 129 points. In basic nonferrous metals, the corresponding figures are 1:1.37 and 137 points.[13]

Although this system was used for the massive reclassification of workers according to skill groups that took place during the reform, the official methodology was somewhat altered in 1961 or 1962. The weighted point system was criticized on two counts. First, the point

10. A survey by the AFL-CIO showed that of those companies having job evaluation plans, "about 80 percent of the larger firms and about 50 percent of the smaller ones used some form of the point system." "Job Evaluation Plans," 1957, p. 34.

Utilization of some sort of weighted point system is by no means new in Soviet wage administration. It was used in the wage reform of 1931–1932. However, the novelty of the present system is that it is intended to be applied in all branches of industry (Kapustin, 1964, p. 146). An example of the point system used in the 1930s may be found in M. M. Krivitskii's *Ekonomika Truda* (second edition, pp. 192 ff, as cited by Bergson, 1944, p. 156).

11. Though not perfectly clear, it seems that the point spreads for industries having six-group scales were standardized according to those of machine construction as presented in table 4.3, in spite of differences in basic wage rates within these scales. Sorochkin and Grishin, 1963 (pp. 37–38) calculate skill groups for "slaughter of large-horned cattle" according to the point spread for machine construction rather than that called for by the food industry skill scale (table 4.2). This is probably a reflection of the importance of the Unified Handbook (discussed later in this chapter) in such industries. The Handbook uses a skill scale identical to that of machine construction.

12. Except for the highest skill group, which is open-ended.

13. See table 4.2.

Table 4.3
A Weighted Point System for Determining Skill Groups

Function	Range of Points According to the Level of Complexity			
	Very Simple	Simple	Average	Complex
Calculations workers must make throughout the work process	0–0	4–4	5–7	10–13
Preparation of the work space	5–5	6–8	10–13	15–22
The work process itself	75–85	95–107	120–135	150–172
Additional skills necessary for servicing machinery	0–0	4–4	5–7	10–13
Responsibility [a]	0–0	5–5	7–10	15–20

Skill group	I	II	III	IV	V	VI
Approximate range of points	80–100	101–113	114–129	130–148	149–172	173–240

Note: The first part of the table is taken from Grigor'ev, 1959, p. 205. Approximate range of points determining the skill group is in accord with information presented by Maier, 1963, p. 69. A slightly different version of this system, as well as a detailed description of each function, can be found in Batkaev and Markov, 1964, pp. 76–84.
[a] Responsibility is usually referred to as a "factor" to be considered rather than as a "function" of the work process. It includes additional qualification necessary for protecting the safety of the worker himself, as well as that of others. However, generally dangerous conditions of work are not included, since they are to be compensated for by a higher basic rate rather than skill group. Kapustin and Mysev, 1961, p. 24.

spreads ascribed to the five functions were said to be subjectively established, there being no objective basis for establishing a weight for the nature of "the work process" at about twelve times the level of that for "servicing machinery." Second, the attempt to relate point spreads to relative basic wage rates was criticized as spurious accuracy.[14]

Maintaining the basic approach, the modification has dropped the explicit point-weighting system. In place of points, the five functions are rated according to four levels of difficulty, and the skill group is determined according to the constellation of ratings for the different functions. This nonweighted system is presented in table 4.4.

This modification eliminates explicit weighting, but is it clear that

14. Maier, 1963, pp. 67–72; Batkaev and Markov, 1964, pp. 90–91; Kapustin, 1964, pp. 146–147.

if it were consistently applied, functions *a, c,* and *e* would be more crucial in skill-group determination. They have a specific value, whereas the grades for functions *b* and *d* are of an "either/or" nature. Furthermore, if the explicit summation of points is dropped, there is no clear rule for establishing skill group when, let us say, a job is rated as (4) for function *b* and (1) for all other functions.[15] However, in spite of such problems, the system is workable, according to reports of a 1961 study done in the Kuibyshev economic region.[16]

The unweighted system's claim to superiority is based upon its greater universality in skill measurement throughout industry. In handbooks developed for occupations specific to particular industries, the weights ascribed to the different factors varied, and changes in the weights could be undertaken only with the agreement of a central organization.[17] The unweighted system is supposedly better suited for making interindustry comparison of the skill levels of workers performing jobs specific to different branches.[18] The system is exclusively for determination of skill levels according to a six-group skill scale, and such a single skill scale was to be made universal throughout industry.[19] A major step in this direction was taken in 1959 with the publication of a new kind of wage handbook.

The Unified Handbook
The general idea that the "quality of labor expended" should influence wage differentiation has long existed in the Soviet literature. However, the first significant industry-wide attempt to standardize pure skill differentials was completed, after more than two years of work,[20] in March 1959 with the compilation of the *Edinyi Tarifno-Kvalifikat-*

15. It is doubtful that such problems often arise in practice, because of what is known in Western job evaluation as the "halo effect," that is, "the tendency of one factor to influence the rating of other factors." Brennan, 1963, p. 444.
16. Two "independent" job evaluations were made according to this system for a number of jobs in twenty-six enterprises belonging to twelve branches of industry. Though the results were not identical, they were considered sufficiently consistent. See Kapustin and Mysev, 1961, pp. 24–26.
17. As of 1962, the Central Bureau of Industrial Labor Norms. Batkaev and Markov, 1964, p. 90. This Bureau was discussed in chapter 3.
18. Batkaev and Markov, 1964, pp. 83–91.
19. This projected policy is discussed in chapter 5.
20. The decision to develop the Unified Handbook was announced by the Government Committee on Questions of Labor and Wages in February 1957. Aganbegian and Maier, 1959, p. 137.

Table 4.4
A Nonweighted System for Determining Skill Groups by Level of Complexity

Functions	Skill Group					
	I	II	III	IV	V	VI
a. Calculations workers must make throughout the work process	(1)	(2)	(3)	(3)	(4)	(4)
b. Preparation of the work space	(1) or (2)	(1) or (2)	(2)	(2) or (3)	(3)	(3) or (4)
c. The working process itself	(1)	(2)	(3)	(3)	(4)	(4)
d. Additional skill necessary for servicing machinery	(1) or (2)	(1) or (2)	(2)	(3)	(3)	(3) or (4)
e. Responsibility	(1)	(2)	(3)	(3)	(4)	(4)

Levels of complexity: (1) very simple, (2) simple, (3) average, (4) complex.
Note: Soviet sources presenting this table are not consistent as to terminology identifying the five functions. However, the differences are not significant. See Mysev and Obolenskaia, 1963, p. 68; Kapustin and Mysev, 1961, p. 25; Maier, 1963, p. 70.

sionnyi Spravochnik Rabochikh Skvoznykh Professii (Unified Wage-Qualification Handbook for Workers of General Occupations, henceforth, Unified Handbook).[21]

A most important assumption, upon which the Unified Handbook is based, is that many different jobs, or occupations (literally, "professions"), may be evaluated in terms of the quality of the labor expended, without reference to the specific branch of industry or the conditions of work where the laborer is employed. Ideally, the skill level of work performed is measured in terms of the work process itself, independent of the actual item being produced.[22]

"General occupation" (*skvoznaia professiia*) refers to those jobs that are found in more than one branch of industry. For example, the operator of a sausage-stuffing machine holds a specific occupation in the meat industry,[23] but the job of keeping the machine greased and oiled (*smazchik*) is considered a general occupation.[24] The Unified Handbook determines the appropriate skill group for all work performed by the general occupations, which allegedly include "more than 60 percent" of all workers employed in Soviet industry.[25]

21. The Unified Handbook, with certain additions and changes, was made available to the public in 1961 in an edition of 25,000 copies. The Labor Institute of the Government Committee was responsible for the compilation of the Handbook, and was assisted by corresponding labor institutes in various branches of industry, the Central Committee of the Trade Unions, and labor specialists from more than 200 separate enterprises. *Edinyi*, 1961, p. 7. Though we are concerned only with industrial workers, two related developments should be noted. In 1960, a Unified Handbook for all construction work, patterned after that for industry, was developed. A description of that handbook may be found in Mitin, 1962, pp. 213–219. In April 1967, a type of unified handbook for all office workers or "employees" was published. which ranked skills according to five groups (for example, a clerk engaged in "routine operations" is classified in the first and a senior bookkeeper in the fifth). *Biulleten'*, no. 8, 1967, pp. 11–30; *Ek. Gaz.* no. 22, 1967, p. 18.

22. Smirnov, 1963, p. 55. With this approach, a significant unification of terminology was accomplished. For jobs covered by the Unified Handbook, 281 different occupations were recognized, replacing more than 2000 occupational designations contained in the separate handbooks. Kuchenev, 1959, p. 65.

23. Sorochkin and Grishin, 1963, pp. 57–58.

24. *Edinyi*, 1961, pp. 662–663.

25. Although it is often repeated in the Soviet literature and accepted by at least two Western scholars writing on Soviet wages (Fearn, 1963b, p. 22; Galenson, 1963, p. 311), I doubt that the general occupations covered by the Unified Handbook comprise "more than 60 percent" of all workers in Soviet industry. This skepticism is based on two points. First, there is the specific statement that general occupations are not to be graded according to the Unified Handbook in several branches of industry, including coal, metallurgy, and chemicals (Kukulevich, 1964, p. 19). These three branches alone (counting only ferrous metallurgy in the second branch and

The different jobs performed in each general occupation are graded according to a six-group skill scale, identical to that established for the machine construction industry.[26] Only six skill levels are recognized for all the work covered. A single occupation usually occupies approximately three consecutive skill groups, that is, one through three, two through four, and so on. A few occupations encompass all six, others only a single skill group.[27] The first part of the handbook is devoted to an alphabetical listing of the general occupations, the skill group(s) covered by each, and the pages on which their respective "skill-group characteristics" can be found. A set of characteristics exists for each skill-group level of a given occupation. The characteristics are divided into three parts: the nature of the work performed, the knowledge necessary to perform the work, and examples of work. If an occupation is graded in, say, the fourth and fifth skill groups, a worker in the fifth must also be able to fulfill the tasks required of workers in the fourth.[28]

At the time of the publication of the Unified Handbook, it was decided that a six-group skill scale was to be imposed in all industries that had not yet undergone the reform.[29] All workers in these branches

---

taking chemicals to include rubber and asbestos) constituted in 1963 better than 13 percent of all industrial workers (*Vest. Stat.*, no. 8, 1964, p. 87).

More significant are the data for percentages of workers classified according to skill scales having different numbers of skill groups. All workers classified according to the Unified Handbook would be in a six-group scale. Of all industrial workers in 1962, 72 percent were paid according to such skill scales. Therefore, if 60 percent of industrial workers were covered by the Unified Handbook, this would indicate that about 83 percent (.60/.72) of all workers classified according to these skill scales are to be considered in the general occupations.

In light of Soviet discussions of implementation of consistent standards in skill measurement, this percentage seems too high. It may be that the "more than 60 percent" refers to the fact that the Unified Handbook was to be utilized in branches of industry that employed more than 60 percent of industrial workers, and that standards established for general professions should be analogously applied to establishing the skill groups for work specific to a given industry. However, the situation is by no means clear.

26. See table 4.2.

27. For example, the occupation of freight elevator operator is classed in the first skill group, and no attempt is made to differentiate skill levels among elevator operators. *Edinyi*, 1961, p. 31.

28. *Edinyi*, 1961, pp. 8–9. The skill-group characteristics existing in previously published branch handbooks were significantly more complicated. Kuchenev, 1959, p. 67.

29. Including machine construction (see table 4.2). According to two Soviet economists, any immediate (1959 or 1960) transformation of all skill scales into six-group scales was considered unwise in industries that had already undergone wage reform. For example, in ferrous metals, the imposition of a standard six-group scale with a

Table 4.5

Relationship in a Typical Branch between Skill Levels and Skill-Group Classification According to Prereform Skill Scale and Skill Scale Introduced with the Wage Reform

	Skill Levels					
	Minimum					Maximum
Skill-group classification according to prereform eight-group skill scale	I–III	IV	V	VI	VII	VIII
Skill-group classification according to skill scale of Unified Handbook and postreform branch skill scale	I	II	III	IV	V	VI

Note: Constructed according to information given in *Edinyi*, 1961, pp. 15–16, and Kuchenev, 1959, pp. 64–65.

who were classified under the general occupations were divided into skill groups according to the Unified Handbook. New branch handbooks were developed for the classification of occupations existing in only one branch. These branch handbooks were supposedly consistent with the Unified Handbook and were constructed simply to "fill the gaps left" by it.[30] That is, if the sausage machine operator was classified in the third skill group by the branch handbook of the meat products industry, his skill level should have been equal to that of the oiler classified in the third skill group by the Unified Handbook.

Thus, from 1959 through the completion of the reform, all workers within a given branch were classified into six-group skill scales:[31] the general occupations according to the scale of the machine construc-

ratio of 2:1 would have meant a large overexpenditure of that industry's wage fund or a reduction in the basic wages of the more highly skilled workers. Either result was considered undesirable. Batkaev and Markov, 1964, p. 64.

30. Kuchenev, 1959, p. 68.

31. In absolute terms, the basic rates of general and specific occupations in a single industry need not be the same, even when they are classified in the same skill group. For example, a worker of an occupation specific to the milk industry, classified in the sixth skill group, received 1.8 times the basic rate of an unskilled (first skill group) worker in the milk industry. If classified in the sixth skill group, a worker of a general profession, even though employed in the milk industry, apparently received 2.0 times the basic rate of an unskilled worker in the machine construction industry. Feokistov, 1962, pp. 129, 132. Unfortunately, the Soviet literature is not at all clear about the actual money rates received by workers of general occupations employed in different branches of industry. The 1968 absolute basic rates in the various branches for the general occupation of "machine operator" (*stanochnik*) is presented in Goberman, 1970, pp. 137–138. Also see footnote 11.

tion industry, and those occupations specific to the given industry according to the new branch scales. Reclassification of workers according to the new skill scales was considerably facilitated by the fact that the first few skill groups of the older scales were virtually empty. Thus, as shown in table 4.5, groups one through three of the older skill scales were subsumed under the first skill group of the newly established six-group scales.

As indicated in the table, the skill-group designation of most workers was lowered when the six-group scale was introduced. Possibly to avoid any widespread decrease in earnings, a special dispensation was made for workers of the general occupations. Any worker of a general occupation who was to have his classification reduced by more than two skill groups could be classified one skill group higher than indicated by the Unified Handbook. This was to be considered an "exception," and classification was to be reduced within a one-year period.[32]

When we turn to those several branches of "heavy" industry where skill scales of more than six groups were established during the early period of the wage reform, the relationship between these branch skill scales and that of the Unified Handbook is most unclear. For example, skill groups six through eight of the eight-group scale in ore mining [33] may, in terms of skill level, correspond to the sixth, or a lower, skill group of the Unified Handbook's scale.[34] However, during the 1960s, the significance of the relationship among such skill scales was rapidly disappearing for reasons that must now be considered.

Prevalence of the Six-Group Skill Scale

By the early 1960s, it became clear that the scales composed of more than six skill groups established in the pre-1959 phase of the wage reform were being transformed into six-group skill scales by upgrading workers out of the lower skill groups. Thus, these scales became more akin to that used in machine construction and for the general occupations.

If we accept a somewhat arbitrary definition of an "effective" skill

32. Urzhinskii, 1962, p. 137; *Edinyi*, 1961, pp. 3–4. No similar dispensation has been reported for workers of the specific occupations. In any event, it seems that reclassification of the worker's skill group was seldom accompanied by a reduction in his earnings. See Galenson, 1963, pp. 314–315.
33. See tables 4.1 and 4.2.
34. *Edinyi*, 1961, pp. 15–16.

group as one that contains more than 2.5 percent of the workers classified according to the skill scale, it becomes clear that, both in terms of the number of skill groups and the ratio of basic wages for workers in the lowest and highest skill groups, Soviet intraindustry skill differentials became considerably more standardized than table 2.3 would indicate. For example, by 1962 the skill scale in nonferrous metals was composed of six functioning skill groups (two through seven) and the basic wage ratio of the lowest to the highest skill group had been reduced from 1:2.6 to 1:2.2.[35]

After the completion of the wage reform, three sets of data concerning the distribution of workers by skill group were published. The first set presented the percentage distribution of workers by skill group within scales consisting of various numbers of skill groups for all industry and for thirty separate branches of industry as of March 31, 1961.[36] No breakdown of the total percentages of workers paid according to each of these various skill scales was then given. Subsequently, similar data, referring to August 1, 1962,[37] and August 2, 1965,[38] were published. These two sets of data were more complete, giving the total percentages of workers paid according to these various types of skill scales within each of the thirty branches and for all industry. The all-industry portion of these data is presented below in table 4.6.

Although the data for 1961 do not give the percentages of workers paid according to scales composed of varying numbers of skill groups, they do indicate the importance of the six-group skill scale at that time. It was the only scale in use in approximately half of the thirty branches of industry presented. In all branches except two,[39] a six-group scale was at least partially in use. In those branches where a scale of more than six skill groups was used, a small percentage of the workers fell into skill groups other than the upper six. Only 2.3 percent of workers paid according to an eight-group scale in ferrous metals were classified in the first two skill groups. Only 1.9 percent of all workers

---

35. See table 4.2, and *Vest. Stat.*, no. 6, 1964, p. 90.
36. *Vest. Stat.*, no. 6, 1962, pp. 90–93.
37. Ibid.
38. Ibid., no. 3, 1966, pp. 92–94; *Trud v SSSR*, 1968, pp. 150–151.
39. The exceptions are coal and wood chemicals. The coal industry is a special case. It alone used what one author calls "simply a system of basic rates," in which there was a most unusual relationship among skill groups. Basic wage rates increased 50 percent between the fourth and fifth, but only 6 percent between the sixth and seventh. See Kapustin, 1964, pp. 219–220, and Peskin, 1959, pp. 7–14.

paid according to a seven-group scale fell in the first skill group, and the corresponding figure for the eight-group scale was 5.4 percent in the first two skill groups.[40] In contrast, 14.1 percent of workers classified according to the six-group scale fell into the first skill group.

The 1962 data directly quantify the scope of the six-group skill scale. Of all workers paid according to any skill scale,[41] 89 percent had their basic wages determined according to a six-group scale. The importance of this type of scale becomes even more impressive by a somewhat different measure. Skill scales with seven, eight, or ten skill groups may be regarded as having six effective skill groups if the first group or groups include a negligible share of the total number of workers. Thus for 1962 the percentage of all industrial workers paid according to the six highest groups [42] of the various skill scales is somewhat greater than 99 percent.[43] More recent data show that the situation was little changed between 1962 and 1965.

We will discuss later both the nature and rationale of the Soviet attempt to establish a single skill scale for determining skill differentials throughout industry. Here we should note that if standardization of the number of skill groups is an essential prerequisite of a consistent system of intraindustry skill differentiation of basic wages, we may say that by the mid-1960s the Soviets had, for the most part, fulfilled this prerequisite. However, this is only one aspect of the problem of standardized skill differentials.

Ideally, for any two branches of industry having a six group scale distribution of workers by skill group should be made according to differences in the quality, or skill level, of labor expended in each branch. Comparison of average skill groups among branches should

40. Only in ferrous metals and machine construction was a ten-group skill scale in partial use. By August 1962 it had been eliminated in the latter branch, and the data for 1965 show that in ferrous metals it had virtually been transformed into a six-group scale with only 2 percent of workers classified in the lowest three skill groups. *Vest. Stat.*, no. 8, 1964, p. 90, and no. 3, 1966, p. 92.
41. See note to table 4.6 concerning those 9 percent who were not paid according to any skill scale.
42. That is, 100 percent of those covered by the six-group skill scale, 98.2 percent of those covered by the seven-group scale, and so on.
43. It might be mentioned that for a given industry, skill scales comprised of more than six skill groups may be significant. For example, in ferrous metals production (excluding ore mining), about 89 percent of all workers were paid according to an eight- or ten-group skill scale in 1962. However, even in this industry, about 95 percent of all workers fall into the six higher skill groups of the various skill scales. *Vest. Stat.*, no. 6, 1964, p. 90.

Table 4.6
Distribution of All Industrial Workers According to Skill Group

Number of Skill Groups in a Skill Scale	Percentage of Industrial Workers Paid According to Each Type of Skill Scale	I	II	III	IV	V	VI	VII	VIII	IX	X
As of March 31, 1961											
6	•	14.1	23.3	29.3	19.6	10.4	**3.3**				
7	•	1.9	8.9	22.1	29.1	23.3	**10.7**	**4.0**			
8	•	0.9	4.5	12.9	22.4	24.9	**23.3**	**8.5**	2.6		
10	•	0.4	2.3	6.1	13.2	24.5	**21.3**	**15.2**	9.5	6.0	1.5
no scale [a]	•	—	—	—	—	—	—	—	—	—	—
As of August 1, 1962											
6	72	14.3	23.4	29.1	19.7	10.3	3.2				
7	7	1.8	9.3	21.7	29.7	24.9	10.4	2.2			
8	10	0.5	4.5	11.2	22.9	24.4	26.0	8.2	2.3		
10	2	0.2	1.2	4.3	11.8	24.2	23.0	17.5	10.8	4.9	1.3
no scale	9	—	—	—	—	—	—	—	—	—	—
As of August 2, 1965											
6	72	12.4	22.4	29.5	20.8	11.4	3.5				
7	11	2.0	12.4	16.8	28.5	29.3	9.0	2.0			
8	6	0.7	5.3	12.4	19.2	22.1	22.8	13.5	4.0		
10	1	0.1	1.4	3.4	9.7	23.5	24.7	18.9	11.5	5.4	1.4
no scale	10	—	—	—	—	—	—	—	—	—	—

Note: Data from *Vest. Stat.*, no. 6, 1962, pp. 90–93; *Vest. Stat.*, no. 6, 1964, pp. 90–93; *Vest. Stat.*, no. 3, 1966, pp. 92–94.
* Not available.
a This includes workers (but not "office workers" or "junior service personnel") who are paid "salaries" determined on a monthly basis (*mesiachnye oklady*). See footnote 72, chapter 1. Also included in this 9 percent are workers paid according to a "group rate" (*gruppaia stavka*). Karinskii, 1963, pp. 78–79; *Raschety*, 1963, pp. 20–21.

provide a meaningful summary comparison of the relative skill levels demanded by the tasks to be performed.[44] After the completion of the wage reform, a significant gap remained between this ideal and reality.

Interindustry Differences in Skill Measurement

After the publication of the Unified Handbook, the Soviet government hoped to proceed with the reform on the basis of consistent standards for determining workers' skill groups in those branches that had not yet undergone the reform. This the Unified Handbook was not able to achieve.

The Unified Handbook is based on jobs performed in the machine construction industry, and is in fact the basic handbook for that branch.[45] Because of both the large number of workers employed in that industry [46] and its intended role, the handbook was constructed with considerable care. Descriptions of occupations and the characteristics for classification according to skill group are highly detailed.

The branch handbooks for classification of occupations specific to other industries were constructed with considerably less care. The characteristics for classification by skill group were less precise and detailed, permitting greater discretion on the enterprise level in the establishment of a worker's skill group. This discretion was generally exercised by placing the worker in the highest possible skill group. Thus, if two workers had the "same" skill level, and one was classified according to the Unified Handbook and the other according to a branch handbook, then the skill-group designation of the latter worker was likely to be higher than that of the former.[47] In part, the problem was that the definition of "unskilled" differed among the branches. Unskilled labor (first skill group) in machine construction in fact turned out to demand a relatively higher level of qualification than in branches such as peat mining, building materials, and meat processing.[48]

Moreover, occupations covered by the Unified Handbook were often renamed, and less demanding skill-group standards were substituted.[49]

44. Aganbegian and Maier, 1959, pp. 216–217.
45. Maier, 1963, p. 192.
46. See footnote 61, chapter 1.
47. Gaile, 1962, p. 46; Maier, 1963, pp. 192–193.
48. Dubovoi, 1967, pp. 57–58.
49. Gaile, 1962, p. 46; Kapustin, 1964, pp. 87–89. In reaction to this development, the

Table 4.7
Calculated Skill Levels and Actual Average Skill Groups in Selected Branches
of Industry

Branch of Industry	Calculated Average Skill Level	Average Actual Skill Group (March 1961)
Milk products	100	2.9
Footwear	115	3.6
Machine construction	120	2.6
Fish products	106	2.9

Note: The calculated skill level is presented for six industries in Maier and Markov, 1958, p. 50. Of these six, the coke-chemical industry and the coal industry are not included in the table. For the former, there are no average skill-group data, and skill groups in the coal industry should not be used in such comparisons. See footnote 39, this chapter. The average skill-group data are from *Vest. Stat.*, no. 6, 1962, pp. 90–93. While there is some difference in nomenclature of the branches in these sources, it is minor. There is approximately a three-year gap between the calculated (published in February 1958) and the actual figures in the table, but it is doubtful that average branch skill levels changed significantly.

In some industries, conditions of work were used as a factor in the determination of skill group.[50] As a result, it became clear as early as 1960 that the average skill group in an industry with a six-group skill scale was no measure of the actual qualifications of that branch's labor force.

At the end of March 1961, the average skill group in light industry was 3.5; in the food industry, 3.0; and in machine construction, 2.6. Data for 1962 and 1965 show no substantial change in these relationships.[51] However, Soviet economists agree that if skill is to be measured according to a consistent methodology, the workers in machine construction must be considered better qualified.[52]

The degree to which the distribution of workers by skill group

Government Labor Committee amended the Unified Handbook to raise the skill groups of some workers in the general occupations. Smirnov, 1963, p. 58.
50. Smirnov, 1963, p. 58; Dubovoi, 1967, p. 58.
51. In 1962, the percentage of workers paid according to such a skill scale was 91 percent in light industry, 86 percent in the food industry, and 89 percent in machine construction. By 1965 the average skill groups in machine construction and the food industry had increased to 2.7 and 3.1 respectively, while in light industry the average skill group had decreased to 3.4. *Vest. Stat.*, no. 6, 1962, pp. 90–93; *Vest. Stat.*, no. 6, 1964, pp. 90–93; *Vest. Stat.*, no. 3, 1966, pp. 92–94.
52. The same problem was discussed in terms of corresponding data for the Republic of Latvia in Gaile, 1962, pp. 45–46. It should be noted that this situation somewhat improved during the five-year period 1965–1969 when the average skill-group classification for all industrial workers increased from 3.1 to 3.2 while the average skill group in machine construction moved from 2.7 to 3.0. Batkaev, 1971, p. 25.

among industries failed to correspond to calculated differences in skill levels may be seen by comparing actual skill groups as of 1961 to a set of Soviet calculations of average skill made by the Labor Institute in 1957.[53] The relative skill levels for several industries were calculated, taking the milk products industry as 100. In table 4.7, the estimated relative differences in skill are compared with the actual average skill groups.

This state of affairs is clearly considered unsatisfactory. In terms of the drive for standardization, the virtual universality of a six-group skill scale is a major accomplishment, but the fact that skill-group standards differ among industries is considered a significant defect of the wage system.[54] By the middle of the 1960s new policies had been developed for further standardization of skill differentials.

The Ongoing Reform of Skill Differentials

According to the Soviet literature, the degree of standardization of skill differentials brought about by the reform was not sufficient. The explicit goal of postreform policy was further standardization through the establishment of a single skill scale for all branches of industry. Other than the fact that this scale was to be composed of six skill groups with a ratio between the highest and lowest of 1:2 or 1:1.8, its exact structure was not clear.[55] Soviet economists have been very explicit as to how this single skill scale is to be imposed throughout industry, and proposed methodology is of considerable interest.

In view of the generally recognized lack of consistency in measuring skills among industries, a new attempt to standardize interindustrial skill-group determination was initiated while the reform was still in

53. Reportedly, the methodology utilized in making these calculations, because of "a series of circumstances," was not consistently applied during the wage reform. Smirnov, 1963, p. 56.

54. Although this fact is not mentioned by the Soviet economists, the different standards for skill-group classification may not be unrelated to the fact that the looser standards were applied in industries that had relatively low wage rates for all skill groups, and, correspondingly, a possible shortage of personnel. Melvin Reder (1955) developed the hypothesis that employers' hiring standards for skilled labor tend to fall when labor is scarce. Also see Robertson, 1960, p. 175.

55. The "single skill scale" was often identified with the skill scale of the general occupations, that is, the one used in machine construction (table 1.2). Several sources proposed a *setka* with a maximum differential of 1:1.8 in place of 1:2 (Kapustin, 1961b, p. 78; Batkaev and Markov, 1964, pp. 60–61). In view of the decrease in skill differentials accompanying the 1968 increase of minimum wages (see chapter 5), 1:1.8 appears to be the most likely ratio of extreme skill groups.

progress. In 1959–1961, the Labor Institute undertook to measure the complexity of labor expended in forty branches of industry located in seven different economic regions.[56]

The basic innovation consisted of grouping occupations specific to a given branch into six theoretical or potential skill groups rather than the six actual functioning skill groups established during the reform. Here, the assumption was that the Unified Handbook covered the total spectrum of skill levels in the economy, while jobs specific to a given branch might not encompass the whole range of skills. Two or three of the most highly skilled occupations specific to each industry were investigated. In order to make interindustrial comparisons, jobs performed by a *slesar'*[57] (henceforth translated as "mechanic") were used to provide consistency in determination of skill levels. Slightly modifying John T. Dunlop's terminology, we may say that the mechanic's job thus served as a "key" skill level, and in each industry a "cluster" of skill levels was determined by the work of the mechanic.[58]

The mechanic's work, rated according to an existing branch handbook, was rerated by an "expert commission" and compared to an "identical" job in the machine construction industry. Then the "branch" mechanic was placed in the skill group that he would have occupied had he been classified in machine construction. Other work specific to the given branch was then rated according to the non-

56. Mysev and Obolenskaia, 1963, pp. 67–72. The most complete discussion of both the scope of this work and its implications for the structure of Soviet skill differentials can be found in Kapustin, 1964, pp. 191–214.

57. The Russian term *slesar'* is very difficult to define, as it encompasses "fitters" and "machinists." The work involves the repair of machinery and the fabrication and installation of specific machine parts. The work performed is considered basically "hand labor" (*ruchnye raboty*). Bakhrakh, 1962b, p. 758; Bliakhman et al., 1965, p. 67; *Entsiklopedicheskii Slovar'*, 1954. vol. 3. p. 234.

In Yanowitch's (1960, pp. 168–171) attempt to measure wage differentials between skilled and unskilled workers, *slesari* are taken to be representative of the former group. It is possible that Yanowitch underestimated this differential in choosing the *slesar'* as representative of skilled workers. In the Unified Handbook, *slesari* are divided into ten separate occupations. Of these ten, the work performed by five occupations covers the whole skill spectrum classified in skill groups one through six. Of the remaining five, two are classified in the four lowest skill groups, and the remaining three perform jobs classified in skill groups one through five, two through six. *Edinyi*, 1961, pp. 40–41, 354–421.

58. Dunlop, 1957. As stressed by Livernash (1957, p. 153), identification of "key" jobs is probably the most difficult step in establishing a job evaluation system.

weighted evaluation method already described [59] and placed in a higher or lower skill group with reference to the branch mechanic, who thus functioned as a transitional step between the machine construction industry and other branches of the economy.[60]

Machine construction appears to be the logical choice as a reference point in the attempt to establish a consistent system of skill determination throughout industry. The heterogeneity of work performed there is indicated by the comparatively large number of piece-rate output norms. During 1964 in the Legingrad region, enterprises producing heavy machinery had about sixty separate output norms per employed worker; enterprises in the chemical and textile industries had a corresponding figure of five or six.[61] Since the machine construction industry has jobs covering the entire skill spectrum, the areas of the skill spectrum and corresponding skill groups occupied by workers in each branch of industry can be determined by this method. Of the forty branches investigated, the coke-chemical industry occupies only the first three skill groups, while three branches cover skill groups one through four. Twenty-three branches are covered by groups one through five, and in only thirteen branches are there workers in the entire skill spectrum, one through six. "In the majority of branches, the evaluations of expert commissions in all economic regions (sovnarkhozi) were in agreement" on these calculations. There was only a small variation for some branches, which is taken to indicate that the results are "more or less objective."[62]

In order to achieve a single six-group skill scale for all industrial workers, work was begun on new types of handbooks in 1964.[63] There

---

59. See table 4.4.
60. Mysev and Obolenskaia, 1963, pp. 67–72; Kapustin, 1964, pp. 191–198.
61. Kotelkin, 1966, p. 71.
62. Mysev and Obolenskaia, 1963, pp. 67–72. It is interesting to note that the first five skill groups are sufficient for work done in ferrous metals, one of the few industries in which most workers were classified according to eight- and ten-group skill scales in 1965. See *Vest. Stat.*, no. 3, 1966, p. 92.
Similar calculations were made at the beginning of 1961 for twelve branches of industry in the Kuibyshev economic region. Here the results of evaluations at the enterprise are compared with those of an expert commission. Although these results also seem objective, the enterprise more often placed a worker in a higher skill group than did the expert commission. Kapustin and Mysev, 1961, pp. 26–27.
63. Kaminer, 1964, pp. 50–51.

were to be fewer of them,[64] and, rather than covering a single industry, they were to deal with "groups" of industries; that is, there would be a handbook for all mining work, a handbook for the food industries, and so forth. To supplement the Unified Handbook, which would remain in operation, separate handbooks for each of twenty-eight "groups of production" were to be published.[65]

A consistent approach to skill-group designation was to be facilitated by the novel structure of these new handbooks. All occupations not covered by the Unified Handbook were to be designated as "general to a group," [66] or as "specific" to one product within a group. For example, in the food industries, 670 occupations are recognized. Of these, 353 are general occupations appearing in several of the subgroups, and 317 are specific to such subgroups as bread baking, meat and poultry, canning, and so on. The corresponding figures for textiles are 200 occupations general to the group and 119 specific to subgroups within the industry. An important technique in the construction of the handbooks was the newly developed "unified enumeration" of all occupations, which reduced the 18,000 occupations listed in the branch handbooks developed during the reform to around 4,000.[67] Taken together, these new handbooks are expected to constitute a single, consistent wage handbook "composed of sections, each of which encompasses one or another [branch of] production or type of work." [68]

By the beginning of 1969, this new set of handbooks, designated as *Edinyi Tarifno-Kvalifikatsionnyi Spravochnik Rabot i Professii Rabochikh Narodnogo Khoziaistva* (Single Wage Handbook for Work and Occupation in the National Economy), was ready for publication, and a handful of copies had been circulated.[69] According to official instructions, its use in determining skill-group classification is to be "mandatory for all enterprises." [70] This all-industry approach to skill-

---

64. It was reported that in the period 1956–61 the Government Labor Committee authorized 235 new handbooks. Smirnov, 1963, p. 51.
65. Ibid., p. 54. This general approach had been suggested earlier by Kapustin (1961b, p. 58).
66. Not to be confused with the "general professions" of the Unified Handbook.
67. Smirnov, 1963, pp. 54–56; Kaminer, 1964, pp. 51–55.
68. Smirnov, 1963, p. 54.
69. Khmirov, 1970.
70. *Biulleten'*, no. 1, 1969, pp. 15–22; Medvedev, 1967.

group classification is based upon a single six-group skill scale and will be implemented during the years 1972–1974.[71] In other words, the goal is to establish within each branch of industry the same structure of relative basic wage rates according to workers' skill levels. The feasibility and economic rationality of this goal as well as the modifications of skill differentials accomplished in 1968 provide the focus of our next chapter.

71. Khmirov, 1970, and Kosygin, 1971, p. 12.

5

Skill Differentials II: Economics of Skill Differentials

Differentiation of Earnings and Basic Rates

The preceding discussion of Soviet policy concerning skill differentials raises several issues. Here, three that seem of special interest to the economist are discussed: the adequacy of the differentials, the economics of attempting to impose a single skill scale throughout industry, and the possibility of utilizing some measure (s) of "training time" to determine a worker's skill level. We also discuss the further changes of skill differentials accomplished in 1968 in terms of these issues. However, we must first deal with a problem originally raised in 1960 by the Western economist Walter Galenson.[1]

Galenson recognized a complex paradox in Soviet reports concerning the wage reform of 1958–1960. On the one hand, Soviet economists consistently stated that the wage reform reduced skill differentials and buttressed their contention by comparing the ratio between basic wages of workers in the highest and lowest skill groups in prereform and postreform skill scales. The ratio in the postreform scales, as was shown in table 4.1,[2] is consistently lower. These same sources also state that virtually no workers were classified in the lower skill groups of the prereform scales. Galenson noted that if the empty skill groups of the prereform scales are excluded, then the postreform scales in fact show constant or possibly increased differentiation of basic wages according to skill levels. We here attempt to show that the "paradox" can be resolved. Even though differentiation of basic rates according to skill levels may well have increased with the wage reform, differentiation of earnings according to skill levels, including payments for norm overfulfillment, decreased.

All available data concerning levels of norm fulfillment in the period prior to the wage reform indicate that average levels of norm fulfillment were positively correlated to classifications by skill group. Thus, at least for those three-fourths of industrial workers then paid according to some form of the piece-rate system, earnings differentiation according to skill level was considerably greater than differentiation of basic wage rates. This relationship can be seen from the data in

1. Galenson, 1960, p. 6, and 1963, p. 307.
2. See columns (5) and (6) of table 4.1.

Table 5.1
Preform Average Relative Basic Wage Rates, Levels of Norm Fulfillment, and
Relative Estimated Piece-Rate Earnings in Twenty-Five Machine Construction
Enterprises

| | Skill Group (no workers classified in first skill group) | | | | | | |
	II	III	IV	V	VI	VII	VIII
1. Relative basic wages skill group II = 100	100	114	130	148	169	193	220
2. Average levels of norm fulfillment	137	147	167	184	226	212	206
3. (1) × (2)	137	168	217	272	382	409	453
4. Relative piece-rate earnings, skill group II = 100	100	123	158	199	279	299	330

Note: Table 5.1 is based upon information provided in Kapustin, 1957, pp. 33–35.
Row (2) is taken directly from the article. It should be noted, however, that Kapustin
performed considerable aggregation in presenting this data. As of 1956, a large number of skill scales existed in the machine construction industry (see table 4.1), and the
author is not explicit as to how he reclassified the workers in these twenty-five plants
into the eight-group skill scale shown here. Row (1) was constructed on the basis of
Kapustin's statement that the "average" scale in these plants had a ratio for skill
groups 1 to 8 of 1:2.6, and a ratio for skill groups 2 to 8 of 1:2.2. Relative basic wage
rates were determined by "fitting" a skill scale having a differential of 14 percent
between skill groups to this information. If a different differential were used, say
13 percent between the lower skill groups and 15 percent in the upper, the results
would not differ significantly. See Aganbegian and Maier, 1959, pp. 129–130 for a
discussion of construction of skill scales.

table 5.1, although there were some methodological problems involved
in their derivation.

The ratio of basic wage rates for piece-rate workers in the second
and eighth skill groups is 1:2.2, while their piece-rate earnings stand
at a ratio of 1:3.3. Rows 3 and 4 of the table presuppose straight
piece rate, and any adjustment for progressive payments should be
expected to make the divergence of these ratios even greater. The
relationships shown in the table reportedly represented conditions in
Soviet industry in 1956.[3]

One source maintained that, on the eve of the wage reform, in the
"majority of branches of industry" it had been "characteristic" for
piece-rate norms to be less tight (easier to overfulfill) for workers in

3. For some reason, Soviet economists do not cite this relationship to support their
argument that the reform brought a decrease in differentiation of earnings by skill.

higher skill groups.[4] Independent data showing differences between the earnings of time-rate and piece-rate workers in given skill groups indicated that the differential in favor of the piece-rate worker was greater in the higher skill groups, or that there was a positive relationship between levels of norm overfulfillment and skill group. This relationship held for both normal and hot and heavy working conditions.[5]

During 1956–1957, a number of experimental attempts to reconstruct wages were undertaken. The skill scales used in these experiments were composed of seven or eight skill groups. Ratios of basic rates between the lowest and highest skill group ranged from 1:2.1 to 1:3.2.[6] It is plausible to assume that these scales, while raising the share of basic wages as a component of earnings,[7] did little to modify existing earnings differentials among workers of various qualifications. On the other hand, the basic scale introduced during the reform—six skill groups with a 1:2 ratio—appears to have reduced skill differentials.

However, even after the reform, piece-rate earnings continued to be more differentiated than basic rates.[8] A positive relationship between skill level and norm fulfillment was found "in all plants where a study of this question had taken place." [9] The results of one sample survey conducted by the Central Statistical Administration are presented in table 5.2. The data reportedly correspond fully to a similar survey made by the Government Committee in 1964.[10]

Comparisons of tables 5.1 and 5.2 must be made with considerable

4. Bliakhman, 1964, p. 144. Earlier, the same author (1960, pp. 21–22) reported than in a Leningrad machine construction enterprise in 1955, the "difference in earnings between categories of workers was excessively high" because of payments for norm overfulfillment. The relationship of earnings for turners (*tokari*) of the fourth and seventh skill groups was 1:4; for mechanics (*slesari*), relative earnings for workers in the third and sixth groups stood at 1:2. According to the established skill scales, basic wages were differentiated at levels of 1:1.65 or less. For discussion of these occupations, see footnote 57, chapter 4; footnote 50, chapter 6.
5. Batkaev and Markov, 1964, pp. 204–205, 196–197.
6. See Fearn, 1963b, pp. 14–15.
7. This increase had been called for by the Twentieth Party Congress in early 1956. See Schwartz, 1965, pp. 78–79.
8. However, it should be noted that Bliakhman (1964, p. 144) maintained that the reform eliminated the difference between differentiation of basic wages and differentiation of earnings. Were Bliakhman correct (the argument in our text indicates that he is not), then the hypothesis that skill differentials were reduced during the reform would have even greater strength.
9. Kapustin, 1964, pp. 113–114. McAuley's (1969, p. 92) on-the-spot experience at three Leningrad enterprises also supports this conclusion.
10. Prigarin et al., 1968, pp. 72–73.

Table 5.2
Postreform Relative Basic Wage Rates, Levels of Norm Fulfillment, and Relative
Estimated Piece-Rate Earnings, 1963 Sample Survey of Machine Construction
Enterprises

	Skill Group					
	I	II	III	IV	V	VI
1. Relative basic wages, skill group I = 100	100	113	129	148	172	200
2. Average levels of norm fulfillment	130	137.2	144.5	148.7	150.0	150.3
3. (1) × (2)	130	155	186	220	258	301
4. Relative piece-rate earnings, I = 100	100	119	143	169	198	232

Note: The first row of the table is the skill scale for the machine construction industry as in table 1.2. The second row is from Prigarin et al., 1968, p. 73.

caution. Most important, we have neither the percentage of workers in
each skill group nor information concerning the distribution of premiums. However, other caveats to such a comparison reinforce what
is apparent: while relative basic rates may have changed little, the
wage reform brought about a reduction in the differentiation of earnings according to skill.

In both tables, calculated piece-rate earnings exclude additional payments for progressive piece rate. Though widespread in the earlier
period, by 1963 this system of wage payments had become of negligible
significance. Had these payments been included, inequality in table 5.1
would probably increase, whereas that in table 5.2 would remain essentially constant.

Between the two periods, the role of premium payments for piece-
rate workers increased dramatically. For the most part, such payments
are based upon the performance of groups of workers of various skill
groups and are calculated as a percentage of a worker's piece-rate earnings. Inclusion of such payments probably would have little effect upon
our measures of inequality.

Speculation on the pattern of inequality that would be shown in
our tables if time-rate workers were included tends further to support
the hypothesis of decreased skill differentials. For these workers, basic
wages, possibly increased by a given percentage for premium payments,

are the basic determinant of earnings. Therefore, their inclusion would have had a dampening effect on differentials in both tables. In the postreform period, because of the considerable increase in the percentage of workers paid according to some form of time rate, this dampening would be greater.

Can we, however, trust that the machine construction industry represents total industry? During the period under consideration, approximately 30 percent of all industrial workers were employed in this branch.[11] Although the reduction in the average level of norm fulfillment was somewhat sharper for machine construction than for industry as a whole (by 1963, as a percentage of prereform levels, the respective figures were 64 and 70 percent), all branches experienced significant reductions in fulfillment levels and a probable decrease in the differentiation of earnings according to skill levels.[12]

Although our concern is with the impact of the reform, the postreform data are from 1963, and the reform was actually completed in machine construction by 1960. During the intervening period, the average level of norm fulfillment grew from 126 percent in 1960 to 133 percent in 1963.[13] Therefore, had table 5.2 referred to the immediate postreform period, both rows 3 and 4 would probably have shown less differentiation.

A definite answer must await the publication of further data. But available information does clearly indicate that the Soviet economists are correct in stating that the wage reform brought a reduction in skill differentials. There remains the question of the rationale behind this reduction and the adequacy of the differentials established during the reform.

Adequacy of Skill Differentials

Recent Soviet literature is rife with arguments about a number of issues and criticisms of numerous aspects of wage setting. There is virtually unanimous agreement on one thing: [14] the reduction of skill

11. *Trud v SSSR*, 1968, pp. 86–87.
12. Table 3.1.
13. Table 3.1.
14. Since 1956, the single exception is Yagodkin (1967, p. 22), who maintained, "Judging by all the evidence, the currently established ratio between the extreme skill groups in machine construction—1:2 in place of the 1:2.43 that existed prior to the

differentials during the reform. Not only is this reduction held to be
economically justified, but further reduction is expected as a result of
certain secular changes in what Western wage theory would call labor
market conditions.[15] The Soviet economist maintains that the skill
scales existing prior to the reform were essentially those that had been
established during the First Five-Year Plan early in the 1930s.[16] At that
time, masses of unskilled workers were entering the industrial labor
force, and the central task of wage policy was the creation of skilled
cadres. High differentials were necessary to motivate millions of former
peasants to develop industrial skills. Moreover, the various branches
of industry were growing at very different rates. The more rapidly
growing branches, that is, producer goods or "Group A," were more
in need of skilled workers, and skill scales with greater skill differen-
tiations were established in these branches. No Soviet economist is currently willing to say that these differentials were too great, but, to
quote E. I. Kapustin again, wage relationships that were "correct for
the 1930s do not answer the demands of today." [17]

By the mid-1950s, according to the Soviet argument, both the rate of
increase in the size of the industrial labor force and its structure had
become relatively stable. Most workers had at least several years of
general education, and the existence of various types of vocational
training as well as opportunities for part-time study had made the
process of acquiring skills easier and more regularized. Furthermore,
the general "cultural level" of those workers currently considered
unskilled is in fact closer to that of the most highly skilled. Finally, the
reduction in the difference between the rates of growth of capital goods
and consumer goods industries permits a single system of intraindustry
skill differentials to be applied in all branches of industry. Although
the relative importance of various branches will still be reflected in

wage reform—is not creating sufficient stimulus for increasing proficiency." He further noted that this conclusion is "confirmed by practice" in Czechoslovakia.

At a conference of administrative personnel held in 1956, a proposed skill scale
with a ratio of extreme skill groups of 1:2.8 was attacked as providing insufficient
differentiation. See Galenson, 1963, p. 307.

15. This is a summary of the positions taken in works by several Soviet economists,
among them, Aganbegian and Maier, 1959, p. 134; Maier, 1963, p. 169, pp. 218–219;
Kapustin, 1961b, pp. 88–90.

16. See table 4.2. It should be noted that there were periodic changes in skill scales
between the 1930s and the wage reform. For an attempt to interpret these changes,
see Yanowitch, 1960, pp. 183–199.

17. Kapustin, 1961a, p. 18.

wage setting, it now may be expressed exclusively in the differentiation of initial basic rates.[18]

In broad outline, the Soviet analysis appears valid and it should be expanded upon. Data are sparse; most likely the relative gap in earnings between the skilled and unskilled worker was somewhat greater on the eve of the wage reform than it had been in 1934.[19] During the intervening three decades, according to one source, data on earnings differentiation were simply not collected.[20] If such differentials were in some sense "right" for the mid-1930s, there is reason to believe that they were too high for the mid-1950s. The narrowing of skill differentials brought by the reform appears to have economic justification.

Before proceeding, it should be noted that the data presented in table 5.2 might be adduced to support an opposite view. The fact that postreform piece-rate earnings show greater differentiation than do basic rates could be interpreted as an indication that the centrally established differentials were inadequate.[21] The difference in structure of basic rates as compared to earnings could be the result of local attempts to correct insufficient differentials by establishing loose norms for work performed by the more skilled worker. However, a more direct explanation for the relatively greater differentiation of earnings shown in table 5.2 can be offered. As has been discussed in chapter 3, technically based and correspondingly tight output norms on jobs performed by skilled workers are difficult to establish. Therefore, because of the nature of Soviet norming practice, the qualified piece-rate worker is less likely to have his job covered by a centrally determined output norm and thus is more likely to receive a greater share of earnings in the form of payments for norm overfulfillment.

By all accounts, occupational differentiation of relative wages in

18. Kapustin, 1961b, p. 78. The initial basic rate is the amount received by a worker in the first skill group under normal working conditions. See discussion accompanying table 1.2, and appendix A.
19. This is the conclusion that Murray Yanowitch (1963, p. 685) draws from data presented by Mozhina, 1961. The Soviet economists Rabkina and Rimashevskaia (1966, p. 88) state that earnings differentials for Soviet workers, as measured by decile ratios, were "somewhat higher" in 1956 than in 1934. See below, appendix B.
20. Rabkina and Rimashevskaia, 1966, p. 88.
21. Rothbaum (1957, pp. 309–310) has noted that in Italy and France the post–World War II wage drift has tended to favor the more skilled workers and "has served as a corrective to levelling tendencies that were considered excessive, whether for market or morale reasons."

Western industrial economies has decreased as these economies have "matured." [22] The measure of wage differentiation usually considered is occupation rather than skill level, though one may assume some correspondence between these concepts.[23] It has been shown that wage differentiation in the Soviet planned economy is by no means immune to the forces operative in a capitalist economy.[24] Thus there is reason to believe that Soviet wage differentials would likewise tend to decrease with industrialization.

Generally speaking, a pure skill differential should be large enough to provide adequate incentive for the unskilled worker to become more skilled. The adequacy of the incentive may be viewed as dependent upon two related considerations. The relative "productivities" of the different types of labor may be said to establish the demand conditions. As for supply conditions, the greater the difficulty, or the "disutility," of the worker's becoming more skilled, the greater the incentive must be in order to be "adequate." In short, the size of the skill differentials should reflect the relative scarcity of workers of different skill levels. Though theoretically possible, it seems doubtful that in the USSR the relative demand for more skilled workers has increased rapidly enough to outweigh the effects of changes in supply conditions, indicating that skilled labor has become relatively less scarce than in the 1930s.

The rate of growth in the number of persons employed in Soviet industry has been considerably smaller in the recent period than during

22. An excellent summary of Western studies concerning occupational differentials is in OECD, 1965, pp. 33–38. We should, however, mention Guy Routh's (1965) well-documented monograph in which he developed the thesis that occupational differentials in Great Britain showed a general long-run stability between 1906 and 1960. He maintained that this is especially true for skill differentials, which tended to narrow during periods of inflation and then widen to their traditional levels during periods of price stability. A most useful discussion of recent empirical and theoretical studies on skill differentials can be found in Perlman, 1969, pp. 80–102.
23. However, the correspondence is by no means complete. In the following quotation from Reynolds and Taft (1956, p. 357), I have italicized those aspects of job content that the Soviets would regard as differences in working conditions rather than skill level: ". . . where our data go back before 1900, occupational differentials have been shrinking throughout the content of the 'skilled' and 'unskilled' categories. There are indications that many skilled occupations are becoming less skilled, *arduous*, and responsible with the *improvement of mechanical equipment and working conditions*. . . . Narrowing of the differential in job content between skilled and unskilled work may partly be responsible for, or at any rate may help to legitimize a narrower differential in wage rates."
24. See Bergson, 1944, especially pp. 194–209.

the first two five-year-plans. The flow of peasants from collective farms into industry has been sharply curtailed, resulting in a relative stability in the size of the industrial work force. The relative wage differential necessary to induce a peasant fresh from the village to become a skilled worker would, one might suppose, be greater than that for a person who has long been exposed to the values of an industrial society.

The general educational level of the current entrant into the industrial work force has been considerably raised. If general education increases a person's ability to acquire industrial skills, a sufficient incentive for raising skill level should be smaller for the worker of today than for the worker of the 1930s. According to Warren Eason, by the end of the 1930s about 92 percent of all Soviet workers had completed no more than elementary school education. By 1959, the figure was reduced to approximately 61 percent.[25]

In a recent book that should be considered a contribution to the "economics of human resources," two Soviet economists attempted to determine the relationship between general education and the rapidity with which a worker moves up the skill ladder. Their conclusions, based upon an innovative methodology and apparently excellent sample data, are of considerable interest. The facilitating impact of a completed high school education upon skill acquisition appeared extremely significant. They concluded that the economy could be best provided with qualified workers not through greater skill differentials but rather through the creation of specific incentives to induce young people to finish high school. One proposed incentive is for new entrants into the labor force to receive a percentage increase in earnings if they have completed their general education.[26]

Equally pertinent to a discussion of the adequacy of skill differen-

25. These percentages are for all "workers," but not collective farmers or "office workers." Our discussion concerning changes in the Soviet labor force relies heavily on Eason, 1963, especially pp. 53–93.

Some of the information gathered in a survey of job changes in the Leningrad region is interpreted by Bliakhman (et al., 1965, pp. 76–77) as indicating that some workers are actually overeducated in terms of their current occupation. Data relating educational level and the likelihood that a worker will change his occupation indicate that "each type of work has, under given conditions, its own optimum educational level (tsenz)." For a description of this survey, see footnote 32.

26. Zhamin and Egiazarian, 1968, pp. 144–218. Similar findings from a less ambitious study were reported by I. Kaplan (1966).

tials is the increase in specialized training. In the abstract, Emily Clark Brown appears correct in stating that "central planning to ensure the needed qualifications and skills in the labor force starts with decisions on the curriculum of primary and secondary schools." [27] According to A. A. Bulgakov, the Chairman of Gosplan's Committee on Professional Technical Education, in the course of the Seven-Year Plan of 1958–1965, 5.7 million "young qualified workers" were graduated from vocational-technical schools. He estimated that in 1964 these schools were able to satisfy something less than one-fourth of industry's "need for new workers. [28]

In comparison with special schooling, on-the-job training has become less important in providing Soviet industry with skilled personnel. Some wage advantage might be necessary to induce a person to postpone entry into the labor force in order to complete his education at a vocational-technical school. However, Soviet educational policies, including student stipends, lead one to assume that such differentials need not be as high as those for on-the-job training. It was reported that in 1964 the number of applications to vocational-technical schools was significantly greater than the number accepted, and "there was just one reason—no room." [29]

On-the-job training itself can be made an easier process. With some success, Soviet policies have attempted to facilitate the process by which a worker can improve his qualifications while remaining a full-time employee.[30] Moreover, according to the results of an "economic

27. Brown, 1957, p. 186.
28. It is difficult to interpret Bulgakov's (1965) statement that "vocational-technical schools provide just less than one-fourth of the need for new workers, and in industry even less." The figure of 5.7 million obviously includes those workers entering construction and agriculture.

The term "vocational-technical schools" refers to the multitude of trade and technical schools that existed under various names until 1958, when all these educational institutions were renamed and uniformly called vocational-technical schools. The hallmark of these schools is that they prepare young people for employment as "productive workers" rather than as administrative personnel. Zelenko, 1962–1965.
29. Tulchinsky (1965, p. 18) reports that on the basis of "incomplete data" in 1964, 768,000 boys and girls applied for admission in urban areas, of whom 569,000 were accepted. For a critique of the current state of Soviet vocational training, see Zhamin and Egiazarian, 1968, pp. 205–218.
30. An International Labor Office delegation was impressed by the facilities provided for on-the-job training as well as by the system of vocational-technical schools. ILO., 1960, pp. 120–122. For a discussion of what Nicholas De Witt calls "an extensive and probably unique system of formal educational facilities for the training of

investigation" reported by Bulgakov, on-the-job training is completed more rapidly by those who have finished vocational-technical schools. The time necessary for a graduate of one of these schools to reach a higher skill group is less than half of that required by a worker lacking such training.[31]

A study of labor turnover in the Leningrad region indicated that Soviet workers did not find postreform skill differentials too narrow. In the Leningrad survey, as it will henceforth be called, 12,000 workers were interviewed to determine motivation for changing their place of employment.[32] No general correlation between skill group level and expressions of dissatisfaction with wage levels appeared in the study.[33]

Reports of "job rationing" [34]—to use Lloyd G. Reynolds's term— provide perhaps the most convincing evidence that postreform skill differentials should be considered adequate, and maybe even excessive. "Job rationing" exists when the number of workers willing and able to perform the more highly skilled tasks exceeds the number of job openings for such work. The Soviet differentials often generate a po-

---

skilled labor" and the "various types of informal on-the-job apprenticeship programs," see De Witt, 1961, pp. 155–295.

Within the Soviet enterprise an imposing collection of forms is filled out to aid in planning yearly needs for workers of various occupations and skill levels. The forms include detailed plans for acquiring such labor through hiring and training. Batyshev, 1965, pp. 217–245.

31. Bulgakov (1965) further notes that when a worker moves to a higher skill group, if he lacks this specialized training he tends to be responsible for from five to eight times more spoiled materials (brak). Also see I. Kaplan, 1966.

32. The Leningrad survey is probably the widest application of the interview technique for analysis of motives for job changing that has even been undertaken in any economy. At twenty-five enterprises, workers who had changed jobs between January 1962 and March 1963 were interviewed. The sample was structured according to percentages of the labor force employed in the various branches of industry in the Leningrad area. A total of 11,000 workers who had changed jobs were interviewed about their motivation for leaving their former places of employment. The authors reporting the results of the survey point out that this sample does not represent a profile of Leningrad workers, but rather of workers who tend to change jobs. Compared to the former, the sample overrepresents women, low-paid workers, and workers of the "general occupations," that is, groups that tend to have a high labor turnover rate, Bliakhman, et al., 1965, pp. 35–40.

33. The pattern of expressed dissatisfaction is most irregular. For lathe operators and mechanics (see note concerning terminology in footnote 4), dissatisfaction was most prevalent among workers of the third skill group; for shoe and leather workers, among those in the sixth; and in the chemical industry, workers in the first and second skill groups were least satisfied. Bliakhman et al., 1965, p. 63.

34. See Reynolds, 1951, pp. 238–240.

tential supply of workers to perform the more highly qualified work that is greater than the number of job openings in the higher skill groups. Thus, workers within some plants must wait for "the freeing of a job in a higher skill group." [35]

A sample study of 3000 workers undertaken by the Moscow Pedagogical Institute attempted to determine the relationship between educational level and the amount of time necessary for a worker to move into successive skill groups. Though a strong relationship was found between educational level and the rapidity of advancement from the first to the fourth skill group, seniority became the determining factor for classification in the fifth or sixth skill group. In the report on this study, it was noted:

It should be said that, as was made clear [by data gathered], the extremely long period for classification [of a worker] into the higher two skill groups was not associated with the training or knowledge of the worker. In the [enterprise's] labor plan, the number of workers in the highest skill groups is strictly limited, and many who are qualified to be classified in the fifth or sixth skill groups continue to work in the fourth or even third.[36]

The findings of the previously mentioned Leningrad survey were similar. The authors reporting the results of that study proposed that a four- or five-group skill scale replace the standard six-group scale established during the wage reform.

Even at the present time, workers of the fourth, fifth, and sixth skill groups cannot be differentiated according to education or training time, but only according to seniority [stazh]. . . . Under such conditions, the skill group ceases to be a measure of a worker's qualification and only characterizes the complexity of the work to which he is assigned.[37]

In short, there is reason to disagree with Walter Galenson's contention that by the mid-1950s "the logical policy was to widen the spread of skill differentials." A long-established theoretical postulate is that the skill differential, as well as other differentials, should be "equalizing." That is, the differential should be sufficient to cover costs incurred by an individual in gaining a certain skill level.[38] As compared

35. Kapustin, 1964, pp. 128–132.
36. I. Kaplan, 1966.
37. Bliakhman et al., 1965, p. 116; Dubovoi, 1967, p. 62.
38. These are basically training costs and income forgone as well as return to investment in acquiring a skill that is equal to the return that might have been received on alternative investments. Rigorously speaking, with a reduction in the

to the situation in the 1930s, these costs appear to have decreased sharply, and by 1956 neither the maintenance of existing skill differentials nor the establishment of higher differentials appeared economically necessary.[39] Nor does there appear to be any reason to question the economic rationality of the further reduction in differentials that took place in 1968.[40]

Thus, if there was an "optimum" skill scale for Soviet conditions in the early 1960s, an extreme skill-group ratio of about 1:2 may have equaled or even exceeded the optimum level of skill differentials. As to the other aspects of the structure of the skill scale, we have no evidence to either prove or disprove E. I. Kapustin's contention that with a maximum differentiation of approximately 1:2, experience demonstrated that the number of skill groups should be six, with an average gap of about 13 to 15 percent between groups. A finer division of the skill spectrum would allegedly not have provided sufficient incentive for the worker to increase his qualifications, whereas classification according to fewer than six skill groups would have made advancement appear excessively difficult to the workers.[41] Even if one were to agree and grant that this in some sense approximated the "optimum" single skill scale, a number of questions remain as to the advisability of using only one standardized scale for establishing skill differentials throughout all of industry.

Standardization of Skill Differentials

Experience in Western economies demonstrates that standard wage scales covering large numbers of employees can be implemented. In the United States, "virtually the entire basic steel industry has . . . been covered by formal intra-company job-wage classification structures." [42]

"costs" associated with obtaining a skill, the "internal rate of return on investment in skill" can remain constant or even increase despite a reduction in skill differentials. See Perlman, 1969, pp. 79–104.

39. Galenson, 1963, p. 307. We should note that Galenson, while recognizing the problem of distribution of incentive earnings, apparently holds that the wage reform widened skill differentials. For reasons already presented, we believe that the evidence points in the opposite direction.

40. Some sort of reduction had been anticipated; see "Direktivy XXIII," 1966, p. 9; Volkov, 1966b.

41. See Kapustin, 1961b, p. 73. The structure of the single skill scale is discussed later in this chapter.

42. Goldfinger, 1957, p. 79. For a comprehensive study of the job evaluation program in the basic steel industry, see Stieber, 1959.

Other industries have also instituted job evaluation systems that tend
to establish identical structures of basic wage rates throughout a given
branch.[43] The experience of the Scandinavian countries and the
Netherlands in the period 1945–1963 demonstrates that an all-industry
system of job evaluation can be implemented.[44]

A further reason for assuming feasibility is that the Soviet system
is intended to determine only relative basic wage rates, rather than
total earnings differentials. A certain amount of flexibility, what the
European economist has come to call "wage drift," is incorporated into
the system. The term refers to the "drift" or gap between basic wage
rates and earnings. This difference is composed of payments for overfulfillment of piece-rate norms, premiums, bonuses, overtime pay, and
so on. In the opinion of a number of Western economists, the wage
drifts and resultant changes in wage structures reflect labor market
conditions that were not properly considered in determining basic
wage rates set through periodic collective bargaining. J. R. Hicks
maintains that "the free market has appeared in a new guise, being
responsible for the determination of the gap between basic 'wages' and
'earnings.' "[45] The possible flexibility in the determination of Soviet
earnings that results from this gap has been and will be further commented upon.[46] Here, we simply note its existence as a factor further
indicating the feasibility of establishing a single skill scale throughout
Soviet industry. Feasibility, however, need not be associated with economic rationality.

The economic implications of the single skill scale must be analyzed
in terms of a very precise type of scarcity. To maintain that the pure
skill differentials expressed by a skill scale should vary among industries, it should be shown that there is variation in what might be called
the pure intraindustry scarcity relationships for workers of different
qualifications. A complaint over the lack of skilled workers in some
geographical region or branch of industry may be the result of an inap-

43. Livernash, 1957, pp. 146–165; A. M. Ross, 1957, p. 196. For a discussion of the
possibility of applying one set of job evaluation techniques, see Brennan, 1963, p. 72.
44. *Incomes*, 1967, chapters 4 and 5 (no consecutive paging), provides a full discussion of West European success in accomplishing such standardization and the
ensuing results.
45. Hicks, 1964, p. 318; OECD, 1965, pp. 21–22; Kerr, 1954, pp. 220–221; Robertson,
1960, p. 128, and 1963, pp. 206–207.
46. See chapters 3, 7, and 8.

propriate wage rate for the first skill group [47] rather than of the relative basic rates received by workers of the various skill groups.

As proposed in the Soviet literature, the single skill scale does not imply that each industry would have the same structure of skill differentials. The percentage of workers in each of the various skill groups would supposedly be dependent upon the skill mix of work performed within the industry. Furthermore, as previously discussed, the ratio of basic wages of the most skilled to those of the "least skilled" in any industry may vary: for example, work performed in the coke-chemical industry is to be rated only according to the first three skill groups of the scale.[48]

However, even after recognizing that the single skill scale standardizes only the pure intraindustry skill differential in terms of existing scarcity relationships, there seems little economic justification for such standardization. In fact, pure scarcity conditions for workers of various skill levels differ significantly among Soviet industries.

Though some Soviet economists view job rationing as a general condition throughout industry, its significance differs sharply among branches. In 1964, it was reported that in the older branches of industry (light and food), which have a relatively stable work force, there is a surplus of workers able to perform the more highly rated jobs. Seniority rather than ability is the basic determinant of a worker's skill group.[49] Thus, for these branches, it would appear that intraindustry skill differentials could be reduced without causing a shortage of skilled personnel.

By contrast, within a rapidly growing branch such as the chemical industry one finds a direct correlation between skill levels and unfulfilled labor requirements. During 1965, in some chemical factories, requirements for workers of the fourth skill group were filled by 80 percent, for the fifth by 55 percent, and for the sixth by only 46 percent.[50] An analogous situation existed in several of the newly settled geographical regions, notably Kazakhstan.[51]

47. The initial rate, above, p. 14.
48. See the section of chapter 4 entitled "The Ongoing Reform of Skill Differentials."
49. Kapustin, 1964, pp. 128–132.
50. Bulgakov, 1965.
51. Vechkanov, 1969. Zhamin and Egiazarian (1968, pp. 14–16) place much of the blame for such conditions upon the network of vocational schools, which, allegedly, do not consider actual or potential shortages within the labor force when planning the occupational composition of graduating classes.

If the single skill scale generates sufficient skill differentials for, let us say, the chemical industry, the same differentials may be considered "too high" in those industries experiencing job rationing for work classified in the higher skill groups. Standardization seems to involve differentials that are "too low" for some industries or geographical areas, and excessively high for others. Thus, there is an apparent divergence between differentials set by the single scale and those that might be considered in accord with scarcity conditions within the various branches. However, such divergence may be mitigated by policies not directly associated with skill differentials. Labor market analysis usually assumes that differentials should and will tend to correspond to scarcity conditions. At least in terms of Soviet wage policy, it is possible to force scarcity conditions to fit established differentials.

In the first place, certain educational policies can serve as a sort of Procrustean bed, making scarcity conditions better fit the established differentials. In the early 1960s, it became possible for the proper economic organs of various industrial branches, with the agreement of Gosplan USSR, to expand vocational-technical schools from the capital investment apportioned to the given branch.[52] One would assume that the economic organs of those branches experiencing a relative shortage of skilled workers would be most willing to utilize their investment funds for increasing worker qualification.

Secondly, the possibility of interindustry transference of skilled workers, both voluntary and directed, might militate against the establishment of standard skill differentials in branches with differing intraindustry scarcity conditions. Job rationing in some branches should tend to induce the worker who is willing and able to increase his skill level to seek new employment in a branch where advancement is more rapid. M. Sonin, probably the leading Soviet authority on the structure of the labor force, states that some industries hire only unskilled workers and rely upon internal promotion and training, while others will tend to hire only those with specific occupations and qualifications.[53] Unfortunately, Sonin specifies neither which industries hire from the base of the occupational ladder nor the direction of inter-

52. When reporting this development, Bulgakov (1965) was highly critical of the way in which such funds were spent. Plans for expanding vocational-technical schools associated with the different branches were fulfilled by only 75 percent during 1964.
53. Sonin, 1959, p. 229.

industry transfer of skilled labor. However, insofar as there is a clear tendency among all workers who change jobs to flow into the more rapidly growing branches of industry, we may assume that voluntary transfer of skilled workers is in the same direction.[54]

There is some directed redistribution of skilled workers in the form of organized recruitment through the official government labor recruiting agency, *Orgnabor (organizovannyi nabor rabochei sily)*, which by 1959 was reported to be increasingly utilized by workers who "have some occupation and qualification." Appeals to patriotism and the operation of social pressures undoubtedly have also played a role in distribution of skilled personnel.[55] However, a special sort of directed labor distribution is particularly important for our purposes. Shortages of skilled labor in any branch may be partially remedied by directing young workers graduating from vocational-technical schools. These graduates have a legal obligation to work at any enterprise to which they are sent for a period of three to four years, though the judicial situation is complicated.[56] Thus, at least in theory, a large group of skilled or semiskilled young workers can be directed to industries where there is a particular need for them.

This legal obligation is a less effective device for distributing young workers among various branches of industry than it might seem, however, since it is apparently seldom enforced.[57] According to information gathered by the Labor Institute in 1958–1960, of those workers who had been employed for less than two years, the one who had finished a vocational-technical school was more likely to change jobs than one who had not undergone this specialized education.[58] The head engineer of a large Leningrad combination of machine construction plants may not have exaggerated when he maintained that it is "very rare" for the graduate to fulfill his obligation.[59]

When enterprises attempt to augment their skilled labor force from the external labor market—as distinct from internal upgrading of

54. Bliakhman et al., 1965, pp. 13, 71.
55. See Sonin, 1959, pp. 217, 222–223, 231–250. Brown (1970) provides a detailed discussion of recent Soviet policy concerning the redistribution of labor.
56. *Labor Law*, 1964, p. 38, Harris, 1964; Voilenko. 1966.
57. Harris (1964) has found that "it is accepted that the obligation to work out a set period should be seen primarily as a normal obligation."
58. The results of the Labor Institute's investigation are given in Bliakhman et al., 1965, p. 20.
59. "Kadry," 1965, p. 19.

employed workers—standard unorganized market mechanisms appear to play a dominant and growing role. According to the current archives of the Central Statistical Administration, in 1950 enterprises hired about 14 percent of new personnel through organized recruitment, 7 percent were accounted for by those finishing some sort of vocational training school, and 79 percent were directly hired by the enterprise. By 1959, the first two percentages had fallen to 4 percent each, and 92 percent were directly hired by the enterprise. Data for 1962 were identical with those of 1959.[60]

In any event, whatever the possibilities for forcing scarcity conditions to fit a single all-industry set of relative skill differentials, the acceptance of such standardization has meant the loss of a policy tool. When the chemical industry experiences a sharp shortage of skilled workers while having an adequate supply of those at lower skill levels, one specialized policy lever for correcting this situation would appear to be a widening of skill differentials within that industry. Use of this policy tool is currently precluded, and other, possibly less precise, tools must be relied upon. From the vantage point of short-run scarcity conditions, the single skill scale lacks economic rationality. However, certain other goals of Soviet wage administration may be realized through such standardization. In addition to skill differentials, these possible advantages apply to other standardized differentials as well. Therefore, that discussion is better postponed until the concluding chapter.

Training Time and Skill Differentials

The relationship between the reproduction of labor power and skill differentials is the most hotly contested question in Soviet wage literature. Two interconnected issues may be identified: first, the possibility of utilizing Marx's "cost of reproduction of labor power" as a determinant of the magnitude of skill differentials; second, the feasibility of applying some measure of "training time" for the establishment of a worker's skill group within a previously determined skill scale.

The idea that skill levels and corresponding wage differentials in some general way depend on the amount of training necessary to perform certain tasks has often appeared in "popular" literature. One widely used textbook states that measurement of relative skill should

---

60. Poletaev et al., 1969, p. 115.

be arranged to facilitate "quantitative comparisons of labor of different qualifications." Hence, "the average expenditure necessary for the training of the employed person of one or another qualification could be used as such a measure." [61] The text does not indicate how this proposal might be implemented.

Though such general statements seem far from radical, one highly competent and original Soviet economist proposes that just such a measure should itself be the determinant of skill differentials. At the very least, V.F. Maier's approach is an interesting attempt to establish Soviet skill differentials in accordance with Marx's analysis of their determination under capitalism:

In order to modify the human organism so that it may acquire skill and handiness in a given branch of industry, and become labor power of a special kind, a special education or training is required, and this, on its part, costs an equivalent in commodities of a greater or lesser amount. This amount varies according to the more or less complicated character of the labor power.[62]

Maier's apparently doctrinaire approach leads him to policy recommendations which, in terms of current wage policy, must be regarded as daringly radical. In his system, determination of skill differentials is based, with impressive consistency, on Marx's concept of "values" created in production by workers of differing skills. Were his system adopted—and he clearly thinks it feasible [63]—the methodology for skill determination, as well as the size of skill differentials, would differ fundamentally from those of current Soviet wage administration.

Maier maintains that in the early stages of Soviet industrialization, skill differentials had to be developed in an ad hoc way to meet the economy's need for skilled cadres. With the relative stabilization of both the size and the structure of the labor force, he believes, the Soviet economy is ripe for a consistent and "scientific" determination of skill differentials. Existing job evaluation techniques for measuring differentials do not meet what he considers to be three basic requirements: objectivity, universal applicability, and quantitative expres-

---

61. *Planirovanie*, 1963, p. 460. An example of the popular literature is the discussion initiated in *Sovetskaia Rossia*, June 9, 1964 (p. 2), and continued in the November 28 issue (p. 2). The topic was how to determine "who gives more" to the national economy. As early as 1924, this same question was taken up by Academician Strumilin (*Izbrannye*, vol. 3, 1963–1965, pp. 101–103) in an article entitled "The Economic Significance of General Education."
62. Marx, 1906–1909, vol. 1, p. 191.
63. Maier (1963, pp. 84–87) even outlines steps to implement this reform.

sion.[64] Furthermore, existing methodology attempts little more than to determine the proper skill group of the worker within some predetermined and hopefully optimum skill scale. Maier's methodology provides the basis of the skill scale itself, that is, the ratio of the extreme skill groups.[65]

Space does not permit a full description of the consistency with which Maier derives his argument from classical Marxist concepts of "value," "surplus value," "rate of exploitation," and "cost of reproduction of labor power." Instead, we truncate his analysis and look only at the last step in his argument, the formulation of the magnitudes that should determine intraindustry skill differentials. The relative quantity of "value" created by a worker is determined by the relative total costs expended in preparing the worker for productive labor.[66] Only a portion, however, of differences in value produced by workers of various qualifications should find expression in wage determination. Maier's operational formula for determining skill differentials is

$$K_i = 1 + \frac{1}{n}(t)$$

where K_i is the coefficient expressing the proper level of remuneration for qualification; n is the number of years a worker remains an active participant in labor force; t is the expenditure of time that the worker himself has made in acquiring the given level of qualification, including only that time of training over and above the average level for unqualified labor. Not included is the labor expenditure of those who have trained the worker and the labor time "embodied" in the mate-

64. Ibid., pp. 74–75, 117–120.
65. Not only could the ratio of the extreme skill groups be determined, but the nature of the skill scale would also change. At present, the basic rate increases by a rising percentage with each higher skill group. Maier's system would increase the rate by a constant, absolute amount; that is, with six skill groups, the percentage increase would be largest between the first and second groups and smallest between the fifth and sixth. His methodology indicates this to be the "normal type of skill scale. Maier, 1963, p. 117.
66. "Values" created in production are proportionate to the "cost of reproduction of labor power" only if each worker produces "surplus value" at a rate proportionate to the value of his labor power, or necessary product. An essential part of the Marxist analysis is that the worker produces a surplus value in addition to his wage or the value of his labor power. Surplus value divided by the value of labor power is Marx's "rate of exploitation." When discussing his own economy, the Soviet economist will refer to this ratio as "rate of surplus" or "norm of product for society." See Marx, 1906–1909, vol. 1, p. 241; Aganbegian and Maier, 1959, pp. 40–41; Maier, 1963, p. 74.

rial goods necèssary for reproduction of the given worker's "labor power."

As an example, Maier applies this formula in determining the skill differential between the unskilled and the most highly skilled workers in the machine construction industry. A value of 25 is assigned [67] to n, the number of years that a worker functions "as a worker." Since five to seven years of experience are necessary for a worker in that industry to be classified in the highest skill group, the value of t is taken as 6. On the assumption that the unskilled (first skill group) worker needs no individual training time ($t=0$ and therefore $K_i=1$), the coefficient showing the proper relationship in relative skill wage would be

$$K_i = 1 + \frac{1}{25}(6) = 1.24.$$

Maier holds that even this rough calculation shows that "the possibility of reducing the difference in pay for qualification is by no means exhausted." In the basic skill scales established during the reform, this coefficient has not been 1:1.24, but rather in the range of 1:2.0–1:1.8. His explanation for the divergence is that the qualified worker currently produces a smaller share of surplus product [68] than does the unqualified worker.

Maier presents similar additional calculations as examples of the general approach that should be used in wage administration. He maintains that the Labor Institute has already collected sufficient data on this aspect of "socially necessary labor time" at least to begin replacing existing job evaluation systems for skill wage differentials.

As might be expected, Maier's theoretical approach and his proposals have been vigorously attacked. On a purely theoretical level, some Soviet economists have objected to applying any variation on the Marxist concept of value to wage determination. These objections rest upon the general idea that under socialism labor power has ceased to

67. Twenty-five years seems an extremely strange figure. Maier uses it because a male worker must work this number of years in order to receive a pension. The median period of time worked, or general labor *stazh*, in industry was about ten to eleven years as of 1963 (derived from data in *Vest. Stat.*, no. 4, 1964, p. 90). Moreover, in terms of Maier's own theoretical framework, the number of years should include only those years that the skilled worker functions as such. Thus, if six years of training are needed, only nineteen years are left to function as a skilled worker. As Maier recognizes, any reduction of n would mean a corresponding increase in the coefficient determining the skill differential.
68. See footnote 66.

be a commodity, and therefore wage determination is unrelated to the concept of value. Since under socialism society carries the burden of expenditure in training workers to become more qualified, value plays no role in determination of skill differentials. Therefore, these differentials simply reflect the necessary stimulation to workers to become more skilled.[69] One critic maintains that the approach is invalid because skill differentials should not be set with reference to past labor inputs, but rather with reference to the current outlays for training young people who are about to become workers.[70]

For the most part, however, criticism of Maier's approach does not center around Marxist economic theory. The discussion narrows and the participants avoid the question of whether proper differentials can be set by "reproduction costs." The issue becomes the possibility of utilizing some measure of training time for classifying workers by skill group within some previously established structure of skill differentials or skill scale. Thus, at the level of wage administration, the usefulness of measures of training time even as an indication of skill levels is questioned on an operational basis:

At first glance, it seems that this would be the most correct and simple method. . . . It would seem that all that need be done is to determine the period of training necessary for fulfilling one or another sort of concrete work.

But it is exactly here that the difficulty begins.[71]

One "difficulty" is how to measure the training period. E .I. Kapustin maintained that it is impossible to find a valid index for expressing necessary training time if it includes formal education as well as work experience. In addition, great differences exist in the time needed by individual workers to obtain a given skill level. Using a most inadequate sample, he attempts to demonstrate the futility of such an approach by presenting a table showing the education and experience backgrounds of eighteen workers of the same occupation and skill group (highest) employed in three different steel plants. On-the-job training prior to classification in the highest skill group ranged from eleven months to over thirteen years. Educational backgrounds were no less varied.[72]

69. Liapin, 1961, pp. 147–148; Gomberg, 1964, p. 23; Batkaev and Markov, 1964, p. 27.
70. Gomberg, 1968, pp. 64–65.
71. Kapustin, 1961b, p. 61.
72. Ibid., pp. 61–64. Maier did not find this table convincing. Using the same data, although questioning its validity as a sample, he attempted to show that the

Generally, Maier's critics maintain that skill measurements are too complicated to be expressed by a single index, and "the fact is that various factors . . . influence qualification in different ways." [73] Therefore, job evaluation methods such as the point system previously described in chapter 4 must remain the cornerstone of skill measurement and corresponding wage differentiation. However, it seems that these critics are too severe. Data on training time could well play a useful role in Soviet wage administration.

Compared to some Western job evaluation procedures, the Soviet methodology for determining skill levels, either through the weighted point system or the unweighted method, does not seem particularly complex. Yet some summary measure of training time as a determinant of skill level would have the virtue of even greater clearness and simplicity.[74] A strong *ex post* relationship between training time and skill group clearly exists. The results of a sample survey of 3284 industrial workers of important (*massovye*) occupations is shown in table 5.3.

This apparent relationship between skill-group level and average training time does not, however, bear upon the feasibility of utilizing training time as a determinant of a worker's skill group. The most important obstacle to testing such a methodology is the absence of some valid index of the three aspects of training time: general education, special technical training, and on-the-job experience.[75]

---

average of total preparation time, including experience and some special education, is a meaningful measure of the complexity of the work performed. Recognizing that there is variation, he goes on to make this interesting statement relating wage policy to price policies: "In the production of identical products, labor expenditures, as a rule, differ to a much greater extent, but this is not an obstacle to the formulation of socially necessary labor time, which finds its expression in a single cost and price for the given product." Maier, 1963, pp. 87–90.

In a later statement, Kapustin (1964, pp. 129–140) continued the argument with greater sophistication. However, judging from an article published in 1965, Kapustin found the application of a Maier-like methodology for establishing skill differentials to be both desirable and practical "at the present time." Kapustin, 1965.

73. Kapustin and Mysev, 1961, p. 23; Gomberg, 1964, p. 29.

74. "Perhaps the clearest and simplest classification scheme [for determining skill levels] uses as its sole criterion the average length of the total training period required to reach average proficiency in the occupation." Ross and Rothbaum, 1959, p. 368.

75. R. S. Eckaus's attempt to project American educational needs on the basis of output projections suffers from a similar defect. As noted by D. F. Ross, Eckaus's measure of "school years" is difficult to defend. This discussion, initiated in 1964 in *The Review of Economics and Statistics* and continued through 1966, has much in common with the Soviet discussion of the significance of training time measurement. See Eckaus, 1964 and 1966; Scoville, 1966; and D. F. Ross, 1966.

Table 5.3
Education, Experience, and Skill Level: Sample Survey Results

Skill Group (1)	Total Preparation Including Middle- School Education (Average in Years) (2)	Work Experience in Given Occupation (Average in Years) (3)	(3) as a Percentage of (2)
I	6.9	0.3	4.3
II	8.6	1.4	16.3
III	10.7	3.6	33.6
IV	13.9	6.8	49.0
V	17.0	9.9	58.2
VI	19.0	11.6	61.0

Note: From Gomberg, 1964, p. 27. The data would be more pertinent if column (3) showed work experience prior to achievment of a given skill group rather than total work experience. The survey was undertaken by the Labor Institute.

As shown in the table, the importance of work experience in terms of total preparation increases with each successive skill group. However, the relationship is not consistent; in the established, slower-growing branches, those achieving the highest skill levels tend to have a great deal of on-the-job training. As noted earlier in this chapter, in rapidly growing branches, especially when enterprises are situated in newly settled areas, the worker moves to the highest skill group more rapidly. This is not to be explained in terms of the skill level of the jobs performed, but appears to be due rather to differences in the age structure of the work force and the relative lack of job openings in the higher skill groups in the older branches.[76] Therefore, if skill is to be measured according to training time, the part of the total skill spectrum occupied by a branch will be significantly influenced by the weights ascribed to each element of training.

R. A. Batkaev and V. I. Markov made a rather crude but interesting attempt to measure a worker's total training time. The authors measured the time necessary to reach the highest skill group in several branches of industry. Special technical education, together with on-the-job experience, were expressed in a single index by assuming that

76. Kapustin (1964, pp. 129–194) maintained that in the more rapidly growing industries young workers form a large share of the work force. These workers, on the average, have a better general and technical educational background and are able to acquire more rapidly the knowledge necessary to advance to the higher skill groups.

Table 5.4
**Most Complex Work in Selected Branches: Unweighted Job Evaluation Technique
and Training Time**

Branch of Industry	Necessary Special Training and On-the-Job Experience in Converted Years (1)	Maximum Skill Group Occupied in Given Branch According to Single Skill Scale (2)
Concrete and rein- forced concrete	3.3	IV
Leather	4.3	V
Bread baking	4.3	V
Meat	4.8	V[a]
Peat	5.2	V
Shoes	5.2	V
Glass	5.2	VI
Oil refining	5.8	VI
Cement	5.8	V
Ferrous metals	6.5	V
Nonferrous metals	6.5	V
Textiles	6.7	VI
Sewing	7.2	VI
Machine construction	7.5	VI

Note: Constructed according to data given in Batkaev and Markov, 1964, pp. 72–74, and Mysev and Obolenskaia, 1963, pp. 69, 72. Though the former source presents data for 20 branches and the latter for 40 branches, correspondence could be found only for the 14 branches listed above. Batkaev and Markov also give the number of skill groups occupied by jobs in each branch according to a "single skill scale," but that scale is determined by their own measures of training time.
[a] Meat and milk.

the importance of the former was three times greater than that of the latter. Thus, one year of special technical education was converted into 1.5 years of training time and one year of on-the-job experience was made equivalent to 0.5 years of training time.[77]

In table 5.4 we compare these estimates of training time necessary to perform the most complex jobs in several industries with the results, already described, of an investigation undertaken by the Labor

77. The eight years of general education that the authors took as necessary in each branch can be disregarded for our calculation. Batkaev and Markov, 1964, pp. 71–74.

Institute to determine the number of skill groups needed to cover the skill levels of work performed in various industries.[78]

A general correspondence between the presumably independently determined columns 1 and 2 of table 5.4 is apparent. Excluding glass and oil refining, the higher the number of converted years of training time, the higher the skill-group classification according to the technique of job evaluation. Were training time in fact the sole method for determining relative skill levels, the results might not differ significantly from those obtained through existing Soviet job evaluation procedures. In terms of equity considerations, especially for Marxists, the explicit establishment of a connection between training time and skill differentials seems attractive. Possible conflicts between equity and efficiency considerations receive attention in our concluding chapter; here we should note that at a minimum, the collection of training time data should prove useful for two purposes.

First, information on training time can serve as a general check on the accuracy of the job evaluation technique itself, although some conflict may be expected. For example, two jobs might be classed in the same skill group according to job evaluation techniques. If, however, one demands little training but a "knack" or special native abilities, that job's skill group would be downgraded were training time used to determine skill level. Still, aside from such "economic rent" elements in skill classification, overall agreement between these two measures should be expected. Then again, training time might be used as an auxiliary consideration in determining the value of one of the functions in the job evaluation procedure itself.[79] A job evaluator collects measurements of average experience and education that surely must influence his estimate of the complexity of such a function as "calculations workers must make throughout the work process." Therefore, the two columns of table 5.4 should perhaps not be considered independently determined.

Second, although it is outside the scope of our study, we should note that such measures may be useful in establishing skill wage differen-

78. See "The Ongoing Reform of Skill Differentials" in chapter 4 and note to Table 5.4.
79. According to Maier (1963, pp. 87–88) it was then serving this function. Gomberg (1964, pp. 29–30) maintains that such measures should exist side by side with job evaluation in determining skill classification.

tials among general occupational and professional groups. Formal job evaluation techniques do not even attempt to compare, let us say, the skill of a bookkeeper with that of a lathe operator.[80] Here, a methodology similar to Maier's could be useful in making some general comparisons of the quality of labor expended by these different groups.

Although Maier, using training-time measures, has urged a reduction in skill differentials, there appears to be no relationship between his proposals and the actual narrowing of differentials that took place in 1968.

Impact of the 1968 Minimum Wage

From approximately the end of 1960 through 1967, minimum basic wage rates in industry were set at a level of 40–45 rubles a month. On January 1, 1968, this minimum wage was raised to 60 rubles a month.[81] The significance of the increased minimum for general measures of inequality is discussed elsewhere.[82] Here we are concerned with its impact upon skill differentials.

Given the decision to raise the minimum rate, two extreme alternatives with respect to skill differentials may be specified. On the one hand, the skill scales established during the reform could have been maintained with an across-the-board percentage increase of all basic wage rates. In each industry, the percentage would be set by the relationship between the 60-ruble minimum and the pre-1968 monthly basic wage rate for workers in the first skill group. In a low-paying industry such as food products, all basic rates would have to increase by approximately one-third.[83] The consequential expansion of the wage fund would be far in excess of the amount needed simply to

80. In a recent discussion of this issue, Kapustin (1968b, pp. 315–316) held that training time data should be used when attempting to compare skill levels of heterogenous groups of workers. See footnote 72.

In Western job evaluation procedures a company almost always has at least two systems of job evaluation. one for wage workers and the other for salaried white-collar personnel. For an excellent discussion of this practice see Wootton, 1962, pp. 140–160.

81. The 40–45 ruble minimum was established when the wages in each branch underwent reform. See Chapman, 1964, pp. 3–4; Kunel'skii, 1968a, p. 83. The original decree concerning the 60-ruble minimum dated November 20, 1967, is in *Builletin'*, no. 1, 1968, p. 3. The Government Labor Committee, along with Gosplan and the Ministry of Finance, played an important role in estimating and distributing the necessary additional wage funds among the various ministries. Vasil'ev, 1967, p. 10.

82. See appendix B. More detailed discussion is presented in Chapman, 1970.

83. As given in table A-1 of appendix A.

increase the minimum. On the other hand, leaving all basic rates above the 60-ruble minimum unaltered would have resulted in what was considered an unacceptable narrowing or elimination of differentials for workers in the lower skill groups.[84]

Soviet policy followed neither of these two extreme alternatives. Rather, the general approach was that with the establishment of the 60-ruble minimum, basic rates greater than 60 but less than 70 rubles a month were also increased.[85] Thus, the degree of compression of skill differentials within a given industry was inversely related to the magnitude of the industry's initial basic rate. Only for underground work in the coal industry, where all basic rates were in excess of 70 rubles, did the skill scale remain unaltered.[86] For other branches, both the ratio of extreme skill groups and relative differentials separating the lower skill groups were reduced. For example, in the low-wage food products industry, the 60-ruble rate for the first skill group was accompanied by a decreasing absolute addition for groups two through four while basic rates for workers in the fifth and sixth groups remained unchanged. The resultant decrease in the ratio of basic wages for groups one to six was from the 1:1.8 established during the reform to 1:1.35 in 1968.[87] In machine construction, the new minimum had a lesser impact: only the first two skill groups were affected, and the ratio of extreme basic rates fell from 1:2.0 to 1:1.8.[88] In several cases, seven- and eight-group scales were converted into a standard six-group pattern through the amalgamation of the first two or three groups.[89]

A long-established pattern in Soviet skill scales has been that the percentage differential separating successive skill groups tends to increase with movement up the skill ladder.[90] That is, taking R_i to represent the absolute basic rate for a given skill group,

84. Pak, 1967; Kunel'skii, 1968a, p. 84, and 1968b.
85. Pak, 1967.
86. Kunel'skii, 1968a, p. 86.
87. These magnitudes are based upon information provided by Kunel'skii (1968a, p. 87) and the light and food industry skill scale as presented in table 4.2.
88. Vasil'ev, 1967, pp. 5–6.
89. Kunel'skii, 1968a, p. 86. Only a minute portion of the work force was thus upgraded. See the discussion of effective skill groups in chapter 4 of this volume.
90. These increases were far more pronounced in the skill scales established during the 1930s. However, in scales implemented during 1927–1928, there was the opposite relationship, that is, relative differentials decreased between successively higher skill groups. See Barker, n.d., p. 47, and Kuznetsova, 1956, p. 17.

$$\frac{R_2 - R_1}{R_1} < \frac{R_3 - R_2}{R_2} < \cdots < \frac{R_n - R_{n-1}}{R_{n-1}}.$$

In skill scales established during the wage reform, the changing relative differentials between successive skill groups were not significant. For example, in machine construction the differential between the first and second skill groups was 13 percent, and between the fifth and sixth, 15 percent. With the 1968 increase of basic rates for workers in lower skill groups, the importance of the inequality signs in the equation, that is, the differentials between lower skill groups were reduced and those separating the upper groups remained unchanged.

In light of previously described scarcity conditions, an appropriate modification of skill differentials would have been in the opposite direction. Job rationing for work classified in higher groups indicates that if differentials were to be lowered, the reduction should have fallen upon the differentials separating these groups. However, given the decision to increase the minimum rate and an obvious reluctance to reduce money wages for any group of workers, a possibly more appropriate alteration of skill differentials would have necessitated a greater aggregate increase of the wage fund.

In short, the 1968 minimum wage increased the heterogeneity of existing skill scales. In relatively low-paying industries there was a considerably greater narrowing of skill differentials. On the other hand, as discussed in appendix A, the new minimum wage should be recognized as a step toward standardization of a different aspect of wage setting. The initial basic rates, or absolute wage levels for workers in the first skill group in the various industries, were brought closer together.

According to expressed Soviet intentions, the 1968 minimum rate has only temporarily deflected policy away from establishing a single skill scale throughout industry. Although it earlier had been reported that basic rates for workers in higher skill groups were to be raised in the first half of the 1970s so as to reestablish a 1:1.8 or 1:2 ratio of rates for the extreme skill groups,[91] apparently these plans have been revised. In 1971 Premier Kosygin announced that the round of wage increases scheduled for the period 1972–1974 would be composed of an increase of the minimum wage to 70 rubles a month and increases in

91. See Pak, 1967; Kapustin, 1968b, p. 330, and 1969, p. 26.

basic rates for workers classified within the unspecified range of "low-
and medium-paid." [92] As previously noted, these changes in rates are
to be accompanied by the establishment of a single skill scale in all
branches of industry. At the time of this writing, the structure of the
scale has not been made available; however, several of its aspects can
be delineated.

The few remaining seven- and eight-group scales will be replaced
by the single six-group skill scale.[93] Much like the 1968 increase of
minimum wages, the new minimum will entail an increase of the
initial basic rates in most branches of industry. However, unlike the
1968 law, the single skill scale most likely will necessitate raising basic
rates for a large percentage of workers in the upper skill groups. This
increase will be sharpest in low-wage industries. For example, in 1970
the basic rate for the first skill group in food products was 60 rubles
a month, and 81 rubles a month for the sixth skill group. Given the
new minimum wage, if the single skill scale has, as will surely be the
case, a ratio of rates for the extreme skill groups greater than 1:1.16
(70:81), workers in the upper skill groups will receive some additions
to their basic rates. Further speculation about the pattern of skill
differentials that will arise from the 1972–1974 changes in rates seems
unwise at this time. We need only stress that implementation of these
plans would signify an enormous step, possibly greater than that taken
during the 1958–1960 reform, toward the standardization of relative
as well as absolute skill differentials throughout industry. We shall
again turn to this issue in our concluding chapter. Although they are
less important as a determinant of differentiation of basic wages, differentials for working conditions must next be discussed.

92. During 1972, these changes are to be acomplished in certain northern regions
of the USSR, in 1973 in some eastern regions including Soviet Central Asia, and in all
remaining parts of the USSR during 1974. Kosygin, 1971, p. 12.
93. Khmirov, 1970.

6

Differentials for Working Conditions

Differentiation of Basic Rates and Earnings

The "law" of distribution according to labor requires that wages be set not only according to the quality or skill level demanded by the work performed, but also according to the "quantity of labor expended." The latter naturally has a time dimension—hours worked. In the Soviet approach, however, the quantity of labor expended in a given work day also differs with working conditions.

As previously discussed, basic wage rates for piece-rate workers are generally set at levels higher than those of time-rate workers.[1] The rationale for this policy is that piece-rate workers' labor is more intensive, and that this difference in quantity should be reflected in basic wages. In this chapter, we turn to the Soviet economist's attempt to quantify through job evaluation the pure wage differential for working conditions.

As compared to the literature on skill differentials, questions related to the quantity of work performed clearly occupy a secondary position. The wage reform produced neither a Unified Handbook nor even a standardized methodology for determination of quantity. There are several reasons for this.

First, the Soviet labor economist is primarily concerned with problems connected with the proper determination of relative money wages. In Soviet theory and practice, remuneration associated with varying skill levels, of qualities of labor, is purely monetary, in that all fringe benefits are directly dependent upon money wage differentials. On the other hand, differences in the quantity of labor expended, or in working conditions, are compensated for by a series of benefits not entering into calculations of relative money wages. Among the most important of these benefits are a reduced working day,[2] periodic rest periods dur-

---

1. For example, see table 1.2, and footnote 42, chapter 2.
2. This may be viewed as a higher monetary wage per hour, but in terms of Soviet wage administration it seems more useful to regard it as a nonmonetary benefit. Basic wages are determined on a monthly basis and hourly basic rates by dividing this monthly wage by the average number of hours worked for different groups of workers. In 1964, the divisor was 174.6 hours for those working according to a normal seven-hour day and 153.6 for those on a six-hour day. See "Elucidation of the Government Committee . . . and the Secretariat of the V.Ts.S.P.C. of September 24, 1964," in *Biulleten'*, no. 11, 1964, p. 31.

Table 6.1
Monetary and Total Compensation for Working Conditions in the Chemical Industry

	Relationship of Basic Monthly Rates (%)	Relationship of Basic Monthly Rates Including Valuation of Special Benefits (%)
For pieceworkers working under		
1. Normal conditions	100	100
2. Hot, heavy, and unhealthy conditions	113	135–140
3. Especially hot, heavy, and unhealthy conditions	133	160

Note: From Markov, 1959, p. 59. Unfortunately, the author does not explain what benefits are included in his calculations. He simply calls them *"l'goty i preimushchestva."*

ing working hours, longer and more desirable subsidized vacations, extra medical care, special foods, and extra pension upon retirement.

Even excluding consideration of differing lengths of the work day, such "hidden emoluments" [3] can add significantly to real differentials dependent on working conditions. A Soviet calculation, reproduced in table 6.1, is an attempt to measure the size of nonmonetary benefits for pieceworkers in the chemical industry according to monthly basic rates in 1959. Had the calculations been made on an hourly rather than monthly basis, the differentials would have been even greater, because of a shortened work day for some jobs.

Perhaps a more important reason for the relative lack of concern with quantity in the Soviet literature is simply that quality is more significant in the system of intraindustry wage determination developed during the wage reform of 1958–1960.[4] For example, as may be seen in table 1.2, for piecework, if quantity (or working conditions) is constant, and the quality (or skill levels) varies, basic rates vary by 100 percent, that is, from 30.5 to 61.0 kopeks under normal conditions, and from 37.8 to 75.6 kopeks for especially heavy and unhealthy working conditions. However, if skill is constant, and only working condi-

3. Dunlop, 1958, p. 357.
4. One Soviet calculation for 1962 showed that only 2.9 percent of the average wage in industry could be attributed to intraindustry differentiation according to working conditions, while 18.8 percent was due to skill differentials. Batkaev and Markov, 1964, p. 228.

tions vary, the maximum difference in base rates is 24 percent, or for unskilled pieceworkers from 30.5 to 37.8 kopeks and for the most highly skilled, 61.0 to 75.6 kopeks.[5]

Unfortunately, a comparison of the size and structure of differentials for working conditions in the periods preceding and following the wage reform is impossible. On the eve of the wage reform, differentials for working conditions were, like much of the system of wage administration, in a most "disorganized" condition. Since the early 1930s, a theoretical principle of Soviet job evaluation has been that differences in working conditions should be compensated for by a percentage addition to basic rates.[6] Nevertheless, the practice of increasing the skill-group classification of a job if it is performed under difficult conditions had also entered the formal system of wage administration. In a wage handbook for the food industry, published in 1947, a worker classified in the first or second skill group who was forced to lift or carry items weighing more than 50 kilograms was to be reclassified into the next highest skill group.[7]

The wage reform succeeded in eliminating such anomalies and in imposing single systems of intraindustry differentiation of basic wage rates for varying working conditions in each of the different branches of industry. Yet, even in the postreform period, data concerning the percentage of workers receiving higher basic rates due to working conditions are sparse and not nearly as extensive as those for differentiation according to skill level. Fragmentary information for the pre-reform year of 1955 and statements from Soviet economists that the scope of these increased rates widened during the reform indicate that more than one-third of Soviet industrial workers were paid according

5. See p. 13.
6. Earlier, the basic practice was to make certain lump-sum additions to the workers' basic rate rather than to include some remuneration for working conditions in the calculation of the rate. Batkaev, 1963, p. 65. Such additions remain widespread only in certain branches of mining industries. Markov, 1959, p. 61. The desirability of some sort of compensation for working conditions has been recognized in the USSR since 1918. Bergson, 1944, pp. 155–160..
7. *Edinyi Pishchevoi*, 1947, p. 5. Through the wage reform reportedly separated skill measurement from working conditions, in some cases the latter continued to influence a worker's skill-group designation. For example, as late as 1968, Dubovoi (1968, p. 18) held that measures had to be taken to "free" the determination of a worker's skill group from the influence of working conditions.

to these higher rates at the conclusion of the wage reform, and that by 1969 the figure was about 40 percent.[8]

The effect of the differentials for working conditions upon total differentiation of basic rates is also difficult to determine. The maximum potential gap in rates increases. For machine construction workers, as was shown in table 1.2,[9] skill differentials indicate a maximum gap of 1:2. Including differences for working conditions, basic rates show a maximum possible gap of 1:2.48. The effect of these differing rates upon any calculation of the inequality of basic rates would be dependent upon the existence of a correlation between skill group and classification according to working conditions. While the published data do not permit us to determine the existence of such a relationship, differentiation of basic rates by working conditions reportedly tends to reduce the inequality of intraindustry basic wages. The percentage of workers in the lower and middle skill groups paid according to increased rates is said to be "significantly higher" than that of the most skilled workers.[10]

Whatever the postreform scope and incidence of the differentiated rates for working conditions, Soviet economists find the system to be inadequate on at least two counts. First, there appears to have been little rationale and certainly no standardized interindustry methodology behind the established differentials. More important, the differentials incorporated in basic rates have not provided adequate incentive to attract workers to jobs performed under difficult conditions.

In three industries—machine construction, chemical, and petroleum refining—three levels of basic rates were established for pieceworkers of a given skill group, according to standards similar to those presented in table 1.2.[11] In the majority of other industries, only two were recog-

8. In 1955, the following rough percentages of workers were paid according to increased rates for working conditions: coal (in mines): 78 percent; ferrous metals: 66 percent; chemicals: 46 percent; machine construction: 25 percent. While not perfectly clear, these figures seem to include both timeworkers and pieceworkers who work under conditions considered to be other than "normal." Markov, 1959, p. 57. For 1962, Batkaev and Markov (1964, p. 26) reported these percentages to be 60 percent in the chemical industry, and "a bit less than one-third" in machine construction. The percentage for 1969 is given by Dubovoi, 1969, p. 58.
9. See p. 13.
10. Kapustin, 1964, p. 261.
11. For machine construction, this differentiation actually created three groups of first skill-group rates. See note to table 1.2.

nized, that is, there was no explicit differential for especially heavy and unhealthy working conditions.[12] In branches of the mining industries, is underground or surface, were established. In the production of concrete and reinforced concrete, the logging industry, and oil extraction, there was no differentiation of rates according to working conditions.[13]

Not only does the number of rates set according to working conditions vary among branches of industry, but there seems no rationale behind the levels at which these rates are set. Thus, the differential between conditions (2) and (3) of Table 1.2 is about 8–9 percent in light and food industries,[14] 13 percent in the chemical industry, and 14 percent in machine construction.[15] No explanation of these various levels of differentiation has been given by Soviet economists, although criticism has been frequent.

The administrative procedure for determining which work is to be paid according to higher rates is also unstandardized. At least until the introduction of the "new system" of economic management in 1965, for each branch of industry with such differentiation, superior planning authorities [16] compiled lists of jobs performed under conditions considered other than normal. In heavy industry, the enterprise director, along with the local trade union committee, may propose additions to these lists for work performed under "analogous" conditions. If confirmed by the economic agency immediately superior to the enterprise, these additional jobs may be paid according to the higher rates.[17] In branches other than heavy industry, such additions are not

---

12. Batkaev, 1963, p. 67.
13. Kapustin, 1961b, p. 89. A compilation of these basic rates for a group of selected industries may be found in Fearn, 1963b, pp. 67–73, and in Batkaev and Markov, 1964. p. 47.
14. This is the maximum increase due to working conditions; conditions described in row 4 of table 1.2 are simply not recognized for light and food industries. This relatively small differentiation for working conditions may help to explain the artificially high average skill group in these industries (see chapter 6). Possibly working conditions were considered in determining a worker's skill group because the explicit differentiation of rates for conditions was inadequate to attract a sufficient number of workers to the less attractive jobs.
15. Kapustin, 1961b, p. 89.
16. The Government Committee and the All-Union Central Council of Trade Unions. For conditions under the "new system" of economic administration, see chapter 7.
17. The lists are supposedly based upon the "unified listing of occupations" discussed in the concluding section of chapter 4. Such a list for machine construction shows 182 types of work classified as "hot and heavy," and 34 as "extremely heavy and unhealthy." Dorokhov, 1962, pp. 237–244. Such lists are also used for determining

permitted.[18] In all cases, the "collective agreements," approved by the enterprise trade union organization, were required to include a list of all jobs within the enterprise that were to be paid at higher rates because of working conditions.[19]

More significant than the lack of standardization is the fact that the differentials are inadequate. Each attempt to measure the relationship between working conditions and wage levels has demonstrated that differentiation of earnings far exceeds differentiation of basic wages. Were the latter relied upon, workers would be unwilling to undertake jobs performed under conditions other than normal. To quote one economist, "it is not difficult to guess" enterprise reaction to inadequate differentiation of basic rates.[20] The enterprise strives to correct[21] the insufficient centrally established differentials, usually by establishing loose norms for work performed under undesirable conditions. The freedom enjoyed by the enterprise in affecting interenterprise differentiation of earnings via the distribution of incentive payments is utilized for this purpose with the following result: "It should be recognized that within an enterprise at the present time, actual wage differentials dependent upon conditions of work are more detailed and more significant than the established basic rates."[22]

As demonstrated by continuing shortages of workers willing to undertake certain unpleasant jobs and a high rate of turnover in such work, the corrections are sometimes not sufficient.[23] Moreover, a "warping" of the formal system of wage determination takes place. The need to establish high-yield incentive systems at certain jobs serves as a barrier both to increasing the importance of basic rates as a determinant

which workers are to receive special clothing and other benefits. See Karinskii, 1963, p. 144, Smirnov, 1963, p. 55, and Kapustin, 1961a, p. 28.

18. Karinskii, 1963, p. 162; Kukulevich and Machikhin, 1961, pp. 32–33. Though formally prohibited, such additions were "not rarely" made without informing any superior economic authority. Batkaev and Markov, 1964, pp. 96–97. One economist proposed that such lists be eliminated, and that the planning authorities limit themselves to establishing standards for work that is to be paid according to the higher rates. Kapustin, 1964, p. 265.

19. Dvornikov and Nikitinskii, 1967, pp. 45–46.

20. Batkaev, 1963, pp. 67–68. The same point is stressed in Kapustin, 1961b, p. 90; Kapustin, 1964, p. 272; Bliakhman et al., 1965, pp. 116–117.

21. The term is Kapustin's (1964, p. 266).

22. Ibid., p. 272.

23. See our discussion of the shortage of operators in the concluding section of this chapter.

of earnings and to the establishment of tight technically based norms. Dissatisfaction with the size and structure of centrally established differentials for working conditions has engendered several proposed reforms as well as an attempt to develop theoretical standards by which proper differentials might be instituted, and it is to these questions that we now turn.·

Soviet Theory and Proposed Reforms

As discussed,[24] changes in the structure of the labor force supposedly indicate that skill differentials should be decreased. No such tendency is recognized for differentiation based upon working conditions. Although automation continually decreases the amount of heavy and unpleasant industrial work,[25] if workers are to be attracted to such jobs through differentiation of basic wage rates, the amount of this differentiation should be increased. The hypothesis that the Soviet worker's standard of living and educational level are inversely related to his willingness to undertake unpleasant jobs gives further reason for the need to increase differentials for working conditions.[26]

The Soviet economist usually begins his discussion of the necessity for differentiation of wage rates by citing differences in the quantity of labor expended, in terms of the physiological needs of the workers. Here, differences can be established with a high degree of precision. The person working under difficult conditions expends more caloric energy than the person working under normal conditions. Therefore, the former needs more food to continue such work, or, in Marxist terminology, a greater expenditure is necessary to reproduce his labor power. The worker laboring under difficult conditions should thus receive some wage advantage, if only to ensure that two workers of a given skill, working under different conditions, enjoy approximately the same level of income, allowing for differences in necessary food purchases.

The physiological aspect of wage differentiation has been quantified several times in the Soviet literature. Table 6.2 is based upon an investigation by the Institute of Nutrition of the Academy of Sciences.

24. Chapter 5.
25. A series of Western studies indicates that along with automation comes improvement in general working conditions as well as the elimination of many types of heavy work. For example, see Shultz and Weber, 1960, pp. 199–201.
26. Dubovoi, 1968, pp. 17–18.

Table 6.2
Physiological Basis of Wage Differentiation for Various Working Conditions

	Relative Caloric Expenditure Per Day (1)	Relative Cost of Market Basket of Food (2)	Relative Wage Differentials to Compensate for Differing Costs of Food in Average Family Budget (3)
Type of work performed:			
a. Not associated with physical labor	100%	100%	100%
b. With mechanized labor	117	106	103
c. With nonmechanized or partially mechanized labor	133	117	106
d. With heavy non-mechanized labor	150–160	129	115

Note: Batkaev, 1963, p. 66. Other calculations appearing in the Soviet literature for "caloric expenditure" differ only slightly from those presented in the first column of the table. See Maier, 1963, pp. 63–67; Aganbegian and Maier, 1959, p. 12, and Markov, 1959, p. 58.

One Soviet economist maintains that the relative "energy units of expenditure," as presented in the first column of table 6.2, provide sufficient basis for differentiating wages by quantity of labor performed. At a given skill level, the person working under condition d should be paid at a basic rate of 150 to 167 percent of that of the person employed under condition a. This forms the theoretical basis for measuring relative quantities, and no other considerations are necessary.[27]

Most Soviet economists, however, hold that calculations such as those in table 6.2 present but one aspect of wage differentiation for varying working conditions. The relationship shown in columns 2 and 3 are taken only as the necessary minimum compensation for physiological differences in working conditions. The second aspect of the problem,

27. Maier, 1963, pp. 63–67. In a sense this is consistent with his idea of setting skill differentials in accord with a measure of the cost of reproduction of labor power (see "Training Time and Skill Differentials" in chapter 5). However, as maintained by other economists and earlier by Maier and his coauthor, differentials for working conditions set in accord with column 3 of table 6.2 are only the minimum considerations. Aganbegian and Maier, 1959, p. 12. A cogent criticism of Maier's approach can be found in Batkaev and Markov, 1964, p. 94.

according to these authors, is the necessity of setting these differentials at a level high enough to "attract workers to the more difficult tasks." [28]

The considerable divergence of Soviet theory and practice from a physiologically determined compensation for differing working conditions is easily demonstrated. Compensation for working conditions is established via a percentage addition to the wages of workers of each skill group. In physiological terms, there is no reason to compensate the highly skilled worker for hot and heavy work with a greater monetary differential than that for the least skilled worker. Both would need the same additional value of food products to "reproduce" the labor expended. However, from table 1.2, it is evident that the unskilled pieceworker (first skill group) under condition 4 receives 7.3 kopeks per hour more than a worker of the same skill under condition 2; on the other hand, for the most highly skilled worker (sixth skill group), this differential amounts to 14.6 kopeks.[29] It is reported that "some economists" maintain that a lump-sum payment, independent of skill level, should be the compensation for arduous working conditions, but such economists are not influential.[30]

The justification for using a percentage addition to the base rate to compensate for working conditions centers around the need to attract both skilled and unskilled workers to the more unpleasant tasks.[31] While such a position seems eminently reasonable, it takes the Soviet economist far away from a physiological basis of wage differentiation for working conditions.

The most interesting attempt to formalize the measurement of quantity, as the weighted point method had formalized quality measurement, was presented in the Government Labor Committee's jour-

28. Markov, 1959, pp. 57–59; also see Dubovoi, 1968, p. 17, and 1969, p. 64.
29. It should be noted that data in table 1.2 refers to 1959, that is, before the reduction in skill differentials caused by a later increase in minimum wages (see "Impact of the 1968 Minimum Wage" in chapter 5).
30. I have not been able to find an example of this position. There are, however, several assurances that it has its advocates. See Aganbegian and Maier, 1959, p. 28, Kapustin, 1961b, p. 88, Maier, 1963, pp. 121–122.
31. The percentage addition "creates material self-interest for workers of any skill group, while an absolute addition that would create material self-interest for workers of the lower skill groups would not provide it for workers of the higher skill groups, or the situation would become such that the wages of workers of lower skill groups, working under undesirable conditions, would approach the wages of workers of higher skill groups, who are working under the same conditions." Kapustin, 1961b, p. 88.

nal, *Sotsialisticheskii Trud,* in late 1963. Unfortunately, there was no indication as to whether this was simply for purposes of discussion, or was actually adopted for implementation at some future date by the Committee. While its operational significance in wage determination is still problematical, the methodology presented is a useful example of recent Soviet thought concerning this aspect of wage differentiation.[32]

The approach to differentiation in basic rates from the standpoint of differing "quantities" of labor in table 6.3 is especially interesting for three reasons. First, it is an attempt to formalize this element of wage determination by means of a methodology completely analogous to that for determination of skill, or quality.[33] If such a system were adopted, all intraindustrial basic rates would for the first time be differentiated according to a standardized system.

Secondly, the number of these rates, as well as their differentiation, is large, compared to current Soviet practice. Under this system, piece-workers at a given skill level could have their wages differentiated at five levels; the current maximum is three. These differentials as established during the reform are set at a maximum of about 1:1.3, whereas under this proposal, the maximum differential would be 1:1.56.

Proponents of this approach hold that no less than five levels are required to account for the variety of industrial working conditions, though not all branches will have to utilize all five rates.[34] The maximum gap of 1:1.56 is not based on any theoretical measurements of "reproduction," but on existing intraindustry differences in average earnings (not basic rates) for work performed under varied working conditions. Thus, increasing the differential based on working conditions only explicitly recognizes conditions that are, in part, expressed in existing wage determination.

The third and most interesting aspect of table 6.3 is the groups of factors to be considered in setting differentials for working conditions.

32. Batkaev, 1963, pp. 65–70. The same methodology, in somewhat greater detail, may be found in Batkaev and Markov, 1964, pp. 91–109. Six years after its original publication, Dubovoi (1969, p. 65) stressed the need for this approach to setting differentials for working conditions. He adds that sociological research has shown that the minimum differential for working conditions should not be under 10 percent because a lower figure would be below the "threshold of recognition."
33. See table 4.3.
34. Batkaev (1963, p. 70) maintained that the first two or three levels should be sufficient for all working conditions in the light and foods industries, while all five levels would be utilized in industries such as coal and metallurgy.

The first two groups of factors lend themselves to objective and quantifiable measurement. "Hot and/or heavy" work is to be measured by considering factors such as weights lifted during the work process, amount of movement, intensity of the work process, and temperature. In determining the number of points for the "unhealthy" category one must consider atmospheric conditions, decibels of noise, tools or materials which are physically harmful, and so on.

The third group of factors, though weighted at only half the level of the first two, deserves special attention.[35] With "unattractive" added to "hot and heavy" and "unhealthy," the Soviet concept of quantity covers many of those considerations that might be grouped under "disutility" in Western economic theory,[36] among them dirtiness, monotony, unpleasant smells, and lack of the opportunity to improve qualifications. Such admittedly subjective considerations were neglected when basic wage rates were established during the reform. While readily admitting that it is difficult to objectively quantify "unattractiveness," the Soviet economist now recognizes the need for providing some wage differential for workers engaged in such tasks.[37]

If this system of differentiation for working conditions were introduced, along with the single skill scale previously discussed,[38] a system of relative intraindustrial basic wage differentials for all branches of industry could be generated. A possible variant of such a system is described in table 6.4. Here, the largest possible gap between the basic rates for workers in a given industry would be 1:3.12 in those branches where the gamut of skill levels and working conditions is recognized. Differentiation of basic rates in other industries would be covered by fewer than the thirty cells of the table.

The tidy schema presented in the table is far from current Soviet differentiation of basic wage rates. Moreover, were such a system established, the 1968 changes in skill differentials [39] would cause the magnitude of the coefficients to be reduced. However, some all-

35. The need for an explicit consideration of such factors in setting basic rates has been expressed by other Soviet economists. Kapustin, 1961b, p. 88.
36. However, the Western economist would tend to include under "disutility" the training time necessary to achieve a certain skill level. See footnote 38, chapter 4.
37. Batkaev, 1963, p. 69; Kapustin, 1961b, p. 88.
38. See chapters 4 and 5.
39. See chapter 5 and appendix B.

Table 6.3
A Weighted Point System for Determination of "Quantity" of Labor Expended, and Corresponding Relative Wage Differentials

	Range of Points (Minimum-Maximum [a])		
	Normal	Significant	Especially Significant
Hot and/or heavy	40–40	48–55	55–62
Unhealthy	40–40	48–55	55–62
Unattractive [b]	20–20	24–28	28–32

	Differentiation of Basic Rates (Skill-group Constant)				
	(1)	(2)	(3)	(4)	(5)
Level of basic rate as percentage of lowest basic rate	1.0	1.12	1.25	1.40	1.56
Range of points for each group	100	100–112	113–125	126–140	141–156

Note: From Batkaev, 1963, p. 69.
[a] Within each range, the number of points ascribed is dependent upon how much of the work day is spent under the designated conditions. The maximum number of points within the range is to be ascribed if more than one of the "groups of factors" are rated at a level other than "normal."
[b] The Russian term is neprivlekatelnost'.

industry system of basic rate differentiation is clearly the goal of wage administration.

Evaluation

There is no need to repeat our previous discussion concerning possible irrationalities involved in attempting to standardize differentiation of basic wage rates throughout industry. With one important modification, considerations similar to those discussed in connection with skill differentials apply to a standardized system of differentials according to working conditions.[40] Independent of the branch in

40. Let us assume that the structure of preference functions of individual workers for work under various conditions is similar in each of two branches of industry. In branch A half the work, and in branch B only one quarter of the work, is performed under hot and heavy conditions. If differentials are set high enough to induce half of the workers in branch A to undertake such work, the same differential in B would be higher than necessary. This point is further developed in our discussion of efficiency considerations in chapter 8.

Table 6.4

Possible Variation of a Single System for Differentiation of Intraindustry Basic Wage Rates

	Quality, or the Six-Group Skill Scale					
	I	II	III	IV	V	VI
Quantity, or relative rates for working conditions	1.0	1.15	1.32	1.52	1.75	2.0
	1.12	1.29	1.48	1.70	1.96	2.24
	1.25	1.44	1.65	1.90	2.19	2.50
	1.40	1.61	1.85	2.13	2.45	2.80
	1.56	1.79	2.06	2.37	2.73	3.12

Note: The skill scale neglects the 1968 minimum wage increase, and is assumed to be as described above. Differentiation of basic rates for working condition is as in table 6.3.

which they are employed, unskilled workers classified in the first skill group assumedly have the same qualification levels. On the other hand, the working conditions described by the term "normal" differ among branches. The "normal" classification in the nonferrous metals industry is taken to delineate a more difficult set of working conditions than in the textile industry. These interindustry differences in normal conditions receive compensation through variations of initial basic rates, that is, the basic wage of an unskilled person working under normal conditions in a given branch. Thus, these differentials have both an intraindustry and interindustry dimension.[41] We are concerned here only with the former.

As already noted, the general methodological approach to intra-industry differentiation of basic wage rates according to working conditions is akin to, but narrower than, the differentiation that the Western economist might explain in terms of the "disutility"[42] of work performed. The Soviet differentials may be viewed as an attempt to establish through job evaluation procedures an *ex ante* equalization of short-run "net advantages"—short-run in the sense that difficulties

41. This matter is further discussed in appendix A.
42. Scitovsky's discussion may be cited as one of numerous exposition of the question of compensation for the relative "unpleasantness" of different types of work. Naturally, to determine for only relative disutilities of various work, other factors, such as levels of income, skills, and training must be held constant. Scitovsky, 1951, pp. 96–104.

involved in acquiring skills through education or training are not to
be reflected. The proposed "weighted point system" for determining
differentials for working conditions [43] may be interpreted as an attempt
to construct an *ex ante* index of "job attractiveness" analogous to that
advocated by the Western labor economist Lloyd G. Reynolds.[44]

The Soviet approach, however, is not strictly *ex ante*. According to
recent literature, determination of the proper level of these differentials both anticipates and reflects scarcity conditions in the labor
market. If these basic rate differentials are set at the correct level, the
supply of workers willing to undertake the unpleasant tasks will be
adequate. On the other hand, Soviet economists have taken actual total
earnings differentials among workers employed under varying conditions as a standard for proper differentiation of basic rates. By contrast
to the literature on skill differentials, a great awareness of short-run
scarcity conditions is shown in discussions of differentiation of basic
wages according to working conditions. The shift in emphasis is explained by the fact that the wage elasticity of labor supplied for, let
us say, hot and heavy work must be assumed to be greater than that for
a given skill level.

We noted previously that scarcity conditions might be adapted to
fit the established structure of skill differentials through various educational policies. Short of militarization of the labor force, it is difficult
to envision similar nonwage policies that might be used to offset inappropriate differentials for working conditions.[45]

J. M. Clark has pointed out that once a laborer has invested time
or money in specialized training, "the result is, in a certain sense, fixed
capital which is useful in one occupation, and in no other, and which
must earn whatever return it can, because the investment cannot be

43. Table 4.3.
44. Lloyd G. Reynolds found the idea of an *ex ante* determination of the degree of
attractiveness of different jobs to be both practical and desirable within the framework of the American labor market. He maintained that "what they [workers] really
want is 'fair treatment' on their present job without moving. They want administrative equalization of job attractiveness rather than equalization through the painful
and uncertain process of mobility. . . . The proper basis for wage setting . . . is
the principle of equalizing the net attractiveness of jobs. . . . The development of
such a rating scale and its application to a variety of jobs throughout the economy
should have a beneficial effect on public thinking about wage determination
stopping short of direct wage regulation by government." Reynolds, 1951, pp. 260,
264–265.
45. However, see table 6.1 and the accompanying discussion of nonmonetary benefits.

withdrawn and moved into some other line of business." [46] If, let us say, skill differentials are too low, one would not expect the skilled worker to decide to become unskilled because of this "fixed investment." However, assuming the availability of other work, it is likely that a worker of any skill level would be unwilling to undertake hot and heavy work if he does not regard the corresponding wage differential as adequate. Thus, if workers in substantial numbers consider these differentials too meager, the inadequacy would be immediately felt and in all probability corrected at the enterprise level. Reportedly, during the wage reform, such corrections were made simultaneously with the institution of the new basic wage scales.[47] While it is possible that such differentiation might be too high, that is, produce job rationing for the work performed under difficult conditions, such a situation has yet to be reported in the Soviet literature.[48]

A Soviet survey of 2665 workers under the age of thirty also indicates that the labor supply for work performed under varying conditions is highly wage-sensitive. While the more skilled workers found factors other than wages to be most important in judging the desirability of a job, the unskilled workers engaged in heavy work tended to consider wages the most important factor. In spite of the fact that this latter group received relatively high wages, they were most likely to change their place of employment, and for this group wages "have a strong incentive influence." [49]

While proposed reforms are a step toward bringing differentials based on working conditions more closely into line with actual intra-industry scarcity conditions, a lacuna continues to exist in the Soviet approach. Both current wage administration and the proposed reforms suffer from an overemphasis on objective measurements of differences in job content. Subjective considerations such as workers' estimations of the desirability of various jobs are virtually neglected. This neglect

46. Clark, 1923, p. 15. Robertson (1960, p. 171) stressed that when we discuss skill differentials, "we are in a market with a very long-run equilibrium."
47. Dubovoi, 1968, p. 17.
48. However, it has been reported that these differentials may be "too high" in a different sense; that is, they may induce the skilled worker to give up his occupation in order to take an unskilled laborer's job that pays greater wages because it is performed under difficult working conditions. According to the Leningrad survey, this is likely to happen only among workers having a very limited educational background. Bliakhman et al., 1965, pp. 74–78.
49. Zdravomyslov and Iadov, 1964, pp. 76–78.

seems not unrelated to the relative scarcity of machine tool operators as compared to mechanics [50] during the period following the wage reform.

According to the reports of a conference held in 1962 by the editors of the journal *Sotsialisticheskii Trud* (Socialist labor) the shortage of operators was not limited to any specific geographical areas.[51] In a group (*kombinat*) of Leningrad machine construction enterprises, the problem had become acute enough to be considered a "serious brake on technical progress" and the basic obstacle to establishing a second shift in these plants.[52] In another Leningrad plant, the need for operators was "exceptionally great," with a labor separation rate for this occupation at about twice the level of any other occupation.[53] A similar situation was reported from a machine construction enterprise in the Latvian city of Elgava,[54] and the shortage was considered "critical for most plants in the Kiev region." [55]

In the Leningrad enterprises, educational policies were not able to ease the shortage. In a two-year period, about as many operators left the plants as entered after graduation from vocational-technical schools. Inplant training also proved inadequate, with only 30 percent of those trained remaining within the plants.[56]

The shortage of operators appears to be specific to the occupation in question rather than general for workers of some skill level. This is reported as a typical occurrence. A young unskilled worker applies for a job involving training as a mechanic. When told that there are no

---

50. A further note on terminology is necessary. Both "mechanic" and "operator" are general occupational designations. The meaning of mechanic (*slesar'*) was discussed in footnote 57, chapter 4. Operator (*stanochnik*) refers to a person operating a stationary cutting or grinding machine tool. Persons working at a drill press (*sverlovshchik*), a horizontal lathe (*tokar'*), or a milling machine (*shlifovshchik*) are all considered types of operators.

A large number of workers are covered by these occupational designations. According to the 1959 census of the almost six million workers classified as "metal workers and workers in radio electronics production" (*metalisty i rabochie v elektroradio proizvodstve*), about 30 percent are classified as mechanics, and 23 percent as various types of machine tool operators. *Itogi Vsesoiuznoi Perepisi*, 1962, p. 146; Bakhrakh, 1962b, p. 58.

51. "Puti," 1962, pp. 40–41.

52. "Kadry," 1965, p. 19.

53. Andreev and Belikanov, 1965.

54. "I Vse-taki Tarif," 1965, p. 11.

55. Zenin, 1966.

56. "Kadry," 1965, p. 19. The two-year period is probably 1963–1964.

openings for mechanics, but vacancies exist for operators, the young worker answers, "I don't want to be an operator—and that's that." [57] In the Latvian plant, out of 100 workers seeking jobs 94 wanted to become mechanics and only 6 were willing to become operators.[58] The Leningrad survey of labor turnover showed that of all mechanics who changed their place of work, 26.8 percent also changed occupation; the corresponding figure for operators was 48.6 percent.[59]

There was no difference in the methodology for determining the skill group for an operator as compared to a mechanic. Measures of training time indicate an insignificant difference between these two occupations. Approximately the same amount of time is necessary to train the unskilled worker for either occupation, and on-the-job training necessary to move into successive skill groups is also the same.[60]

Until 1968, Soviet economists usually maintained that the sole reason for this shortage of operators involved norm setting. The piece-rate norms for the mechanic are easier to fill, and therefore their earnings tend to be higher than those for operators. While this explanation has some validity and has been commented upon,[61] an alternative, or rather an additional explanation, was not discussed in the Soviet literature.[62]

A machine-tool operator's job, while often demanding a high level of qualification, is tedious and repetitious and usually involves being tied to a single work space. In contrast, the mechanic is called upon to fabricate a variety of single machine parts, to keep a number of machine tools in repair, and to move about the work shop while performing such tasks. Western studies of workers' preferences, or "job satisfaction," indicate that the mechanic's work is more desirable.[63]

57. "Kadry," 1965, p. 19.
58. "I Vse-taki Tarif," 1965, p. 11.
59. Bliakhman et al., 1965, pp. 72–73. This survey is described in footnote 20, chapter 3.
60. This is based upon the data presented by Batyshev (1965, pp. 231–234) for training time for a mechanic as compared to that for a horizontal lathe operator (tokar'), which is by far the most important type of operator. Itogi Vsesoiuznoi Perepisi, 1959, p. 146.
61. See chapter 3.
62. However, see footnote 66.
63. Walker and Guest's (1952, pp. 38–80) study of workers in an auto plant documents that "men who had nonrepetitive jobs liked the varied nature of their work, and that those whose jobs were repetitive disliked that aspect of the job" (pp. 52–53). Also see Mayo's (1933, pp. 81–85) comments on the relationship between monotony and

Lack of "job interest," or simply, boredom, did not play any role in the system of wage differentials for working conditions established during the reform. While "monotony" does appear in the proposed weighted point system for determining these differentials, its weight seems negligible. Monotony, along with dirtiness, odors, small chance of advancement, and other disadvantages, is to be evaluated as a part of the group of factors designated as the "unattractiveness" of work. If a job is "normal" in terms of the temperature of the work place, weights moved, and health hazards, the maximum differentiation of basic rates to allow for "especially significant unattractiveness" is only 12 percent.[64] However, according to the results of the Leningrad survey, the portion of workers who specified that they changed jobs for reasons included under "unattractiveness" was 14 percent. "Dirty work" constituted the motivation for 2.2 percent of those who left; "monotony," for 2.0 percent; and absence of prospects for increasing qualifications, for 9.8 percent.[65]

In Soviet job evaluation procedures, there appears a bias against adequate consideration of subjective factors that fit neatly neither into the category of "skill" nor into that of "working conditions." The shortage of operators was, in large measure, explained by this bias. The ease with which centrally established, technically based output norms could be applied to jobs performed by operators seriously constrained the enterprise's ability to correct the inadequate level of basic wages.[66] In recognition of the problem, but not of its cause, new regulations were implemented in an attempt to increase the incentive yield on jobs performed by workers in this occupation. In addition to the establishment of various special premiums, enterprise managers were given the authority to lower centrally established output norms for an operator by as much as 40 percent during the first three months of his employment, and by as much as 20 percent in the succeeding three months. Such measures proved inadequate.[67]

---

job satisfaction, especially his discussion of boredom being "fairly prevalent among operatives employed on repetitive processes."

64. Above, table 6.3.

65. Bliakhman et al., 1965, p. 54. It is notable that on the strength of the result of the survey, these authors proposed (pp. 82, 124–125) that the basic rates for work performed at a constant pace should be set at a level higher than that for mechanics and others whose work is classified as hand labor.

66. See chapter 3.

67. Parfenov and Shor, 1968, p. 28; Kunel'skii, 1967, p. 13.

In an earlier version of this study, it was stated that "operators will probably remain a deficit occupation until their relative basic rates are systematically increased." [68] In September 1967, a general increase was announced. Average basic rates were increased by 15 percent, and, while more complicated in detail, the general pattern was a 32 percent increment for those in the first skill group, 20 percent for the second, and 12 percent for operators classified in skill groups three through six. By May 1968, the new rates had been put into effect for all of the approximately 1,400,000 operators working in industry.[69] In addition, several new premium regulations especially advantageous to operators were instituted.[70]

It is too early to determine the effect of these measures on the shortage of operators. The fact that an across-the-board increase in the basic wages of a single occupation was deemed necessary does, however, indicate a lack of flexibility in, and a certain ineptness of, Soviet centralized wage determination. Issues such as these are broader than the question of differentials for working conditions, and may be better discussed in our concluding chapter.

68. Kirsch, 1967, p. 214.
69. In fact, two sets of basic rates were established. The percentage increases given in our text were derived by comparing the new "group two" rates with those presented in table 1.2. The classification of machine construction enterprises into two groups (see note to table) was not changed. In branches other than machine construction, the higher "group one" rates apply to operators working in those branches generally designated as heavy industry. The absolute basic rates appear in *Biulleten'*, no. 2, 1968, pp. 3–4; and the classification of industries, in Goberman, 1970, pp. 137–138. Simultaneously with the establishment of the new rates, operators who had been paid according to seven- or eight-group skill scales were transferred to one of the two new six-group scales. For further information on these new rates, see *Ek. Gaz*, no. 39, 1967, p. 2 and no. 2, 1968, p. 18; *Trud*, December 3, 1967 and February 27, 1968; *Rabochaia Gazeta*, September 12, 1968; Kunel'skii, 1968a, p. 87; and Parfenov and Shor, 1968, pp. 28–29.
70. These involved an increase of both the level of and ceiling on premium payments to operators working according to technically based norms. In addition, enterprises were given the right to pay operators double time for night work. Kunel'skii, 1968b and Parfenov and Shor, 1968, p. 29.

7

The Role of the Enterprise and the "New System" of Economic Management

The "New System"

Two concerns provide the focus for this chapter. First, in light of several changes in Soviet economic administration initiated in 1965, some further delineation of the enterprise's administrative role in wage determination is in order. Second, the "material incentive fund" established by these changes and its possible impact upon earnings determination for workers in industry must be discussed. The modifications of economic administration, involving an increase in the enterprise's autonomy as well as a restructuring of its "success indicators," have been described by a Western economist as "an economic revolution in the U.S.S.R." [1] More modestly, Soviet economists refer to them as the "new system." [2] By the middle of 1969, enterprises producing approximately 80 percent of industrial output were working in accordance with the new regulations. [3]

Often associated with the proposals developed by the Kharkov economist Evsei Liberman, the "new system" properly refers to the changes in planning announced by Premier Kosygin in 1965. [4] Virtually simultaneous was the publication of the Statute on the State Productive Enterprise (henceforth, Enterprise Statute) and the announcement that the regional economic councils created in 1957 were to be eliminated in favor of reestablished branch ministries. [5] Several tentative and intriguing attempts to delineate the implications of these measures for the entire system of centralized planning have already appeared. [6] Our discussion is equally tentative but, because of the apparently minor impact of these measures upon earnings determination, un-

1. This is the title of Goldman's (1967) article. A more moderate appraisal of the import of this reform is presented by Bergson (1967). The most detailed treatment of the background of these reforms appears in Felker, 1966.
2. A shortened form of the official designation "The New System of Planning and Economic Stimulation."
3. *Ek. Gaz.*, no. 29, 1969, p. 1.
4. Kosygin, 1965.
5. "Polozhenie," 1965; Kosygin, 1965. While most of the provisions of the Statute immediately went into effect with its publication, the new system was to be gradually expanded. See *Ek. Gaz.*, no. 3, 1966, p. 16.
6. Campbell, 1968 is especially stimulating.

fortunately less intriguing. The basic outline of workers' wage determination described in previous chapters remains essentially unchanged.

Still, several issues deserve discussion. First, it should be stressed that the ministries established in 1965, unlike their pre-1957 counterparts, have little control over the distribution of earnings among workers within their administrative jurisdiction. With the exception of establishment of centralized piece-rate output norms, none of the authority that had come to reside with the Government Labor Committee has been transferred to the ministries. All decrees, instructions, and explanations concerning wage setting continue to emanate from the Government Labor Committee and the All-Union Central Council of Trade Unions. The conflicts that existed between the Labor Committee and the various ministries prior to 1957 have not reappeared.[7]

In 1968, authority in establishing centralized piece-rate output norms was transferred from the Government Labor Committee to the individual ministries. Determination of the importance of or rationale for this shift of administrative jurisdiction is not yet possible. Prior to 1968, such norms became operational and, in some cases, mandatory [8] on being issued by the Government Labor Committee and a trade union organization that "corresponded" to the group of workers covered by the norm. According to the 1968 statute, the ministry and a "corresponding" trade union organization become responsible for issuing output norms for jobs performed by workers within the given ministry,[9] as well as for organizing the process of norm reviewing.[10] It is not clear whether the separate ministries will now develop their own norming bureaus or whether this work will remain with the Government Labor Committee and only official approval will be given by the affected ministry. In view of the previous performance of ministries in this sphere of wage administration, one hopes that the latter is the case.[11]

The ambiguous wording of regulations concerning the new system, especially that of the Enterprise Statute, makes it too easy to overstate

7. See "The Wage Reform: A Brief History" in chapter 1.
8. See chapter 3.
9. Lifshits and Sorinskii, 1968, pp. 109–110, p. 116.
10. "Obshchee Polozhenie o Ministerstvakh," 1967.
11. See the first section of chapter 3.

the autonomy of the enterprise in the determination of systems of
wage payments and the distribution of the wage fund. The Enterprise
Statute of 1965 states that the enterprise has the right to decide if
piece rate or time rate is to be used in wage determination for different
groups of workers.[12] At first glance, the Statute seems to follow the
recommendations of several economists who have maintained that only
at the enterprise "can all important aspects of this problem be studied." [13] The importance, or lack thereof, of this provision can best be
gauged in terms of both the previously established role of the enterprise and the interpretation of the provision since the Statute's
publication.

Prior to being replaced by regional economic councils in 1957, the
various ministries drew up lists of jobs that were to be covered by the
different systems of wage payments.[14] Subsequently, these lists were
replaced by a number of "model" enumerations of jobs to be paid
according to either time or piece rate issued by the Government Labor
Committee. Officially, these were only "methodological guidelines." [15]
With the exception of progressive piece rate, for which the approval
of a superior agency was mandatory,[16] formal authority to decide
which wage system was to be used rested with the enterprise. The
meaning of this formal right was, however, questionable. In 1962, the
head of the labor division of the Kirov regional economic council reported that his division had put together a list of occupations that had
to be paid according to either time rate or piece rate throughout that
economic region.[17] Moreover, the "model" rules appear to be less
discretionary than the term implies. In 1961, one economist held that
enterprise independence in determining premium payments should
be "greater than exists at the present time," [18] and in 1963 another
economist found it necessary to stress that the "model" rules should be
interpreted as no more than "suggestions." [19]

Despite the wording of the Statute, since 1965 the enterprise's free-

12. "Polozhenie," 1965.
13. Kapustin, 1961a, pp. 53–54; Shkurko, 1961, pp. 104, 151; Bliakhman et al., 1965,
p. 128.
14. Karinskii, 1963, pp. 148–149.
15. Kapustin, 1961a, pp. 53–54.
16. Karinskii, 1963, p. 148.
17. Podolskii, 1962, p. 94.
18. Shkurko, 1961, p. 151.
19. Maier, 1963, p. 235.

dom in this sphere of wage administration has remained limited. In a
few branches of industry there are enumerations of occupations that
are to be paid according to specific types of time-plus-premium and
piece-plus-premium systems. These must be followed and can in no
way be altered at the enterprise level.[20] More important, a 1968 collection of legal commentaries on the Statute simply states that enterprise authority in choice of wage systems is defined by a regulation
of 1958, which remains fully in effect, and that "now these [enterprise]
rights are reflected in the Statute." [21] In other words, the situation remains as hazy as it was prior to 1965.

As to authority in determining which groups of workers are to be
paid the higher basic rates for unusual working conditions, the Statute
indicates no change in established procedure. The increased rates are
to be paid only "in accordance with the established typical enumerations of occupations and types of work that exist in the various
branches of production." [22] In some cases, with the approval of the
Government Labor Committee, jobs that are "analogous" to those
specified in the enumeration can be paid at the higher rates.[23]

Although the Statute indicates no expansion of enterprise authority
in establishing premiums paid out of the wage fund,[24] indirect and
tentative evidence indicates that the new system has in fact resulted in
an enhancement of enterprise autonomy in this area. Premiums continue to be established "on the basis of" the typical regulations that
exist for each branch of industry, but the literature stresses that these
regulations are "highly flexible" and should be viewed simply as an
attempt "to ensure uniform procedure for awarding premiums without narrowing the right of the enterprise to utilize one or another
method of stimulation." [25] A more important indicator of increased
enterprise authority is the wording of the typical premium regulations
in branches that had been transferred to the new system as compared

20. Laptev, 1968, p. 220. Earlier it was reported that these enumerations existed only
in the coal and ferrous metals industries. Karinskii, 1963, p. 149.
21. Laptev, 1968, p. 211.
22. "Polozhenie," 1965. For example, see *Biulleten'* (no. 11, 1969, pp. 25–34) for this
enumeration in construction materials.
23. Laptev, 1968, p. 216. Earlier, it was reported that the approval of the ministry was
necessary. *Ek. Gaz.*, no. 3, 1966, p. 16.
24. Premiums originating from the material incentive fund are discussed later in this
chapter.
25. These regulations are distinct from the mandatory enumerations.

to branches not transferred. For the latter industries, the regulations are considerably more detailed and, from the point of view of the enterprise, more confining.[26]

As in the past, the wage fund remains an essential component of control in wage administration. Several "experiments" are currently being conducted that significantly increase enterprise autonomy in the use of the wage fund, among them the highly publicized Shchekino experiment. As of yet, they have proven to be inconclusive and are discussed in a long footnote.[27] Here we are concerned with the impact of the new system, which has brought only some apparently minor and easily overestimated [28] departures from past regulations. Before 1965, superior agencies determined or affirmed the enterprise's total wage fund as well as the average wages to be paid to each of the three groups employed by the enterprise: workers, office workers, and managerial-technical personnel. For enterprises transferred to the new system, only the global wage fund is now determined by the superior agency, and thus the share of the fund going to each of the three classes of personnel is determined by the enterprise.[29]

26. *Ek. Gaz.*, no. 43, 1967, pp. 16–17. The "Standard Regulations Concerning Premiums" appeared in February of the same year, no. 8, pp. 9–10 and in *Biulleten'*, no. 4, 1967, pp. 1–10. Also see Laptev, 1968, p. 219; Izmenenia, 1966; and *Biulleten'*, no. 9, 1966, pp. 6–47.
27. For example, see Felker, 1966, pp. 95–96.
28. Shchekino is a large chemical complex near the city of Tula. Begun in 1967, the experiment essentially consisted of guaranteeing that the enterprise's wage fund would not be changed for a period of three years. Therefore, if the number of employed personnel was reduced, there would be no corresponding reduction of the wage fund, and part of the saving could be divided among those continuing to work at the complex. In fact, employment was reduced, and earnings increased considerably faster than the average for industry. The experiment, with serious modifications, has been expanded. By 1970, about 70 enterprises employing more than 400,000 persons were included. However, it appears that the increasing scope of the experiment was accompanied by increasing restrictions on enterprise freedom as well as serious dilution of the innovative importance of the "Shchekino method." For one of the latter groups of enterprises included in the experiment, the "98 enterprises," the change appears minimal. For these plants, the material incentive fund is determined according to standard regulations (shortly to be discussed), but the size of the fund is increased with fulfillment of plan targets if the enterprise has incorporated within its plan an increase in labor productivity greater than a certain "norm" established for the given type of enterprise. See Goldman, 1970; Volkov, 1970; "Stimulirovanie," 1970; *Ek. Gaz.*, no. 10, March, 1970, p. 11; *Pravda,* January 23, 1970, p. 2; Baranenkova, 1970; and Brown, 1970.
29. This is not a provision of the Enterprise Statute, which states that the size and structure of the staff of office workers and managerial-technical personnel and their average wages emanating from the wage fund must be in accord with the "estab-

On the surface, this is a major expansion of enterprise prerogative. While centrally determined wage and salary scales remain mandatory, in formal terms the enterprise becomes able to determine both the distribution of the given wage fund among the three types of personnel and the skill and occupational mix within each group. However, the importance of the wage fund within the system of enterprise success indicators as well as the procedures by which the fund is determined indicate that in practice enterprise discretion is less than regulations suggest.

Within the Soviet system of enterprise "success indicators" and corresponding managerial bonuses, the wage fund continues to play a pivotal role. For each quarter of the planning year, the enterprise is permitted to pay out a given wage fund if the gross output target is met. If gross output is, let us say, 2 percent short of this target, the enterprise's wage fund is reduced by the same percentage. On the other hand, for each percentage point overfulfillment of the gross output plan, the wage fund is increased by between 0.6 percent and 0.9 percent, depending on the branch of industry. Thus for each level of output there is a corresponding maximum sum of wages that can be paid out. While the penalties for overexpenditure of the wage fund were made somewhat less severe in 1966, there remains little question that Soviet managerial personnel avoid overexpenditure of the fund when possible. Before 1966, overexpenditure in any quarter of the plan year entailed no bonuses to be paid to managerial personnel until the overexpenditure was repaid to the Government Bank (Gosbank). Currently, overexpenditure entails a 50 percent reduction of bonus payments that would otherwise be received by managerial personnel until the overexpenditure is repaid, but such reduction is to be continued for a period not greater than 18 months. The single source for such

lished typical structure" and authorized by a superior agency. Only enterprises working according to the new system are freed from this regulation. See "Polozhenie," 1965; Laptev, 1968, pp. 246–247.

It should be further noted that, according to Karpukhin (1963, pp. 135–136), since 1959 enterprises have had the "right" to determine both the composition of employment among classes of personnel and the share of the wage fund going to each group; in other words, only the aggregate fund and total employment were to be determined by superior agencies. If this "right" was granted, it clearly was not exercised. For example, in 1963, Proshko (1963, p. 104) specifically requests that enterprises be granted this authority. For further discussion of the wage fund and managerial motivation, see Bergson, 1964, pp. 78–80.

repayment is "economizing" the wage fund—that is, at some future date paying out less than the permitted maximum. The procedures, time limits, and penalties for overexpenditures are complex; [30] here it is sufficient to stress that the regulations are such that managerial personnel will attempt to avoid overexpenditure whenever possible.

Despite the new system, enterprise discretion in distributing the global wage fund among the various categories of personnel appears severely limited. Wage fund disimbursements are closely monitored by superior agencies that are to receive data on the planned and actual monthly, quarterly, and yearly relationship between wages and productivity disaggregated according to classification of personnel; [31] monthly reports on the fulfillment of the enterprises's labor plan; [32] periodic information on the average amount of wages paid to workers (other categories of personnel are excluded) per unit of output; [33] and numerous other types of reports relating specifically to the three categories of personnel. [34]

Monitoring wage fund expenditures in itself need not entail constraints on enterprise discretion. Dynamic considerations, however, indicate that this is the case. Superior agencies set the planned wage fund on the basis of an evaluation of disaggregated indices of current wage fund expenditures. According to the highly authoritative book issued by Gosplan in 1969, *Methodological Instructions Concerning the Compilation of the State Plan . . .*, enterprises submit estimated "element by element" changes in the wage fund for the planned period, and the "ministries make a detailed analysis of these changes." For determining the actual magnitude of the planned fund, "the structure of wages during the base period is taken as the foundation for this calculation, and changes are made in individual elements as a

---

30. As of 1964, only the Government Labor Committee has the power to free the enterprise from the obligation to repay overdrawn wage funds. For general descriptions of wage fund regulations see "Zarabotnaia Plata," 1964; Maier, 1963, pp. 142–143; "Puti," 1962, pp. 144–145; Karpukhin, 1963, pp. 163–164; *Ek. Gaz.*, no. 50, 1964, p. 39. Discussions of the effects of the new regulations upon the enterprise's wage fund appear in Laptev, 1968, pp. 250–255; *Ek. Gaz.*, no. 10, 1966, p. 31, and no. 43, 1967, p. 17; Kurskii and Slastenko, 1966, p. 14; and Batukhtin, 1969.
31. See "Letter of Instruction" issued by Gosplan, the Government Labor Committee, the Ministry of Finance, and the Central Statistical Administration in *Biulleten'*, no. 5, 1966, pp. 8–9.
32. *Metodicheskie Ukazaniia*, 1969, p. 321.
33. That is, *trudoemkost'*, most often translated as "labor intensiveness."
34. See Gur'ianov and Kostin, 1967, especially pp. 272 ff.

result of anticipated increases in labor productivity, changes in the structure of personnel, and elimination of various additional payments." [35]

We can little more than speculate about the constraints that such disaggregated evaluation of wage fund disbursements places upon the enterprise. Such speculation leads one to believe that even under the new system, if the enterprise is to obtain a wage fund that it views as satisfactory for the planned year, in the current year it must strive for a pattern of wage expenditures among classes of personnel that superior authorities will find to be "proper." [36]

The Material Incentive Fund

In contrast to previous policy, by which virtually all profits reverted to the government budget, under the new system a portion of profits earned by the enterprise remains at its disposal. The regulations for determining the actual amount kept by the enterprise are enormously complex, and there is little need to catalogue them here. They differ not only according to industrial branch, but even among enterprises within a given branch. In most general terms, the amount of profits remaining with the enterprise is a function of enterprise performance measures in terms of certain "normed" or expected returns on fixed and working capital (the "profitability index"), as well as the total value of goods sold by the enterprise. Profits remaining with the enterprise are then distributed, again in accordance with complex and specific regulations, among three funds: the "social-cultural fund," to be used for creating social amenities, including housing for enterprise personnel; the "fund for development of production," which is to be utilized by the enterprise for the expansion of capital investments; and the "material incentive fund."

Here, our concern is limited to the last fund. Enterprises have the right to transfer monies between the first two funds, but no such transfers can be made to or from the material incentive fund, which, in large part, is determined according to independent standards.[37] As im-

35. *Metodicheskie Ukazaniia* (1969, pp. 292–294) has been translated into English; see bibliography for citation.
36. Our previous discussion of possible bargaining about the size of the wage fund (above, chapter 3) would fully apply to enterprises working under the new system.
37. The general pattern seems to be that from 80 to 90 percent of the material in-

plied by its name, this fund is established to provide a relationship between an individual's earnings and the performance of the enterprise
in which he is employed.

For workers, any payments received from the material incentive
fund are additional to normal premiums and other incentive payments
emanating from the wage fund. On the other hand, all premiums and
bonuses received by office workers and managerial-technical personnel
originate from the material incentive fund. Therefore, norms for determining the magnitude of the fund are set so as to ensure that if the
enterprise meets its planned targets, employees and managerial-technical personnel will receive their customary premium payments.[38] In
contrast to the constraints on wage fund expenditures, at least until
1969 the enterprise enjoyed almost complete freedom in distributing
the material incentive fund. Unlike previously discussed premium or
bonus payments, there is no ceiling on the amount that an individual
might receive from the material incentive fund.[39]

Reportedly the enterprise's use of this discretion has caused an
undesirably meager portion of the material incentive fund to be
distributed among workers. For enterprises working under the new

---

centive fund is dependent upon the profitability index and the remaining portion
dependent upon the value of goods sold. Acharkan, 1966.

As of October 1965, the norms used for determining this fund were developed
jointly by the Government Labor Committee, the Ministry of Finance, and the All-
Union Central Council of Trade Unions. It is reported that in 1967 the Labor Committee temporarily ceased to play a role in this process "until more experience has
been accumulated." Shkurko, 1967, p. 21; "Rabotnikam Predpriiatii," 1967, p. 49.
The Shkurko article is a lucid and critical discussion of procedures for determining
the material incentive fund.

38. Shkurko (1967, p. 20) reports that for enterprises operating on the new system
in 1967, norms were established so that at plan fulfillment the material incentive
fund would be at a magnitude equal to 9 percent of the wage fund. In that all
their premiums originate from the material incentive fund, this standardized approach operated to the disadvantage of office workers and managerial-technical personnel working in branches where they constituted a higher-than-average share of
the labor force. The role of normal premium payments for these personnel is
specified in *Biulleten'*, no. 5, 1966, pp. 8–9.

39. Mirgaleev and Peshkin, 1966, reported that at one Kharkov tractor factory, a
professor of psychology was called in to provide expert advice as to what sort of
distribution of this fund would be "psychologically most effective in providing
incentives."

The necessity of guaranteeing complete enterprise autonomy in the distribution
of this fund was even stressed by a representative of the Ministry of Ferrous Metals
in *Trud*, September 21, 1966. Also see Volkov and Grishin, 1966, p. 31.

system during the first half of 1966, the average amount received by workers from the material incentive fund was only 50 kopeks a month.[40] According to several articles appearing in the trade union newspaper *Trud* during 1966, the problem was not that the amounts distributed were inadequate, but rather that an inordinately high share of the payments went to the enterprise's office workers and managerial-technical personnel.[41]

Though workers constitute more than 80 percent of those employed in industry, they received only about one-fourth of all monies paid out of the fund.[42] In one glass-producing factory, technical and clerical personnel received a quarterly bonus out of the material incentive fund equivalent to 97.8 percent of their normal monthly earnings; the figure for higher administrative personnel was 147.2 percent. Payments to workers from this fund were "not even considered." [43] Some sources hold the trade unions responsible in that the local union does not take its assigned active part in decisions concerning the distribution of the fund. According to a member of the Labor Institute, properly "the trade unions are, in the full sense of the word, the masters (*khoziaeva*) of this fund." [44]

Two factors are to be considered in evaluating the significance of reports that the workers' share of the material incentive fund is inadequate. First, up until February 1969, neither initial announcements of the new system nor the various "clarifications" indicated that the central authorities had a conception of "proper" proportions in the distribution of the fund among classes of personnel.[45] Second, all premiums for office workers and managerial-technical personnel emanate from the material incentive fund, while workers continue to receive such payments from the wage fund as well. Therefore, simply in order to stabilize given earnings differentials among classes of personnel, the

---

40. Mirgaleev and Peshkin, 1966.
41. Acharkan, 1966; Lavruk, 1966; Vardimiandi, 1966; Mirgaleev and Peshkin, 1966; Rykov, 1966.
42. Mirgaleev and Peshkin, 1966.
43. Rykov, 1966. Also see Oblomskaia, 1968.
44. Acharkan, 1966; Mirgaleev and Peshkin, 1966; Vardimiandi, 1966; *Metodicheskie Ukazaniia*, 1969, p. 296.
45. For example, see the highly authoritative "methodological instructions" signed by Volkov and Grishin (1966) who were, respectively, Chairman of the Government Labor Committee and Chairman of the All-Union Central Council of Trade Unions.

Table 7.1
Growth of Earnings between 1965 and 1966 in Enterprises Transferred to the
New System, by Category of Personnel

	Average Earnings as a Percentage of 1965	
Category of Personnel	1. Net of payments from material incentive fund	2. Including payments from material inventive fund
Workers	103	104
Office workers	102	110
Managerial-technical personnel	102	108

Note: From *Vest. Stat.*, no. 5, 1967, p. 94.

share of the material incentive fund going to workers should be
smaller than their share of the labor force.

In fact, however, differentials were not stabilized. Scattered data
firmly indicate that the earnings of office workers and managerial-technical personnel have fared better under the new system than have
those of workers. In 1966, about two million persons worked in industrial enterprises operating under the new system.[46] As shown in
table 7.1, at these enterprises between 1965 and 1966 earnings net of
payments from the material incentive fund grew at close to the same
rate for each of the three categories of personnel. However, when payments from this fund are included, earnings of office workers and
managerial-technical personnel show a rate of growth of about twice
that of workers' earnings.

Several controls aimed at increasing the workers' share of the material incentive fund have been proposed. At one extreme these include
a sweeping regulation that the percentage of the material incentive
fund distributed among workers be pegged at a value equal to the
percentage of the wage fund received by workers.[47] At the other end
are more modest calls for the creation of some standard regulations
directed at "the expansion of the circle of recipients." [48]

In February 1969, Gosplan reacted to the problem. A regulation was
issued that defines the maximum annual rate of growth of premiums
paid to office workers and managerial-technical personnel as the rate
of growth of the material incentive fund. Thus, a floor equal to the

46. *Vest. Stat.*, no. 5, 1967, p. 94.
47. Rykov, 1966; Mirgaleev and Peshkin, 1966; Oblomskaia, 1968, pp. 134, 137.
48. Shkurko, 1967, pp. 27–28; Sukharevskii, 1967, p. 15; Shkurko, 1970, p. 163.

1968 level is placed under the share of the fund that must be distributed among workers.[49]

Payments from the fund take various forms, and as we have been using the term, "premium payments" properly refers only to a portion of these. Data for all enterprises working under the new system showed that only about 45 percent of the total fund was distributed as premium payments, and less than one-fifth of this amount as premiums to workers.[50] Workers' premiums from the fund appear to be based upon indexes not directly related to measurements of output, that is, for keeping equipment in good repair, not producing defective parts, high quality of output, and so on.[51]

Another portion of the incentive fund is distributed according to criteria that have no relationship to an individual's productive activity; it takes such forms as "awards to outstanding personnel" and lump-sum assistance to enterprise personnel suffering from temporary financial problems. One study reported that the "awards" represented about 8 percent of all payments from the incentive fund and were made for a variety of activities, including participation in sports, theatrical activity, and, for young workers, good marks in school.[52]

The third and largest portion of the material incentive fund distributed among workers takes the form of a year-end bonus. Data for all enterprises covered by the new system in 1968 show that 2.7 percent of workers' average wages were accounted for by payments from the material incentive fund. Of this amount, 40 percent was received in the form of the year-end bonus, 31 percent in the form of premium payments, and the remainder in various types of lump sum payments.[53] The year-end bonus is of special interest in light of innumerable articles in the Soviet press about "excessive" labor turnover. Since the

49. *Biulleten'*, no. 7, 1969, pp. 4–5.
50. Shkurko, 1968, pp. 357–358. The data apparently refer to 1967 or 1968. His definition of "premium" is not explicit. However, according to Oblomskaia (1968, p. 131), only that part of the fund distributed monthly can properly be considered as premiums.
51. Kunel'skii, 1967, p. 12.
52. Labkovskii, 1967. Also see *Metodicheskie Ukazaniia*, 1969, p. 296.
53. Shkurko, 1970, pp. 55, 169. Earlier, the proportion distributed as a year-end bonus may have been higher. Sukharevskii (1968, p. 10) and Oblomskaia (1968, p. 134) had complained that too great a portion of the fund was being distributed as year-end bonuses, and the latter source maintained that 40 percent would be appropriate. Kurskii and Slastenko (1966, p. 13) reported that three-fourths of payments received by workers was in the form of year-end bonuses.

system of seniority bonuses was downgraded during the wage reform, no specific policy tools existed for reducing turnover. While some social benefits are dependent upon the length of "uninterrupted work" (*nepreryvnyi stazh*) within the economy or within a specific branch of industry, virtually no benefits other than the level of sick pay are dependent upon uninterrupted service within a given enterprise.[54]

Soviet economists have expressed the hope that by making the size of the year-end bonus at least partially dependent upon a worker's seniority within a given plant, the "stability of cadres" will be increased. The new Soviet labor code,[55] published in 1970, indicates that if these year-end bonuses are to be paid, seniority within the given enterprise must be considered in determining their magnitude. Therefore, even in the face of highly fragmentary data, usually of a "for instance" nature, some discussion of this bonus seems in order.

Generally, the distribution of the material incentive fund is decided at the enterprise level, but if workers are to receive year-end bonuses, the minimum value of such payments is to be not less than ten days' wages.[56] Despite continual urging that "the individual contribution" of the worker should be considered, reports indicate that the magnitude of the bonus received is usually simply a function of seniority. If not always in practice, at least potentially this bonus can be made a highly precise policy instrument aimed at reducing turnover. For example, one enterprise was criticized for distributing the bonus only among those workers who had been at the plant for more than three years; yet this group accounted for only about one-fourth of the enterprise's turnover.[57]

While possibly fulfilling similar goals, the year-end bonus should not be identified with the system of seniority payments existing prior to the wage reform. The latter were centrally determined according to branch of industry or geographical region or both. More important,

54. Minimum sick pay is 50 percent of earnings for those with less than five years employment, and the maximum is 100 percent for those with more than eight years. Madison, 1968, p. 202. Both Brown (1966) and McAuley (1969) give detailed information concerning Soviet labor turnover.
55. "Osnovy Zakonodatel'stva," 1970, section 5, article 38.
56. Interestingly, this was apparently the only conclusion reached by a commission on the "Transfer of Enterprises to the New System," Oblomskaia, 1968, p. 133. Rykov (1966) had previously proposed a similar standard.
57. Mirgaleev, 1967. Also see Lavruk, 1966; Kurskii and Slastenko, 1966, p. 13; Rykov, 1966.

they were a guaranteed part of earnings, while all payments from the material incentive fund are dependent upon the success of the enterprise in which the worker is employed. According to A. Volkov, Chairman of the Government Labor Committee, any attempt to reinstitute the previous type of seniority bonus would have proven too expensive, and a reduction of labor turnover can be achieved more economically through the enterprise's judicious use of the material incentive fund.[58] Though Volkov may be correct, two questions are yet to be answered: will the sums distributed turn out to be in some sense adequate, and if so, can the individual enterprise be relied upon to distribute them judiciously?

A further issue concerning the size of the material incentive fund is the long-established dictum in Soviet policy that within any economic unit, except under highly unusual conditions, labor productivity must grow faster than wages. Previously discussed regulations ensure that growth in payments from the wage fund will not outstrip increases in productivity.[59] No similar regulations had been established for earnings distributed via the material incentive fund. Thus it became possible for total earnings to grow faster than productivity.[60] In early 1969, Gosplan eliminated this possibility. The new regulation, in essence, ensures that total average earnings (including payments from the incentive fund) cannot increase more rapidly than labor productivity; and payments from the incentive fund may be reduced in order to maintain this relationship.[61]

Here we cannot pursue certain microeconomic implications of this regulation. However, it should be noted that much of the thrust of the new system has been toward construction of enterprise success indicators that are based upon "net" or "value added" indexes in place of the previous "gross output" indexes. In so far as productivity is generally now measured by the gross output of goods sold divided by the number

---

58. Volkov, 1965. In 1971, an article in *Ekonomicheskaia Gazeta* stressed that enterprises experiencing high rates of labor turnover should increase the share of the material incentive fund distributed as year end bonuses. "Voznagrazhdenie," 1971.
59. That is, the wage fund regulations discussed earlier in this chapter.
60. Sukharevskii, 1968a, p. 10; Orlovskii, 1968, pp. 17–18; Kapustin, 1967, pp. 70–72.
61. *Biulleten'*, no. 7, 1969, pp. 3–4. Similar regulations are incorporated in Gosplan's statement on developing long-term "stable" norms for determining the size of the material incentive fund. See "O Stabil'nykh Normativakh," 1969.

of persons employed by the enterprise, a gross output constraint on the material incentive fund is introduced.

For the Soviet economy, predictions as well as extrapolations of current trends are notoriously precarious. However, it appears that the new system will not essentially alter the patterns of wage determination presented in the previous chapters. The recent regulations just mentioned limit both the rate of growth of the material incentive fund and enterprise discretion in its distribution. No authority has questioned "the necessity of maintaining the decisive role of basic wage rates in earnings determination." [62] Moreover, an important policy statement appearing as an editorial in *Pravda* during early 1970 indicates that the Soviet planner may have lost some of his earlier enchantment with the new system.[63]

When he has gone to some pains to describe a phenomenon such as Soviet wage determination, an author is psychologically disposed to believe in its importance and stability. In so far as it concerns the argument that the new system is of minor significance for industrial workers' earnings, this predisposition appears to be rooted in reality.

62. Sukharevskii, 1968a.
63. *Pravda*, Jan. 13, 1970; New York Times, Jan. 17, 1970, p. 1.

8

Soviet Wages: An Evaluation

Soviet Wage Theory

During the past decade or so, economic literature in the USSR has been marked by an increased concern with "the market" and with decentralization. However, if a central theme is to be found in our preceding chapters, it is that of increased centralization and consistency in the determination of earnings for workers in industry. Both theory and policy share this emphasis, and, in fact, the Soviet approach to wage determination precludes the usefulness of any attempt to separate questions of theory from those of policy. The relationship between theory and practice intriguingly is here the reverse of the Western situation. In *New Concepts in Wage Determination* (an excellent collection of essays by some of the ablest labor economists in America), the editors explain that "when an eminent economist was recently asked to evaluate the present state of wage theory, he replied by denying that there was any theory to evaluate." [1] Even when taken with the proverbial grain of salt, the retort points to the lack of agreement among economists as to what constitutes wage theory. In large measure the problem revolves around the cleavage between the "empiricists" and the "theorists" in questions of wage setting. Frank C. Pierson has stated the problem as follows:

One factor contributing to the muddled state of wage economics is the gap that has come to exist between deductive and inductive wage analysis. An axiom of all scientific endeavor is that these two methods of inquiry should closely parallel one another, each enriching and forwarding the other. The study of wage phenomena, however, is marked by no such mutuality. Theorists frequently appear to be dealing with one subject, empiricists with another, the work of each suffering as a result.[2]

The "eminent economist's" retort might with equal justification, if

1. Taylor and Pierson, 1957, p. vii.
2. Pierson, 1957, p. 3. Of the many discussions of the nature of wage theory, or more accurately, the applicability of conventional theory, two direct confrontations between an empiricist and a theorist might be mentioned. The Lester-Machlup discussions, which appeared in the *American Economic Review*, were concerned with the adequacy of marginal analysis in wage determination. Almost ten years later, a formidable defense of the theorists by Simon Rottenberg was no less formidably answered by Robert Lampman for the empiricists. Lester, 1946 and 1947; Machlup, 1946 and 1947; Rottenberg, 1960; Lampman, 1960. Of the attempts to synthesize these approaches, we might mention Dunlop, 1957 and Reynolds, 1951, pp. 207–257.

not for different reasons, have been made by one of his Soviet colleagues. Excluding those dogmatists who simply repeat empty phrases,[3] Soviet "empiricists" and "theorists" are usually the same persons. A theoretical position is often defended (or attacked) in terms of its correspondence (or lack of it) with the existing wage system. The gross overlapping of wage theory and policy may be a necessary result of the Soviet economist's view of himself as what might be called an "endogenous variable" in wage analysis. Not only does the economist seek to analyze wage determination, but if possible, significantly to influence the process.[4]

Thus, among the publications we have relied on most heavily throughout this study are those published under the aegis of the Labor Institute, officially designated as the Scientific Research Institute of Labor. In addition to being the center of analytical work on the structure of earnings, the Institute is charged with developing proposals in the general area of labor and wage administration. Moreover, the Institute is directly subordinate to the Government Labor Committee —the agency directly responsible for the changes in wage policy discussed in previous chapters. Hence, the phrase "Soviet wage theory" must not be taken as designating a body of pure theory. Rather, as we use the phrase, it refers to the economists' general approach to problems of wage determination. In the remainder of this chapter, we argue that this approach is appropriate to its institutional framework, attractive in terms of some widely accepted equity criterion, and clumsily inflexible.

The hallmark of the Soviet economist's approach to wage determination is the concept of a wage structure determined according to a number of pure wage differentials. Several shortcomings of this approach have been discussed and will shortly receive further comment. Here we propose that given the general framework of planning in the USSR, the Soviet approach to earnings determination has considerable virtue both in terms of generating pertinent economic data and facilitating control.

As stressed throughout this study, in practice the established pure

3. The articles by I. I. Kuzminov (1961a and 1961b) are among the more depressing examples of this genre.
4. For example, note how E. I. Kapustin (1968a), the director of the Labor Institute, spells out the tasks facing the Soviet labor economist.

differentials have tended to lose some of their purity. However, an enormous body of usefully structured data, generally not available in Western economies, can be generated from the wage system that existed during the mid-1960s. Such data may be expected to become even more pertinent if the attempt further to specify each differential continues. Though Western statistics provide information on levels of earnings, we recognize that such levels are the result of the interaction of a number of different types of differentials. The results of an attempt, let us say, to compare average wages in two branches of industry net of geographical differentials are often of dubious value. Any attempt to compare these levels net of differentials for intraindustry working conditions or skill differentials seems doomed to failure. The Soviet approach lends itself better to making just such measurements, and the information thus provided would not be without pertinence for understanding wage structures in Western economies.

Assuming that the current approach to "pure" differentials is further refined, the average earnings for workers in two branches of industry within a given geographical area [5] might be disaggregated in the following way. Any statistical difference in average wage levels will be explained as the result of four types of wage differentials, with the effect of each differential readily quantifiable. The effect upon earnings levels of a difference in the initial basic rate [6] in each industry constitutes the pure interindustry differential. The addition to earnings generated by the distribution of workers according to a single six-group skill scale measures the effect of the pure skill differential. Similarly, the classification of jobs according to working conditions, with the corresponding additions to basic wages, constitutes the pure differential for working conditions. Finally, levels of payment for norm overfulfillment and premiums constitute the pure incentive differential.

Thus, simply in terms of generating data about wage structure, the Soviet approach has much to recommend it. More important, the determination of earnings levels via a set of distinct and standardized all-industry set of pure differentials enormously facilitates the

5. We thus avoid consideration of the coefficients used for increasing earnings in various regions. This pure geographical differential could, however, easily be integrated into the analysis. See chapter 2.
6. This is the basic rate for a pieceworker of the first skill group, working under normal conditions. See chapter 1 and appendix A.

planning of and control over the process of wage determination. Referring to the complex and multitudinous skill scales existing during the 1930s, conditions not dissimilar to those that have been described as prereform conditions, Franklyn D. Holzman stated, "It is not only difficult to apply correctly so complex a system; it is almost impossible, and very costly, to audit it properly." [7]

The system described in our previous chapters, because of its simplicity and standardization, lends itself to proper auditing. For example, the components of workers' average monthly wages within any given enterprise may be disaggregated according to a formula such as the following: [8]

$$W = B_1 \times D_s \times D_c \times D_i \times D_g \times M$$

where:

W is workers' average monthly wage

B_1 is the daily basic rate for a worker of the first skill group under normal working conditions—the initial basic rate

D_s is a coefficient corresponding to the average skill group in an enterprise—a measure of the pure skill differential

D_c is a coefficient corresponding to the increase in basic rates due to working conditions other than normal—a measure of the pure differential for working conditions

D_i is a coefficient corresponding to the percentage of earnings in excess of basic rates due to premiums and norm overfulfillment by piece-rate workers—the "pure" incentive differential

D_g is a coefficient that will be greater than unity if the enterprise is located in an area having a regional differential—a measure of the pure geographical differential

M is the number of workdays in a given month.

Methodology similar to the above can be applied for *ex post* or *ex ante* analysis at various levels of aggregation, for example, a shop

7. Holzman (1955, p. 33, pp. 31–44) further argues that the cumbersome nature of the wage system was in part responsible for "unanticipated inflationary pressures" during this period. Also see Granick (1954, pp. 179–181) for a discussion of wages as a source of inflation during the 1930s.
8. This is an adaptation of the methodology presented by Gal'tsov (1957, p. 22), which included a coefficient—always less than unity—accounting for the average percent of absence during the given month.

within an enterprise, an entire branch of industry, and even the total wage fund for workers throughout the national economy.[9]

Equity Considerations

A continually reappearing theme in the Soviet literature has been that under socialism, wages are determined according to the amount of labor performed, and that thus the fulfillment of the rule of equal wages for equal work is ensured. On the eve of the wage reform, the theme was little more than an incantation. Despite evident and oft-cited inequities and inconsistencies in wages, there was no attempt to define proper differentials in terms of concepts exogenous to the existing structure of earnings.[10]

The Western economist would easily dismiss Soviet attempts to find an equity basis for the pattern of prereform wages in a rather primitive concept of productivity wage—in the idea that, because of the absence of capitalist exploitation, what a worker gets in wages is proportional to what he gives society in terms of additional products. However, the essential theoretical underpinnings of the concept of productivity wage—not even to speak of "marginal productivity"—have been absent within the context of Soviet economic processes. Markets for industrial products were (and remain) sellers' markets, with prices received by enterprises generally constructed according to variations of cost-plus formulas.[11] Still, even given this context, it may be useful to speak of productivity wages for broad groups of workers—that is, skilled workers as compared to unskilled, workers in high priority branches compared to those in low priority branches, and so on.[12] At lower levels of aggregation, the link between productivity and earnings is most tenuous. A more cogent explanation is advanced by those Soviet economists who maintain that by the early 1950s the pattern—or lack thereof—of earnings is best understood as being the

9. The Soviet economists Batkaev and Markov (1964, pp. 227–229) presented a disaggregation of the 1962 wage fund according to the pure differentials presented in table 1.1. Calculations were given for "all industry" and nine separate branches. Because their methodology is unspecified, these data are of dubious value. However, see Chapman's (1970, pp. 53–61) discussion of these calculations.
10. See chapter 1 for a discussion of the condition of Soviet labor economics in the prereform period.
11. For example, see Bornstein, 1962.
12. See Bergson, 1944; Yanowitch, 1960; Schroeder, 1966; and Chapman, 1970.

result of the accumulation of numerous ad hoc regulations and enter-prise practices.

In contrast, the approach to earnings determination established dur-ing the reform of 1958–1960, an approach stressing pure differentials as the essential determinant of earnings, has definite attraction in terms of equity considerations. The approach provides a relatively simple and universal methodology, ideally exogenous to existing wages, by which the equality or inequality of work may be quantified. The assumption that it is proper to compare kinds of work in terms of job content rather than by some measures of productivity is an assump-tion shared by most Western trade unions.[13] Even if serious equity questions are raised concerning the relative magnitudes of the pure differentials, the framework of the Soviet approach retains its appeal.

"Equal pay for equal work" is a rule that also plays a part in tradi-tional Western wage theory. A. C. Pigou's classic *The Economics of Welfare* stressed that fair wages must meet criteria of both efficiency ("wages . . . equal to the values of the marginal net product") and equity ("between similar persons . . . the relation of equality").[14] However, as Albert Rees aptly states, "The [Western] economist puts primary emphasis on efficiency, and views "equal pay for equal work" as a pleasant by-product of achieving efficient allocation.[15]

In broad outline, the theoretical postulate is that under conditions of perfect markets, each worker attempts to maximize his "net advan-tages." Without any direct attempt to measure job content, the re-sultant distribution of wages will fulfill not only the equity rule of

13. Goldfinger (1957, pp. 52–56), shows that the "equal pay for equal work" rule "is deeply ingrained in the thinking and tradition of trade unions" and has had significant impact upon wage patterns established through collective bargaining. Also see Douty, 1963, pp. 225–245.
  The Soviet economist has attempted to quantify this equity rule via specific defi-nitions of terms, and it should be noted that quantification of equity rules is under-taken not only in Soviet wage administration. For example, few would object to the rule that "a fair day's work" is expected from all workers. In negotiations with the United Steel Workers Union, a negotiator for United States Steel Corp. insisted that the rule be quantified, and the resultant contract (1946) defined a fair day's work as "that amount of work that can be produced by a qualified employee when working at a normal pace . . . a normal pace is equivalent to a man walking, without load, on a smooth level ground at a rate of three miles per hour." The definition remained in subsequent contracts. Bell, 1960, pp. 707–708.
14. Pigou, 1932, pp. 549–550.
15. Rees, 1962, p. 63.

equal pay for equal work, but it will be an efficient distribution of labor in which the worker's wage is determined by his marginal productivity or "marginal revenue product." Here we need not discuss the possible merits of this theoretical approach. Rather, for our purposes, it need only be stressed that unlike the Western theoretical model, the Soviet approach to "equal pay for equal work" is not a result of, nor can it be identified with, an efficient distribution of labor and wages.

Efficiency Considerations

The fact that recent Soviet practice grossly deviates from Pareto optimality efficiency standards that have developed in Western welfare economics will come as no surprise to the reader, and at least one attempt to gauge the magnitude of this deviation has proved to be of considerable theoretical interest.[16] But a detailed discussion of Soviet practice in terms of Pareto efficiency would be out of keeping with the focus of this study. The magnitude of labor market imperfections stressed by the empiricist wage theoreticians forces the author to question the usefulness of these precise efficiency standards for understanding the operation of any existing wage structure. Moreover, one is sorely pressed to find evidence indicating that the Soviet economist and planner share the normative goals of Pareto optimality. Though it may be argued that he should seek just such a goal, that discussion would range far from the central concern of this study.

Still, without specification of explicit standards, the word "efficiency" (as Gordon Bloom said of "exploitation") ceases to be a noun and becomes a noise.[17] Our proposed standard, though less theoretically tractable than those postulated by Pareto optimality, appears more pertinent to existing Soviet wage determination. For us, the index of "efficiency" (henceforth without quotation marks) is measured in terms of how well the wage system performs the task of inducing workers toward those courses of action that are desired by "society" or the economic authorities. In other words, our discussion of efficiency takes the goals and framework of Soviet economic institutions as given.

16. See the section entitled "Principles of Socialist Wages," in Bergson, 1966, pp. 175–191, and Bergson, 1964, pp. 106–126. For a lucid statement of Pareto optimality for the labor market, see the chapter entitled "The Worker and the Efficiency of the Labor Market" in Scitovsky, 1951, pp. 83–108.
17. Bloom, 1941, p. 413.

Much of our analysis is centered on the question of aggregation, a term that should not be identified with centralization. A system of wage determination might have both a high degree of centralization and a low degree of aggregation; that is, there might be a single central authority determining a specific set of differentials for each separate enterprise in accordance with the authority's view of the need of each individual enterprise. Aggregation refers to scope of application. In the case of a wage differential, disregarding geographical considerations, the level or degree of aggregation may be viewed as proceeding from the individual enterprise, to enterprises within a narrowly defined branch, to a broadly defined branch, to all industry. We first consider the level of aggregation used in setting differentials; and then, taking this level as given, the ability of economic authorities to establish an efficient set of differentials.

Recent Soviet policy aimed at increasing the level of aggregation from branch to all industry in determination of skill differentials received detailed discussion in chapter 5. Much of that argument readily applies to other pure differentials. Here is a general rule: *at a given degree of aggregation,* any pure differential may be said to be at an efficient level if it provides adequate differentiation at the significant marginal economic unit. By significant marginal economic unit, we mean some unit—branch, group of enterprises, or even single enterprise—that is considered significant by the center's wage-setting authorities, and that lies at the upper margin in terms of the average magnitude of the differential required to meet the needs of that unit.[18] Differentials for working conditions provide an example that helps to clarify the rule.

Assume that the minimum wage rate in each industry is fixed and that a 10 percent differential for hot and heavy work is sufficient in the chemical industry to induce an adequate flow of workers in that industry to undertake jobs classified as hot and heavy. Further assume that in the ferrous metals industry, with the same definition of hot and heavy

18. Note that we here refer to the average rather than the marginal level necessary within the economic unit. If our significant units are defined at a branch level, the adequate level would be that generally needed within that branch rather than the level required by some single enterprise within the branch. Were we concerned with the single enterprise requiring the highest differential within the branch, then the significant economic unit would be defined as the enterprise rather than the branch.

work, the greater prevalence of such jobs necessitates a differential of 50 percent. If set on a branch level, an efficient differential for working conditions would be 10 percent in chemicals and 50 percent in ferrous metals. However, if this differential were set on an all-industry basis and ferrous metals identified as the significant marginal unit, the differential would be excessive in all branches other than ferrous metals. For example, the chemical industry, following all-industry standardization, would pay a 50 percent addition to basic wage rates to workers performing hot and heavy work, while a sufficient number would have undertaken these jobs if the differential had been only 10 percent.[19]

The argument is not novel. It is closely related to the standard Western theoretical concept of "marginal" and "intramarginal" workers at a given wage rate, and for our purposes its further formalization would belabor the obvious. Assume that the minimum money wage rate has been established. If the scarcity conditions for various types of labor differ among enterprises, each enterprise theoretically would have its own unique set of "equilibrium" money differentials. If standardized differentials are set within a group of enterprises, say a branch, then, from the standpoint of the separate enterprise, equilibrium conditions are violated. Further assume that each enterprise is identified as a significant unit. Then any single differential, if it is to

19. Although our approach deals with average adequate levels, the essence of the problem is more neatly stated if, for the moment, we turn to marginal levels as presented in the diagram. On the vertical axis, Wa/Wn expresses the differential in basic wages for work performed under abnormal as compared to normal working conditions. The supply schedule of workers willing to undertake the abnormal work is designated as S_{La} and is assumed to be identical in the ferrous metals and chemical industry. In the former a flow of n_f workers is needed to fulfill these jobs, and n_c is needed in the latter. If the all-industry differential is set at the level needed in ferrous metals, the cost of the differential will be $onmn_f$ in ferrous metals and $onqn_c$ in chemicals. However, had the differential been set on a branch level, its cost would have been only $orpn_c$ in chemicals. Thus, $rnqp$ represents expenditures due to the all-industry differential.

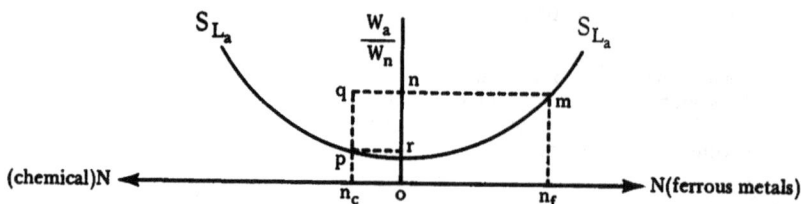

be efficient according to our use of the term, would be at a level adequate for that enterprise within the group that requires the maximum differential to assure the needed flow of labor of a given type. Thus the standardization entails excessive wage expenditures in the sense that each differential will be too high in all but one enterprise. If the level of aggregation is further increased from branch to all-industry, there will be an analogous increase of excessive wage expenditures. Such excessive expenditures necessitated by setting a single differential or all differentials at higher levels of aggregation must be viewed as an opportunity cost, or at least as something akin to it. For a given total wage fund, if the pure differential is excessive in a series of economic units, that part of the fund expended for this excessive differentiation might have been utilized for such alternative purposes as increasing other pure differentials or raising the minimum wage.

There is, however, a further consideration, which, in terms of Soviet practice, blunts the importance of this analysis. With each increase of the level of aggregation it is possible (and in practice likely) that the definition of the marginal significant unit will be altered. That is, at a branch level of aggregation, differentials might be set according to the needs of some large enterprise or complex of enterprises within the branch; at an all-industry level, according to the general needs of an entire branch. Excessive wage expenditures for a pure differential might be reduced by setting it at a level not sufficient for those economic units that might be, or were, previously identified as significant.

As often mentioned in the course of this study, the individual enterprise has some autonomy in the distribution of payments for norm overfulfillment and premiums. Therefore, those economic units finding the all-industry (or branch-wide) differential inadequate might be able to supplement the centrally determined differential through judicious utilization of incentive payments. However, as also previously stressed, the larger the share of the wage fund represented by incentive payments, the weaker the central control over earning determination.

Not only does widespread utilization of incentive payments to correct differentials weaken central control, but it also undermines the entire rationale of earnings determination through pure differentials. According to Soviet wage theory, the sole function of incentive payments is to induce a worker to work "harder" or "better." However, both individual enterprises and central authorities [20] have used premiums and norm overfulfillment payments to adjust structural inadequacies in the set of basic wage rates established during the reform. By the late 1960s, most incentive payments were not utilized for establishing on-the-job incentives. The complaint voiced by Premier Bulganin in 1955,[21] that incentive additions have little to do with incentive but exist in order to maintain earnings levels, was repeated a decade later in almost the same words by a Soviet economist.[22]

Enterprises are able to utilize incentive payments for correcting only certain types of defects in the structure of basic wage rates. The consequences of too meager branch-wide differentials for working conditions were generally avoided by increasing the incentive yield on jobs performed under undesirable conditions. The significance of these corrections is underscored by the results of a 1967 study in the metallurgical industry, which showed that even though the centrally determined basic wage rates called for a *maximum* increase of basic wages of about 18 percent for working conditions, various incentive payments resulted in an *average* increase of earning at jobs having other than normal working conditions of about 36 percent.[23] The previously described shortage of operators throughout the 1960s stands in sharp contrast. Here, specific centrally determined output norms for piece-rate workers made it impossible for the enterprise sufficiently to correct the inadequate level of basic rates.

In short, given the minimum wage rate and some degree of aggregation above the enterprise level, Soviet wage policy faces a dilemma. On the one hand, centralized differentials can be set at an efficient level for highly specified significant units only with excessive wage expenditures. Alternatively, at the same level of aggregation, the role of central control in earnings determination is reduced if the significant units are defined with less specificity. Then, efficient centralized differentials can be established at lower levels with the expectation that in some units incentive payments will be used to compensate for the inadequate differential. The significance of the dilemma is posi-

20. For example, as noted in chapter 3, centrally determined output norms were consciously set at "loose" levels for workers in machine construction.
21. Bulganin, 1955, p. 12.
22. Karpenko (1965, p. 13) states that "the existing system of wage payments makes not norms of work, but norms for wages."
23. Dubovoi, 1969, pp. 64–65.

tively related to the degree of aggregation. The "cost" of moving from branch to all-industry differentials thus appears to necessitate either an increase of excessive wage expenditures or a reduction of the precision and importance of centralized wage policy, or both.

Up to this point, our discussion has focused upon the relationship between degree of aggregation in basic wage determination and efficiency. We have assumed that at the given level of aggregation, the centrally established set of differentials is at least appropriate to that level, though perhaps not efficient in the sense of economizing wage costs. The decade following the wage reform indicates that this assumption is untenable. A clumsy inflexibility in the determination of basic wage rates has become a source of inefficiency.

For any level of aggregation, two indexes are readily available to measure the appropriateness of centrally established differentials. First, if the wage system generates a shortage of workers willing to undertake a specific type of job such as that of machine operator, one or more of the established differentials is inappropriate. However, if enterprises are able to correct the centralized differentials, a long-term inordinately high number of job vacancies for a specific type of work need not accompany inappropriate differentials. Therefore, a second and less direct index may be proposed. A differential or set of differentials should be considered inappropriate if corrections at the enterprise level result in a "warping" of other differentials.[24] Thus, in the period following the wage reform enterprises were forced to utilize norm over-fulfillment payments to supplement the meager differentials for working conditions. This, in turn, meant that indices relating to the quality of piece-rate norms lost their rationale. Given the structure of basic wage rates, any attempt by the enterprise to increase the percentage of technically based norms would result in a shortage of workers willing to accept jobs performed under other than normal working conditions.

A major shortcoming of the Soviet approach is that the centralized differentials, once established, are ponderously inflexible and insensitive to labor market conditions. Since the completion of the wage reform, there has been a continuous stream of reports that differentials for working conditions are too low. Despite these reports and the policy

24. See "Differentiation of Basic Rates and Earnings" in chapter 6.

guidelines set by the Twenty-Third Party Congress in early 1966,[25] these differentials remained essentially unchanged. With considerable cogency, one Soviet economist maintains that even had the differentials been adequate for 1960, by 1970 they would have outlived their accuracy. The age structure, general level of education, and tastes of the labor force had changed during this period, and, correspondingly, workers' definitions of what constituted "unattractive" working conditions had become more encompassing.[26] During the second half of 1969, basic wages in the construction materials industry were increased, and so was the relative differential for working conditions. Reportedly, this is a harbinger of a coming expansion of the pure differential for working conditions.[27] It is long overdue.

For further illustration of the inflexibility of the Soviet approach, we again turn to the shortage of machine operators. Previously we argued that the shortage was not due to centralized wage determination per se, but rather in large part to the simple boredom and lack of prospects for advancement that accompany that job. These factors had not been considered in the job evaluation procedure used for determining basic wage rates. By the late 1960s, the shortage reportedly has resulted in a widespread disruption of production. However, a change in job evaluation procedure would have had repercussions throughout the wage system. Instead, the basic wages of machine operators were increased, thus creating an abnormality in a supposedly consistent system of wage determination.[28] Thus, much of the inefficiency of the wage system appears to stem less from the existence of standardized job evaluation procedures than from the fact that once established, the specific job evaluation procedures and the resultant set of basic wage rates have proven to be too rigid. If wage setting is viewed as a policy tool for distribution of the labor force, high levels of aggregation and inflexibility have blunted the effectiveness of this tool. If, however, our frame of reference is widened, the macroeconomic consideration of price

25. "Direktivy XXIII," 1966.
26. Dubovoi, 1969, p. 58.
27. *Rabochaia Gazeta,* March 4, 1969. According to several sources, the change in basic rates in that industry should be viewed as the initial step in the wage reform scheduled for 1972–1974, which was discussed in the concluding section of chapter 5. Also see Batkaev, 1971, p. 27 and Khmirov, 1970.
28. See "Evaluation" in chapter 6.

stability might make the blunted tool more attractive than a precise one.

The price stability issue can be clarified by assuming that the sources of inefficiency mentioned earlier in this chapter are eliminated as follows: pure differentials are set on an enterprise level of aggregation, and if the set of differentials appears inappropriate for the specific labor market conditions facing the enterprise, one or more of the differentials are increased. The constraint that modifications can be made only in an upward direction is not simply an acceptance of Keynesian "sticky" wage rates. Rather, apparently for political as well as economic reasons, virtually all Soviet wage theory and policy is based upon the notion that modification of wage differentials is to be effected without the reduction of money wages for any significant group of workers.[29] Given "sticky" wage rates, a positive relationship arises between the flexibility of differentials and the size of the aggregate wage bill. If one or more differentials are raised in response to a short-term inadequacy in the flow of workers willing to undertake certain vacant job classifications, this increased differential becomes a part of the enterprise's long-run internal wage structure, and, no less important, an element in the external wage structure for all those enterprises that are in some way affected by the altered differential.[30] This change in wage structure is "washed out" only by an equal relative increase in the wages of workers in all other job classifications.

Considering the long-standing condition of full employment (even chronic overemployment) in the USSR, the flexibility described here should be expected to lead to continuous and rapid upward adjustment of differentials. However, most clearly since the end of World War II, a stable or declining consumer price index has been a goal of Soviet policy.[31] To ensure a stable consumer price index without sup-

29. In an interview with Victor Perlo (1961, pp. 48–49), A. I. Mikoyan stated that wages are "easy to raise, tough to cut." An excellent discussion of this issue during earlier periods of Soviet industrialization appears in Holzman, 1955, pp. 22–75 and Holzman, 1960.
30. Most directly, other enterprises within the same labor market would be affected.
31. The goal is not stability of the general price level, but rather of retail prices of consumer goods. Thus, in 1967, a price reform resulted in a general increase of wholesale prices while retail prices were left essentially unchanged. See Bornstein, 1966, and Sitnin, 1968.

pressed inflation, the "goods coverage of the aggregate wage fund" [32] must be assured. In other words, total wages are not to increase more rapidly than the output of consumer goods, or, more precisely, the output of wage goods.[33] Were individual economic units permitted to increase a specific differential in response to transitory or local labor market pressures, a type of wage inflation not unlike the phenomenon of "structural inflation" analyzed by Charles L. Schultze would ensue.[34] In 1966, Alec Nove wrote:

Before leaving the subject of wage drift in the Soviet Union, one must emphasize that it has been fairly successfully held in check in the most recent years. Whereas in every previous five-year plan the average wage was exceeded, sometimes by a wide margin, the seven-year plan which ended in 1965 presented a contrast in this respect. . . . Given the shortage of foodstuffs (consequent upon agricultural shortcomings), and the underfulfillment of plans for some categories of industrial consumers' goods, it was therefore hardly surprising that average real wages were below expectation. It remains both surprising and unusual, however, that *money* wages were held down, in the face of what must have been considerable pressures.[35]

This success in regulating money wages is in no small part due to the strict enforcement of regulations concerning enterprise wage fund expenditures [36] and the imposition of relatively inflexible centralized differentiation of basic wage rates. Because of "sticky" wages and an a priori decision on the share of national income to be devoted to consumption, attempts to increase the flexibility and efficiency of the structure of relative earnings may succeed only at the cost of inflationary pressures. The problem would be mitigated if a wage structure better reflecting labor market conditions would tend to increase output (thus maintaining the "goods coverage" of a greater total wage fund). Still, the apparent magnitudes involved in the necessity of "washing out" an increased differential that becomes superfluous leads the author to believe that there is some trade-off between an efficient, malleable earnings structure and a planned economy that is able to avoid inflationary pressures.

32. Kapustin, 1969, p. 24.
33. The term wage goods is taken to exclude that part of consumption distributed as "free" social goods.
34. In general, the term denotes inflation caused by changes in the composition of demand rather than by overall excess demand. Schultze, 1959.
35. Nove, 1966, pp. 218–219.
36. For a far more pessimistic evaluation of the efficacy of Soviet ability to control wage inflation than we presented in chapter 7, see Fearn, 1965.

Within the institutional framework of the USSR's economy, the question of whether a proper balance has been struck between inflationary pressures and an efficient determination of earnings structure can be answered only in accordance with a series of subjective value judgments. In addition to possibly furthering price stability, the virtues of a centralized and relatively stable system of earnings determination that were discussed earlier include the following: facilitating worker understanding of wage determination; furthering the equity rule of equal pay for equal work; and an enormous simplification of accounting and auditing procedures throughout the economy. On the other hand, a more flexible system might entail greater output with concomitant possibilities for increasing standards of living and the growth rate of national income.

The existence of incentive payments that permit firmly centralized control of basic wages with a degree of enterprise autonomy tends to blunt the sharpness of the choice. In any event, because of his possibly vestigial trade unionist value system, this author finds the recent Soviet tendency to strike a balance closer to centralization to be appealing. Any attempt to elucidate the preference function leading to this conclusion would be boring to the reader and embarrassing to the author. Rather, in conclusion, it would be better again to quote Nove:

Not only is there a great deal more information we would like to have about Soviet wages, but there are also many labor problems of the greatest interest which ought to attract the attention of western labor economists. . . . Now that the Soviet side is beginning to relax its statistical silence in respect to wages, a real dialogue between east and west, and perhaps even some joint research, seems to be entering the area of possibility. We surely have something to learn from each other. Certainly no one in Britain will claim that we have found a satisfactory answer to the many extraordinarily difficult problems of wages and income policy.[37]

The British are not alone in finding no "satisfactory answer." If this study has furthered the dialogue, it should be considered a success.

37. Nove, 1966, p. 221.

Appendix A:
A Note on Interindustry Wage Differentiation

The concern of our study is intraindustry wage determination. Here we briefly turn to two aspects of interindustry wage differentiation: differences in the initial basic rate among branches, and levels of average earnings.

The initial basic rate has been defined as the basic money wage rate for a piece-rate worker of the first skill group under normal working conditions. The rate differs among industries, and, according to Soviet wage theory, its level is determined by making two additions to the minimum wage. The first increment is for differences in what are considered normal working conditions among branches. For example, normal work in ferrous metals presumably entails a greater quantity of labor expended because of burdensome conditions than is the case for normal work in the textile industry. Methodology for the determination of the proper size of such additions is much like that used in specifying intraindustry differentials for working conditions.[1]

No similar "objective" method for determining the size of the second increment exists. Rather, Soviet economists simply hold that the initial basic rate should be further adjusted for a branch's importance or its expected growth so that certain industries are "first in line" in hiring additional workers.[2] Reportedly, because of a narrowing of differences in the rates of growth among branches, notably that between producers' and consumers' goods industries, the relative magnitude of this addition has tended to decrease during the past decade.[3] The calculations presented in table A.1 provide one example of Soviet evaluation of the significance of these additions in determining the initial basic rate.[4]

In 1964, two leading Soviet labor economists, R. A. Batkaev and V. I. Markov, developed a system for determining the initial basic rates for twenty branches of industry. Their proposals are presented in the first four columns of table A.1. As shown in column (1), they assumed the establishment of a minimum wage of 50 rubles a month. Their pro-

1. It should be noted that "working conditions" do not include a consideration of the geographical distribution of enterprises within a branch. For a detailed discussion of interindustry wage differentials, see Kaplan, 1970, pp. 16–32.
2. Aganbegian and Maier, 1959, pp. 15, 47–48; "Zarabotnaia Plata," 1964, p. 4; Kapustin, 1961b, p. 94; Batkaev and Markov, 1964, p. 108. Orlovskii, 1961a, p. 96.
3. Aganbegian and Maier, 1959, p. 175; Maier, 1963, p. 169; Bliakhman, 1964, pp. 151–152; "Zarabotnaia Plata," 1964, p. 4; Kapustin, 1961b, p. 94, and 1961c, pp. 7–8.
4. Similar calculations can be found in Aganbegian and Maier, 1959, pp. 126–129 and *Planirovanie,* 1963, p. 463.

posed additions to the minimum for differences in normal working conditions are given in column (2) and those for the importance of the branch in column (3). Column (4), the proposed initial rates, shows the sums of the first three columns. According to their evaluation, only in the oil extraction, oil refining, and chemical industries does the importance of the branch outweigh adjustments for differences in normal working conditions.

These proposed rates may be compared to those in column (5), which are the actual postreform basic wages according to what we called the "effective" initial basic rate. As outlined in the note to the table, allowance is made for the fact that as of 1962 an insignificant number of workers were classified in the lower or lowest skill groups of some branch skill scales established during the reform. Columns (6) and (7) present respectively the effective and the proposed initial basic rates as percentages of those in coal. Although the rates proposed by Batkaev and Markov weer consistently higher than the actual effective rates, their relative levels with coal taken as 100 percent are remarkably similar. The proposed rates, however, set at only six levels, show considerably more standardization.[5]

The final colum (8) in the table gives average workers' earnings in 1962 as a percentage of those in coal. If these entries are compared to similar data for the prereform year 1955, a slight narrowing of interindustry differentials appears to have been accomplished during the wage reform.[6]

Comparison of the percentages in column (8) with those in columns (6) and (7) is striking. Differentiation of actual interindustry earnings far exceeded the differentiation of the proposed or actual initial basic rates. For example, were the initial basic rate the sole determinant of interindustry differentiation, wages in the sewing industry, as a percent-

---

5. Like most Soviet economists, Batkaev and Markov (1964, pp. 110–118) find standardization of basic wage rates most desirable. They propose that with further reform of wage determination, a maximum of 40 absolute levels of basic rates should be established for all industrial workers. In 1959, Aganbegian and Maier (1959, pp. 234–238) advanced a similar proposal.

6. For nine major branches of industry in 1955, three showed workers' earning levels within 95 to 105 percent of the average level. In 1962, five fell within these percentages. However, because of the rapid growth of wages in the coal industry (from 161 to 181 percent of the average), the range between the highest- and lowest-paying branches increased. *Trud v SSSR*, 1968, pp. 140–144. For a detailed discussion of changes in statistical measures of interindustry wage differentiation, see Chapman, 1970, pp. 46–64, and Kaplan, 1970, pp. 16–32.

Table A.1
Initial Basic Monthly Rates in Rubles and Kopeks for Pieceworkers: Proposed, Actual, and Average Earnings Compared for Selected Industries

| Branch of Industry | Proposed | | | | Effective Postreform Initial Rate (Rubles) (5) | Initial Rates as a Percentage of That in Coal | | Average Earnings as Percentage of Those in Coal, 1962 (8) |
	Minimum in Industry (Rubles) (1)	Addition for Conditions (Rubles) (2)	Addition for Importance (Rubles) (3)	Proposed Initial Rate (Rubles) (4)		Effective (6)	Proposed (7)	
1. Coal	50	18.5	14.8	83.3	69.4[a]	100%	100%	100%
2. Ore mining	50	18.5	14.8	83.3	65.8[b]	95	100	(—)
3. Ferrous metals	50	18.5	14.8	83.3	65.5[c]	94	100	68.9
4. Nonferrous metals	50	18.5	14.8	83.3	67.8[d]	98	100	76.7[u]
5. Oil extraction	50	10.9	13.1	74.0	68.8[e]	99	89	(—)
6. Oil refining	50	8.5	7.3	65.8	52.0[f]	75	79	61.7[v]
7. Chemicals	50	8.5	7.3	65.8	52.0[g]	75	79	55.9
8. Peat mining	50	10.9	4.9	65.8	50.0[h]	72	79	(—)
9. Machine construction (I)	50	8.5	4.8	63.3	53.8[i]	82	79	
10. Machine construction (II)	50	8.5	4.8	63.3	53.0[j]	76	76	55.2

11. Cellulose and paper	50	8.5	7.3	65.8	52.0[x]	75	79	57.1
12. Cement	50	8.5	7.3	65.8	60.9[l]	88	79	58.5
13. Mining of building materials	50	18.5	5.5	74.0	61.1[m]	88	89	(—)
14. Production of building materials	50	8.5	4.8	63.3	48.0[n]	69	76	52.7[w]
15. Timber	50	10.9	4.9	65.8	55.9[o]	81	79	58.9
16. Woodworking	50	8.5	4.8	63.3	48.0[p]	69	76	49.0
17. Textile	50	8.5	4.8	63.3	51.0[q]	74	76	44.5[x]
18. Sewing	50	6.3	4.6	60.9	48.0[r]	69	73	38.5
19. Food products	50	6.3	4.6	60.9	45.0[s]	65	73	45.7
20. Local dairy (outside cities)	50	0.0	0.0	50.0	40.2[t]	58	60	(—)

(—) Not available

Columns (1), (2), (3) and (4) are from Batkaev and Markov, 1964, p. 116. An "effective initial rate" is the rate for the first skill group (basic shops, pieceworkers, normal conditions) if that skill group contains more than 2.5 percent of the total workers covered by a given skill scale in 1962 according to the data in *Vest. Stat.*, no. 6, 1964, pp. 89–95. If not otherwise specified, the rate refers to the first skill group of a six-group skill scale. In the sources identified below, these rates are sometimes given in hours or days and converted into monthly basic rates in accord with the instructions of the Government Labor Committee, that is, 25.6 days and 174.6 hours per month. *Biulleten'*, no. 11, 1964, p. 31. See footnote 2, chapter 6. When the first skill group of any scale included less than 2.5 percent of workers, the rate for first skill group was multiplied by the coefficient of the lowest skill group containing more than 2.5 percent of the workers. See "Prevalence of the Six Group Skill Scale" in chapter 4.

(*Continued*)

Column (8), except as noted below, is calculated from data in *Trud v SSSR*, 1968, pp. 140-144. Ruble figures were there given rounded to the nearest ten kopeks, and our percentages are rounded to one decimal place.

a Second skill group of an eight-group skill scale. Rate from Maier, 1963, p. 141, multiplied by coefficient presented in table 4.2.

b Second of an eight-group skill scale. Rate from Maier, 1963, p. 141, multiplied by coefficient as in note a. The rate is for underground work in mining of iron ore.

c Third of an eight-group skill scale. Rate from Maier, 1963, p. 141, and skill group coefficient derived from data in same source. This does not refer to the skill scale presented in table 4.2. By 1962, more than 60 percent of workers in that industry were classified according to an eight-group scale and only 30 percent according to the ten-group scale.

d Second of a seven-group skill scale according to skill group distribution in mining of nonferrous ores. Druze and Mashkov, 1961, p. 21.

e For those directly employed in oil drilling and extraction brigades, Belenkii, 1959, p. 53. Maier (1963, p. 143) gives this rate as 69.0.

f Maier, 1963, p. 143.

g Second of a seven-group skill scale. Rate from Maier, 1963, and skill-group coefficient derived from same source, p. 142.

h Peat mining and processing in enterprise administered by local authorities. Kukulevich and Machikhin, 1961, p. 22.

i Maier, 1963, p. 143. Corresponds to the higher rates discussed in note to table 1.2.

j As in note i, but here corresponds to rate presented in table 1.2 (30.5k. per hour).

k The rate for enterprises administered by local authorities. Kukulevich and Machikhin, 1961, p. 21. This rate corresponds to that given in *Lesnaia Promyshlennost'* (March 30, 1960), as cited by Fearn, 1963, pp. 71, 87.

l Second of a seven-group skill scale. Arkhipov, 1961, p. 124.

m Underground work in mining and processing nonore construction materials in enterprises under local administration. Kukulevich and Machikhin, 1961, p. 21.

n Enterprises under local administration. Kukulevich and Machikhin, 1961, p. 21. This rate does not cover concrete, reinforced concrete, building glass, building ceramics, and several other industries that might be considered as "building materials." It is not clear if Batkaev's and Markov's proposed rates include these industries.

o For those employed in logging camps and the floating of lumber. Popov-Cherkasov, 1962, p. 39.

p Popov-Cherkasov, 1962, p. 54.

q A higher rate (54.1), under special procedure, can be applied in some plants in Moscow, Leningrad, and the Baltic Republics. Severianova, 1959, p. 48.

r A higher rate much like that in note q exists. *Shveinaia Promyshlennost'*, no. 2, 1960, pp. 1-5, as cited in Fearn, 1963b, pp. 73, 87.

s For meat, sugar, bread baking, canning, alcoholic and nonalcoholic beverages, in cities and workers' settlements. Somewhat higher rates exist for tobacco and meat slaughtering plants. The rate is for enterprises administered by local authorities. Kukulevich and Machikhin, 1961, pp. 25-26.

t Kukulevich and Machikhin, 1961, p. 26. Maier (1963, p. 144) gives the rate as 40.

u As calculated by Chapman (1970, pp. 47-48) from data in Batkaev and Markov, 1964, p. 228.

v As cited in Chapman, 1970, pp. 47-48.

w Includes cement and possibly mining of building materials.

x Includes sewing.

age of those in coal, would have been about 70; they were, however, somewhat less than 40 percent.

Despite the substantial difference between interindustry differentiation of initial basic rates and that of average earnings, it is at least conceptually possible that the initial basic rate was the sole expression of the pure interindustrial differential. That is, *ceteris paribus,* initial basic rate levels essentially explained the effect of employment within a given branch upon workers' earnings; and the greater differentiation of average wages was caused by other pure differentials such as higher average skill levels in coal than in sewing. Although theoretically possible, in light of the evidence presented in the course of this study, this explanation must be rejected. For work that is considered identical as to job content, such things as skill-group classification, incentive payments, additions for working conditions and increments for geographical area [7] differ according to industrial branch. In short, as of 1962, any measurement of the pure (as distinct from the statistical) interindustry differential is exceedingly complex if not impossible.

Although average branch wage levels for 1968 are not yet available, the increase of the minimum wage accomplished in that year tended to further reduce interindustry differentials, and, as compared to the data in column (6) of table A.1, dramatically lowered the variation of initial basic rates among branches. These rates were increased in all branches other than coal, and the new rates stood within the range of 60–70 rubles a month. This narrowing of interindustry differentiation probably reduced earnings inequality among Soviet workers, a subject discussed in appendix B.

7. Between 1966 and 1968 these differences were sharply reduced. The regional wage differentials that had existed only for certain "important" industries were extended to all branches in the far east and north. Kunel'skii, 1968a, p. 82.

Appendix B:
A Note on Earnings Inequality

Changes in wage structures, or interoccupational wages, are customarily measured in two ways. The skill differential is measured in terms of the ratio between the earnings of skilled and unskilled workers. The evidence presented in chapter 5 indicated a recent tendency toward the narrowing of skill differentials in Soviet industry. Here we turn to a second and broader measure of inequality: the occupational wage structure measured by the dispersion, or variation of the entire structure of earnings.[1]

Simon Kuznets has emphasized that a distinctive aspect of Soviet economic development was the rapid, almost violent, shifts that took place in the composition of output during the 1930s.[2] The effect of this upheaval upon the structure of earnings has been documented and analyzed.[3] The upheaval appears to be over, and the Soviet economy has entered a period of relative "normalcy." Comparisons of the distribution of the wage fund in recent years with those distributions presented by Bergson for 1934 or 1928 would be extremely valuable. Such comparisons, unfortunately, are not currently possible. For unknown reasons, recently available Soviet data are not consistent with those in Bergson's work.[4]

Therefore, we here rely exclusively upon Soviet sources, which report that in 1956, inequality in the distribution of workers' earnings was greater than it had been in 1934. The reported indexes are quartile and decile ratios. In general terms, the quartile ratio as defined in Soviet statistical practice is the quotient of the wage of the worker whose earnings are higher than those of 75 percent and lower than those of 25 percent of workers divided by the wage of the worker whose earnings are greater than 25 percent and less than those of 75 percent

1. For a discussion of these two measures, see Perlman, 1969, pp. 81–102.
2. Kuznets, 1963, especially pp. 367–368.
3. Bergson, 1944.
4. As noted by Yanowitch (1963, pp. 685–686), in Mozhina's (1961) study of wage inequality for 1934, 1956, and 1959, data for the earliest date indicate considerably less inequality than is shown by Bergson (1944, pp. 120–129) for that year. Mozhina does not indicate any change in the coverage of her data for the three years she is comparing. Even more perplexing is the laconic presentation by Rabkina and Rimashevskaia (1966b, p. 88) of decile ratios for the earnings of industrial workers. According to their data, with the exception of 1930, wage inequality by this measure consistently decreased in the years between 1924 and 1934. Furthermore, their data show a significantly greater change in decile ratios—towards equality—between 1927 and 1934 than do those of Mozhina. Bergson's study, however, shows an increase in wage inequality during this period.

of workers. The decile ratio is similarly determined, with the relevant percentages in the frequency distribution of earnings being 10 and 90.[5] For industrial workers in 1934, quartile and decile ratios are given as 1.82 and 3.17. In 1956, these ratios were 1.85 and 3.38, indicating a slight increase of earnings inequality.[6]

It is probable that any attempt to trace the patterns of changes in wage inequality between 1934 and 1956 will prove unsuccessful. Such data were simply not collected during the period. A few Soviet economists have tentatively advanced the hypothesis that inequality reached its peak on the eve of World War II and then either remained constant or decreased somewhat during the decade following the war.[7]

Since 1956, information on the distribution of earnings has been systematically collected by the Central Statistical Administration through periodic sample surveys.[8] Though the results of these studies have been made available only in a scattered piecemeal fashion,[9] the evidence clearly points to a significant reduction of wage inequality among industrial workers since 1956. Among the pieces of evidence pointing in this direction are earnings data for individual enterprises

5. Here we follow Soviet practice in measuring quartile and decile ratios as Q_3/Q_1 and D_9/D_1. Therefore, these measures of inequality must be greater than, or equal to, unity. In Western studies, the inverse relationship is often reported as the ratio(s). For a fuller discussion of these measures, see Bergson, 1944, pp. 51–56.

6. Mozhina, 1961, pp. 24–25; Rabkina and Rimashevskaia, 1966b, p. 88. However, Mozhina also reports a decrease in a measure of skewness which she calls quartile and decile coefficients of skewness. In 1934 these were, respectively, 1.55 and 2.14. In 1956, these indices had fallen to 1.28 and 1.82. The indices are defined in Karpetian, 1958, pp. 143–150 as follows:

$$K_q = \frac{Q_3 - Q_2}{Q_2 - Q_1} \text{ and } K_d = \frac{D_9 - D_8}{D_2 - D_1}$$

where K_q and K_d are measures of quartile and decile skewness; Q_i is the absolute value of the indicated quartile; and D_i is the absolute value of the indicated decile. Therefore, if these coefficients are greater than unity, the distribution of earnings is skewed to the right, and to the left if they are less than unity. Accordingly, while wage inequality measured by quartile and decile ratios increased between 1934 and 1956, the distribution of earnings in the latter year more closely approximated a normal curve.

7. Rabkina and Rimashevskaia, 1966b, p. 88; Mozhina, 1961, pp. 21, 25.

8. Labok (1966, pp. 270–272) describes several of these surveys. The most detailed one was taken in 1963 and included 10 percent of workers in each branch of industry.

9. Among others, Maier (1963, p. 126) has called for the publication of earnings distribution data. In a study by the Soviet economist V. P. Gruzinov (1968), there is an attempt to compare wage structures in several socialist countries. Because of lack of data, most of the tables exclude information about the USSR. See especially pp. 237–269.

and branches; calculated distributions of basic wage rates; a roughly
drawn chart of the distribution of industrial workers according to
earnings levels; a number of dispersed statements about changes in the
distribution of industrial workers according to wage levels; and some
data on income differentiation for all employed personnel.[10] Janet
Chapman has compiled and judiciously analyzed these diverse data.
She concludes, for the period 1956–1960:

The evidence presented suggests that the wage reform led to a significant reduction in variation in earnings among industrial wage earners.
The evidence, however, is incomplete and provides no basis for quan-
tifying the extent of the decline in wage variation.[11]

After careful analysis, however, Chapman finds a tentative calculation
indicating a decrease in the decile ratio for earnings of industrial workers from 3.38 in 1956 to less than 2.8 in 1961 to be "quite plausible." [12]
This, as well as further reductions of inequality that have taken place
since 1961, are in large part due to extremely rapid increases in minimum wage rates.

The policy of reduced income inequality was set at the Twentieth
Party Congress in early 1956,[13] and the minimum wage established on
January 1, 1957, appears to have initiated the implementation of this
policy. The previous minimum wage of 10–12.5 rubles [14] per month
for industrial workers had been established in 1937 and was altered by
the "bread allowance" of 1946. In order to reduce the impact of increased retail prices accompanying the abolition of rationing, the
wages of those in low and middle pay ranges were increased. The
increase was determined according to a sliding scale with the maximum
addition being 11 rubles for those having a basic wage of less than
30 rubles, and the minimum addition set at 8 rubles for those with
basic wages between 70 and 90 rubles a month. No increase was
granted to high-paid workers receiving more than 90 rubles.[15] Inas-
much as the average wage in 1946 was only about 45–50 rubles, this
adjustment probably produced only a modest narrowing of absolute

10. See footnote 25.
11. Chapman, 1970, pp. 90–91.
12. Chapman, 1970, pp. 66, 91–94.
13. Specifically, A. Mikoyan announced the policy. *Pravda,* February 18, 1956, as cited
in Yanowich, 1963, p. 684.
14. We continue to express all values in terms of the post-1960 "heavy" ruble, which
equals 10 "old" rubles.
15. Aganbegian and Maier, 1959, pp. 220–221; Schwarz, 1951, p. 220.

differentials among workers.[16] With this 11-ruble addition, the minimum wage for industrial workers became 21–23.5 rubles a month.

On January 1, 1957, the minimum wage for industrial workers was established at 30–35 rubles. During the wage reform, the minimum was again increased,[17] and by the end of 1960 it had become 40–45 rubles, the higher rate applying to virtually all industrial workers except for those employed in small rural processing plants of the food industry.[18] At the beginning of 1968, the minimum was set at a flat 60 rubles for all industrial workers.[19]

It must be assumed that these increases have tended to compress the range of wage dispersion. In 1968, average money earnings for industrial workers were reported to be approximately 156 percent of their 1955 level.[20] For minimum wages, the corresponding figure is in the range of 255–286 percent. Moreover, the Soviet minimum provides a floor on basic wage rates. The worker whose basic wage is equal to the minimum may receive additional payments in the form of premiums, bonuses, and, if a piece-rate worker, payments for norm overfulfillment. In the latter case, with underfulfillment of the output norm, earnings can be less than the minimum wage.[21] Highly fragmentary data for 1962 indicate that possibly one or two percent of industrial workers who worked a full month received earnings below the established minimum.[22] Conversely, it is reported that for workers in the first skill group, the only ones who could be paid the minimum, aver-

16. The compression of differentials resulting from this adjustment seems to have been overestimated by several Western scholars. Galenson (1963, pp. 306–307) maintains that as a result of the 1946 additions, by the mid-1950s "the logical policy was to widen the spread of skill differentials." Also see Chapman, 1970, p. 10. On the average monthly wage in 1946, Fearn's (1963a, p. 2) calculation of 51 rubles in 1945 seems to have turned out to be an overestimate. According to *Trud v SSSR* (1968, pp. 137–138) the 1945 figure for industrial workers is 45 rubles, and other data in the same source indicate a range of 45–50 for 1946.

17. See "The Wage Reform: A Brief History" in chapter 1.

18. For all workers and employees the minimum range established in 1957 was 27–35 rubles. See Chapman, 1964, pp. 2, 8; and Kunel'skii, 1968a, p. 83.

19. "Bigger Pay Packets this Year," 1968; Chapman, 1970, pp. 126–135; Kunel'skii, 1968a, p. 83.

20. *Nar. Khoz.*, 1968, p. 554; *Trud v SSSR*, 1968, pp. 138–139.

21. Before 1934, workers were entitled to two-thirds of basic wages regardless of norm fulfillment level. In the West, piece-rate workers almost universally are guaranteed a minimum earnings level that is most often equal to the hourly basic rate. Glicksman, 1960, p. 19; Mangum, 1962, pp. 257–259.

22. Maier, 1963, pp. 110–111; Chapman, 1964, pp. 7–8.

age earnings were from 15 to 20 percent higher than basic wage rates.[23]

Each increase of the minimum directly affects those workers who had basic wages below this level, and the effect upon other workers appears to be inversely related to their wage levels. As previously discussed, in all but one branch of industry the 1968 minimum entailed upward adjustments of basic wages for workers in the lower skill groups. These rates were increased to levels of between 60 and 70 rubles a month.[24] Thus, the 1968 increase and probably those of 1957 and 1959–1961 have tended to change the shape of the frequency distribution of workers according to earnings; that is, the left portion of the distribution was shifted toward the center while the right remained largely unchanged. In 1963, Murray Yanowitch advanced the thesis that an "income revolution" was taking place within the Soviet Union. Given the incompleteness of available data, one might hesitate to apply such a dramatic title. However, newly available information and recent Soviet policy, especially the further increase of the minimum wage to 70 rubles planned for 1972–1974, indicate that for industrial workers, and even more so for total employed personnel, Yanowitch's phrase has a new appropriateness.[25]

23. Kunel'skii, 1968c, p. 17.
24. The exception was underground work in the coal industry, where the basic wage for the first skill group was in excess of 70 rubles. Kunel'skii, 1968a, p. 86. See "Impact of the 1968 Minimum Wage" in chapter 5.
25. Loznevaia (1968, p. 129) reports that the decile coefficient for all workers and employees fell from 7.24 in 1946 to 3.26 in 1966. There is some indication that since 1955 the earnings of very highly paid personnel have been generally frozen and in some cases reduced. Mikoyan stated that the wages of approximately 100,000 individuals were reduced. See Perlo, 1961, pp. 48–49; Varga, 1957, p. 105; Schwartz, 1965, p. 78; Ageeva and Tyklin, 1961, pp. 34–35; Maier, 1963, pp. 133–134.

During the period under consideration, policies concerning taxation and pensions also tended to reduce income inequality. Information concerning changes in the distribution of income for all employed personnel is to be found in Chapman, 1970, pp. 95–125; Raitsin, 1967; Rabkina and Rimashevskaia, 1966a and 1966b; and Rimashevskaia, 1965.

Appendix C:
Notes to Table 2.1

Several of the column headings in the table should be further specified. We have chosen to call entry 7 "bonus" rather than "payment" for overtime work because the Soviet term *doplata* (rather than *oplata*) seems to indicate that for work paid at a time-and-a-half rate, only the "half" is entered as overtime pay. The time-rate worker receives time and a half for the first two hours and double time for all additional hours of overtime work in a given work day. The piece-rate worker receives his normal piece earnings for the additional hour(s) plus a bonus. This bonus is equivalent to half the basic rate of a time-rate worker of the same skill group for each of the first two hours and, for each additional hour, the full basic rate of the time-rate worker.[1]

Entries 8 and 9 both refer to time lost and/or output not produced as a result of factors for which the worker is not considered responsible.[2] Included under the former are payments to compensate for the piece-rate worker's being provided with poor quality raw materials or improper equipment. He is paid according to (entry 9) two-thirds of his basic wage rate if, because of circumstances beyond his control, work is not performed.

Entry 10 may include items as diverse as a free apartment; fuel; electricity; the difference between the price of goods purchased at the enterprise outlet and the retail price; an amount of money equivalent to the value of services the worker is entitled to but does not receive; free food, and so on. Not included in this category is special work clothing that the worker may receive.[3]

Finally, it should be noted that because of Soviet terminology, entry 1*b* is sometimes mistakenly taken to be part of basic wages rather than payments for norm overfulfillment.[4]

Table 2.1 was constructed from the following sources:
1950 and 1955: *Promyshlennost' SSSR*, 1957, p. 28. The relationship between *a* and *b* of the first entry is from Aganbegian and Maier, 1959, p. 66. The data refer to workers in enterprises subordinate to All-Union and Union-Republic Ministries.

1. Iu. Orlovskii, 1961, pp. 140–141. In any event, overtime work does not appear to be substantial. In 1962 it was about one-half of one percent of total time worked. See Feshbach, 1966, p. 724.
2. "O Sostave," 1964, pp. 5–6.
3. "O Sostave," 1964, pp. 6 and 8.
4. Fearn (1963b, p. 34) apparently makes this mistake in his interpretation of the data presented in Kapustin, 1961a, p. 45.

1957: entries 2 through 11 are from Karpukhin, 1963, p. 61. Entry 1, *a* and *b* are from Batkaev and Markov, 1964, p. 221. In the latter, these data are presented in a more aggregate form (as in the column for 1961), except for division of piece-rate wages into two components. The percentages presented in these two sources are clearly compatible. Karpukhin identifies the data as being for workers in the industry of the *sovnarkhoz*.
1958: Karpukhin, 1963, p. 61. For workers of industry of the *sovnarkhoz*.
1959: As for 1958.
1961: Batkaev and Markov, 1964, p. 221. Though not identified, probably for workers of industry of the *sovnarkhoz*. It should be noted that Karpukhin also presents data for 1960. However, because of an apparent typographical error, this information cannot be utilized. For that year, his figures show that the sum of all the components of the wage fund, including "other," total only 96 percent.
1963: *Vest. Stat.*, no. 8, 1964.

Bibliography

As explained in the Preface, all sources are alphabetized according to the shortened citations used throughout this study.

Acharkan, 1966

Acharkan, V., "Vozmozhnosti Pooshchreniia" [Possibilities for Stimulation], *Trud*, October 6, 1966, p. 2.

Aganbegian and Maier, 1959

Aganbegian, A. G., and Maier, V. F., *Zarabotnaia Plata v SSSR* [Wages in the USSR]. Moscow, Gosplanizdat, 1959.

Ageeva and Tyklin, 1961

Ageeva, A., and Tyklin, A., "Analiz Sokrashcheniia Razlichii v Oplate Truda Nizko- i Vysokooplachivaemykh Rabotnikov Elektrotekhnicheskoi Promyshlennosti" [An Analysis of the Reduction of the Difference between the Wages of Low-Paid and High-Paid Personnel in the Electrotechnical Industry], *Biulleten' Nauchnoi Informatsii*, no. 12, 1961, pp. 30–38.

Aleksandrov, 1958

Aleksandrov, N., Latov, B., and Pogostin, I., "Uporiadochenie Normirovaniia Truda i Zarabotnoi Platy Rabotnikov Khimicheskoi Promyshlennosti" [Reforming the Norming of Work and Wages of Those Employed in the Chemical Industry], *Sots. Trud*, no. 7, 1958, pp. 33–39.

Amel'chenko, 1962

Amel'chenko, M., "Obiazannosti i Rol' Normirovshchika na Proizvodstve" [Responsibilities and Role of the Normer in Production], *Sots. Trud*, no. 7, 1962, pp. 78–80.

Andreev and Belikanov, 1965

Andreev, V., and Belikanov, G., "Po Sobstvennomu Zhelaniiu. . ." [By One's Own Desires . . .] *Pravda*, February 2, 1965, p. 2.

Arkhipov, 1961

Arkhipov, A. V., "Sovershenstvovanie Zarabotnoi Platy na Tsementnykh Zavodakh" [Improving Wages at Cement Factories], in *Sovershenstvovanie Organizatsii Zarabotnoi Platy* [Improving the Organization of Wages], edited by S. I. Shkurko, pp. 118–146. Moscow, Ekonomizdat, 1961.

Bakhrakh, 1962a

Bakhrakh, I. M., "Brigada Proizvodstvennaia" [The Productive Brigade], in *Ek. Entsik.*, vol. 1, pp. 177–181.

Bakhrakh, 1962b

Bakhrakh, I. M., "Professiia" [Occupation], in *Ek. Entsik.*, vol. 2, pp. 756–761.

Baranenkova, 1970

Baranenkova, T., "Tekhnicheskii Progress i Dvizhenie Kadrov v Promyshlennosti [Technical Progress and Cadre Turnover in Industry], *Voprosy Ekonomiki*, no. 2, 1970, pp. 50–61

Barker, n.d.

Barker, G. R., *Some Problems of Incentives and Labor Productivity in Soviet Industry*. Oxford, England, Basil Blackwell, n.d.

Batkaev, 1958

Batkaev, R., "O Sootnosheniiakh v Oplate Truda Rabochikh-Sdel'-shchikov i Povremenshchikov v Mashinostroenii" [Concerning the Relationship of Wages for Piece-Rate and Time-Rate Workers in Machine Construction], *Sots. Trud*, no. 10, 1958, pp. 71–76.

Batkaev, 1963

Batkaev, R. A., "O Differentsiatsii Zarabotnoi Platy Rabochikh v Zavisimosti ot Uslovii Truda" [Concerning Wage Differentiation Dependent upon Working Conditions for Workers], *Sots. Trud*, no. 10, 1963, pp. 65–70.

Batkaev, 1971

Batkaev, R. A., "Rost Zarabotnoi Platy v Vos'moi Piatiletke" [Growth of Wages in the Eighth Five-Year Plan], *Sots. Trud*, no. 7, 1970, pp. 23–33.

Batkaev and Markov, 1964

Batkaev, R. A., and Markov, V. I., *Differentsiatsiia Zarabotnoi Platy v Promyshlennosti SSSR* [Wage Differentiation in Industry of the USSR]. Moscow, Ekonomika, 1964.

Batukhtin, 1969

Batukhtin, I. L., *Analiz Truda i Zarabotnoi Platy na Predpriiatii* [Analysis of Labor and Wages at Enterprises]. Moscow, Ekonomika, 1969.

Batyshev, 1965

Batyshev, S. Ia., *Podgotovka i Povyshenie Kvalifikatsii Rabochikh na Proizvodstve* [On-the-Job Training and Raising the Qualification of Workers]. Moscow, Vysshaia Shkola, 1965.

Belcher, 1960
Belcher, David W., "Employee and Executive Compensation," in *Employment Relations Research*, edited by Herbert G. Heneman, Jr., et al., pp. 73–131, New York, Harper & Brothers, 1960.

Belenkii, 1959
Belenkii V., "Novye Usloviia Oplaty Truda v Neftianoi i Gazovoi Promyshlennosti" [New Conditions for Wages in the Oil and Gas Industries], *Sots. Trud*, no. 7, 1959, pp. 52–58.

Bell, 1956
Bell, Daniel, *Work and its Discontents*. Boston, Mass., Beacon Press, 1956.

Bell, 1960
Bell, Daniel, "The Subversion of Collective Bargaining," *Commentary*, March 1960, pp. 697–714.

Bergson, 1944
Bergson, Abram, *The Structure of Soviet Wages*. Cambridge, Mass., Harvard University Press, 1944.

Bergson, 1961
Bergson, Abram, *The Real National Income of Soviet Russia Since 1928*. Cambridge, Mass., Harvard University Press, 1961.

Bergson, 1964
Bergson, Abram, *The Economics of Soviet Planning*. New Haven, Conn., Yale University Press, 1964.

Bergson, 1966
Bergson, Abram, *Essays in Normative Economics*. Cambridge, Mass., Harvard University Press, 1966.

Bergson, 1967
Bergson, Abram, "Planning and the Market in the USSR," in *Planning and The Market in the USSR*, edited by A. Balinsky, pp. 43–64. New Brunswick, N.J., Rutgers University Press, 1967.

"Bigger Pay Packets This Year," 1968
"Bigger Pay Packets This Year," *Soviet News*, January 23, 1968, p. 44.

Biulleten'
Biulleten' [Bulletin], Gosudarstvennyi Komitet Soveta Ministrov SSSR po Voprosam Truda i Zarabotnoi Platy, Moscow.

Biulleten' Nauchnoi Informatsii

Biulleten' Nauchnoi Informatsii Trud i Zarabotnaia Plata [Bulletin of Scientific Information Concerning Labor and Wages] published monthly from 1958 to 1962 by the Labor Institute of the Government Labor Committee.

Bjork, 1953

Bjork, Lief, *Wages, Prices and Social Legislation in the Soviet Union.* London, England, Dennis Dobson, Ltd., 1953.

Blaug, 1962

Blaug, M., *Economic Theory in Retrospect.* Homewood, Ill., Richard D. Irwin, Inc., 1962.

Bliakhman, 1960

Bliakhman, L. S., *Uporiadochenie Zarabotnoi Platy v Promyshlennosti SSSR* [The Wage Reform in Industry of the USSR]. Leningrad, Obshchestvo po Rasprostraneniiu Politicheskikh i Nauchnykh Znanii RSFSR, 1960.

Bliakhman, 1964

Bliakhman, L. S., *Proizvoditel'nost i Oplata Truda v Period Razvernutogo Stroitel'stva Kommunizma* [Productivity and Wages during the Period of the Further Construction of Communism]. Leningrad, Lenizdat, 1964.

Bliakhman et al., 1965

Bliakhman, L. S., Zdravomyslov, A. G., and Shkaratan, O. I., *Dvizhenie Rabochei Sily na Promyshlennykh Predpriiatiiakh* [Labor Force Dynamics at Industrial Enterprises]. Moscow, Ekonomika, 1965.

Bloom, 1941

Bloom, Gordon F., "A Reconsideration of the Theory of Exploitation," *Quarterly Journal of Economics*, vol. 55, 1940–1941, pp. 413–442. Reprinted in *Readings in the Theory of Income Distribution*, edited by William Fellner, and Bernard F. Haley. pp. 245–277. Homewood, Ill., Richard D. Irwin, Inc., 1951.

Boborykin and Zelikson, 1967

Boborykin, S. G., and Zelikson, M. Ia., *Voprosy Organizatsii Zarabotnoi Platy (na predpriiatiiakh Mashinostroitel'noi, sudostroitel'noi i Metalloobrabatyvaiushchei Promyshlennosti SSSR) Spravochnoe Posobie* [Questions of the Organization of Wages (at Enterprises of Machine Construction, Shipbuilding and Metalworking Industries), a Handbook]. Leningrad, Sudostroenie, 1967.

Bornstein, 1962

Bornstein, Morris, "The Soviet Price System," *American Economic Review*, vol. 52, March 1962, pp. 64–103.

Bornstein, 1966

Bornstein, Morris, "Soviet Price Theory and Policy," in *New Directions in the Soviet Economy*, part 1, pp. 65–94. Washington, D.C., Joint Economic Committee, U.S. Government Printing Office, 1966.

Breitman, 1968

Breitman, M., "Organizatsiia Zarabotnoi Platy na Stanochnykh Avtomaticheskikh Liniiakh" [Organization of Wages for Machine Tool Operators on Automated Assembly Lines], *Voprosy Ekonomiki*, no. 6, 1966, pp. 139–141.

Brennan, 1963

Brennan, Charles W., *Wage Administration*. Homewood, Ill., Richard D. Irwin, Inc., 1963.

Brezhnev, 1966

Brezhnev, L., "Report of the Central Committee of the Communist Party of the Soviet Union to the Twenty-Third Congress of the CPSU," *Twenty-Third Congress of the CPSU*, pp. 7–160. Novosti Press Agency Publishing House, 1966.

Brown, 1957

Brown, Emily Clark, "The Soviet Labor Market," *Industrial and Labor Relations Review*, vol. 10, January 1957, pp. 179–200.

Brown, 1960

Brown, Emily Clark, "The Local Union in Soviet Industry: Its Relations with Members, Party, and Management," *Industrial and Labor Relations Review*, vol. 13, January 1960, pp. 193–215.

Brown, 1966

Brown, Emily Clark, *Soviet Trade Unions and Labor Relations*. Cambridge, Mass., Harvard University Press, 1966.

Brown, 1970

Brown, Emily Clark, "Continuity and Change in the Soviet Labor Market," *Industrial and Labor Relations Review*, vol. 23, January 1970, pp. 171–190.

Bugrov and Chubarov, 1964

Bugrov, A. P., and Chubarov, G. C., *Otraslevye Normy Truda* [Branch Labor Norms]. Moscow, Ekonomika, 1964.

Bugrov and Semenkevich, 1964

Bugrov, A., and Semenkevich, S., "Normativno-Issledovatel'skaia Rabota v 1964–1965 gg" [Norming Research Work during the Years 1964–1965], *Sots. Trud,* no. 5, 1964, pp. 81–86.

Bulgakov, 1965

Bulgakov, A. A., "Rastet Sem'ia Rabocraia" [The Worker's Family Grows], *Trud,* September 10, 1965, p. 2.

Bulganin, 1955

Bulganin, N. A., "Concerning Tasks in the Further Advance of Industry, Technical Progress and Improvement of Production Organization," *Current Digest of the Soviet Press,* August 24, 1955, pp. 3–20. Translated from *Pravda,* July 17, 1955.

Campbell, 1968

Campbell, Robert W., "Economic Reform in the USSR," *American Economic Review,* vol. 58, May 1968, pp. 547–558.

Chapman, 1963

Chapman, Janet G., "Consumption," in *Economic Trends in the Soviet Union* edited by Abram Bergson and Simon Kuznets, pp. 235–282. Cambridge, Mass., Harvard University Press, 1963.

Chapman, 1964

Chapman, Janet G., *A Note on the Soviet Minimum Wage.* Santa Monica, Calif., The Rand Corporation, March 1964, no. P-2880.

Chapman, 1970

Chapman, Janet G., *Wage Variation in Soviet Industry: The Impact of the 1956–1960 Wage Reform.* Memorandum RM–6076–PR, Santa Monica, Calif., The Rand Corporation, 1970.

Chirkov, 1965

Chirkov, A., "Eta Forma Oplaty Sebia Opravdala" [This Form of Wages Has Justified Itself], *Ek. Gaz.,* August 18, 1965, p. 11.

Chirkova, 1967

Chirkova, A., "Ne Prosto Nadbavka" [Not Simply an Addition], *Ek. Gaz.,* no. 21, May 1967, p. 15.

Clark, 1923

Clark, J. Maurice, *Studies in the Economics of Overhead Costs.* Chicago, Ill., University of Chicago Press, 1923.

Deutscher, 1950

Deutscher, Isaac, *Soviet Trade Unions*. London and New York, Royal Institute of International Affairs, 1950.

Deutscher, 1957

Deutscher, Isaac, *Russia in Transition*. New York, Coward-McCann Inc., 1957.

Dewar, 1962

Dewar, Margaret, "Labor and Wage Reform in the USSR," *Studies on the Soviet Union*, n.s., vol. 2, no. 3, 1962, pp. 80–91.

De Witt, 1959

De Witt, Nicholas, "Upheaval in Education," *Problems of Communism*, January–February 1959, pp. 25–34.

De Witt, 1961

De Witt, Nicholas, *Education and Professional Employment in the USSR*. Washington, D.C., National Science Foundation, 1961.

Direktivy, 1957–1958

Direktivy K.P.S.S. i Sovetskogo Pravitel'stva po Khoziaistvennym Voprosam [Directives of the CPSU and the Soviet Government on Economic Questions], 4 vols., Moscow, Gospolitizdat, 1957–1958.

"Direktivy XXIII," 1966

"Direktivy XXIII Sezda K.P.S.S. po Piatiletnemu Planu . . . na 1966–1970 gody" [Directives of the Twenty-Third Congress of the CPSU on the Five-Year Plan . . . for the Years 1966–1970], *Ek. Gaz.*, no. 8, February 1966, pp. 3–13.

Dobb, 1959

Dobb, Maurice, *Wages*. Cambridge, England, James Nisbet & Co., 1959.

Dorokhov, 1962

Dorokhov, M. P. (ed.), *Trud i Zarabotnaia Plata v Zhilishchno-Kommunal'nom Khoziaistve*, Chast' I [Labor and Wages in Housing and Municipal Services], Moscow, Ministerstvo Kommunal'nogo Khoziaistva R.S.F.S.R., 1962.

Douty, 1963

Douty, H. M., "The Impact of Trade Unionism on International Wage Structures," in *Internal Wage Structure*, edited by J. L. Meij, pp. 222–259. Amsterdam, North Holland Publishing Co., 1963.

Druze and Mashkov, 1961

Druze, I. D., and Mashkov, A. N., *Organizatsiia Zarabotnoi Platy na Zavodakh Tsvetnoi Metallurgii* [Organization of Wages at Nonferrous Metals Plants]. Moscow, Metallurgizdat, 1961.

Dubovoi, 1967

Dubovoi, P., "Obespechenie Mezhotraslevogo Edinstva v Oplate Truda Odinakovoi Slozhnosti" [Providing Interindustrial Unity in the Pay for Work of Identical Complexity], *Voprosy Ekonomiki*, no. 9, 1967, pp. 55–65.

Dubovoi, 1968

Dubovoi, P., "Usloviia Truda i ego oplata" [Working Conditions and Payment for Labor], *Ek. Gaz.*, no. 27, July 1968, pp. 17–18.

Dubovoi, 1969

Dubovoi, P., "Usloviia Truda kak Faktor Differentsiatsii Zarabotnoi Platy" [Working Conditions as a Factor in Wage Differentiation], *Voprosy Ekonomiki*, 1969, no. 9, pp. 57–66.

Dunlop, 1957

Dunlop, John T., "The Task of Contemporary Wage Theory," in *New Concepts in Wage Determination*, edited by George W. Taylor and Frank C. Pierson, pp. 117–139. New York, McGraw-Hill Book Company, Inc., 1967.

Dunlop, 1958

Dunlop, John T., *Industrial Relations Systems*. New York, Henry Holt and Company, Inc., 1958.

Dunlop and Healy, 1955

Dunlop, John T., and Healy, James J., *Collective Bargaining*. Homewood, Ill., Richard D. Irwin, Inc., 1955.

Dvornikov and Nikitinskii, 1967

Dvornikov, I. and Nikitinskii V., "Pravovye Normy v Kollektivakh" [Legal Norms within the Collective], *Sovetskie Profsoiuzy*, no. 19, 1967, pp. 45–47.

Eason, 1963

Eason, Warren W., "Labor Force," in *Economic Trends in the Soviet Union* edited by Abram Bergson and Simon Kuznets, pp. 38–95. Cambridge, Mass., Harvard University Press, 1963.

Eckaus, 1964

Eckaus, R. S., "Economic Criteria for Education and Training," *The Review of Economics and Statistics*, vol. 46, May 1964, pp. 181–190.

Eckaus, 1966

Eckaus, R. S., "Economic Criteria for Education and Training: Reply," *The Review of Economics and Statistics,* vol. 48, February 1966, pp. 105–106.

Edinyi, 1961

Edinyi Tarifno-Kvalifikatsionnyi Spravochnik Rabochikh Skvoznykh Professii [Unified Wage-Qualification Handbook for Workers of the General Occupations]. Moscow, Gostoptekhizdat, 1961.

Edinyi Pishchevoi

Edinyi Tarifno-Kvalifikatsionnyi Spravochnik dlia Rabochikh Pishchevoi Promyshlennosti [Single Wage-Qualification Handbook for Workers of the Food Industry]. Moscow, Pishchepromizdat, 1957.

Ek. Entsik.

Ekonomicheskaia Entsiklopediia Promyshlennost' i Stroitel'stvo [Economic Encyclopedia: Industry and Construction], vols. 1–3. Moscow, Sovetskaia Entsiklopediia, 1962–1965.

Ek. Gaz.

Ekonomicheskaia Gazeta, weekly organ of the Central Committee of the Communist Party of the Soviet Union.

Ekonomicheskie Nauki

Ekonomicheskie Nauki [Economic Science], monthly publication of the Ministry of Higher and Middle Special Education of the USSR.

Enke, 1963

Enke, Stephen, *Economics for Development.* Englewood Cliffs, N.J., Prentice-Hall Inc., 1963.

Entsiklopedicheskii Slovar', 1954

Entsiklopedicheskii Slovar' [Encyclopedic Dictionary], 3 vols., Bol'shaia Sovetskaia Entsiklopediia, Moscow, 1954.

Ermakov, 1962

Ermakov, I., "K Pobede Kommunisticheskogo Truda" [Toward the Victory of Communist Labor], *Molodoi Kommunist,* no. 9, 1962. pp. 71–75.

Fakiolas, 1962

Fakiolas, R., "Problems of Labor Mobility in the USSR," *Soviet Studies,* University of Glasgow, vol. 14, July 1962, pp. 16–40.

Fearn, 1963a

Fearn, Robert M. ("prepared by"), *Average Annual Money Earnings of Wage Workers in Soviet Industry*. Washington, D.C., CIA/RR ER 63–19, July 1963.

Fearn, 1963b

Fearn, Robert M. ("prepared by"), *An Evaluation of the Soviet Wage Reform*. Washington, D.C., CIA/RR ER 63–22, August 1963.

Fearn, 1965

Fearn, Robert M., "Controls Over Wage Funds and Inflationary Pressures in the USSR," *Industrial and Labor Relations Review*, vol. 18, January 1965, pp. 186–195.

Felker, 1966

Felker, Jere L., *Soviet Economic Controversies*. Cambridge, Mass., The MIT Press, 1966.

Feoktistov, 1962

Feoktistov, A. M., *Organizatsiia Truda i Zarabotnoi Platy v Molochnoi Promyshlennosti* [Organization of Labor and Wages in the Dairy Industry]. Moscow, Pishchepromizdat, 1962.

Feshbach, 1960

Feshbach, Murray, *The Soviet Statistical System: Labor Force Recordkeeping and Reporting*. Washington, D.C., International Population Statistics Reports, Series P–90, no. 12, 1960.

Feshbach, 1966

Feshbach, Murray, "Manpower in the USSR: A Survey of Recent Trends and Prospects," *New Directions in the Soviet Economy*, part 3, pp. 703–788. Washington, D.C., Joint Economic Committee, U.S. Government Printing Office.

Figurnov, 1961

Figurnov, S. P., "Ekonomicheskii Zakon Raspredeleniia po Trudu i Oplata Truda pri Sotsializme" [The Economic Law of Distribution according to Labor and Wages under Socialism] in *Politicheskaia Ekonomiia Sotsializma*, edited by I. I. Kuzminov, pp. 315–324. Moscow, Izdatel'stvo V.P.Sh. i A.O.N. pri Ts. K. K.P.S.S., 1961.

Figurnov, 1962

Figurnov, S. P., *Stroitel'stvo Kommunizma i Rost Blagosostoianiia Naroda* [The Construction of Communism and the Growth of the People's Welfare]. Moscow, Sotsekgiz, 1962.

Gaile, 1962

Gaile, G., "Vsemerno Ukrepliat' Printsip Material'noi Zainteresovan-nosti" [Totally Strengthen the Principle of Material Self-interest], *Sots. Trud,* no. 2, 1962, pp. 45–50.

Galenson, 1960

Galenson, Walter, "The Soviet Wage Reform," *Proceedings of the Thirteenth Annual Meeting of Industrial Relations Research Association,* December 1960, pp. 250–265. Reprinted, 16 pages.

Galenson, 1963

Galenson, W., "Wage Structure and Administration in Soviet Industry" in *Internal Wage Structure,* edited by J. L. Meij, pp. 300–334. Amsterdam, North Holland Publishing Co., 1963.

Gal'tsov, 1957

Gal'tsov, A., "Voprosy Normirovaniia i Oplaty Truda v Novykh Uslo-viiakh" [The Question of Norming and Wages in New Conditions], *Sots. Trud,* no. 4, 1957, pp. 20–24.

Gerschenkron, 1962

Gerschenkron, Alexander, *Economic Backwardness in Historical Perspective: A Book of Essays.* Cambridge, Mass., Harvard University Press, 1962.

Gerschenkron, 1964

Gerschenkron, Alexander, "Study of the Soviet Economy in the USA," *Survey,* January 1964, pp. 82–89.

Gintsburg, 1958

Gintsburg, L. Ia., *Trudovoi Stazh Rabochikh i Sluzhashchikh* [Seniority of Workers and Office Workers]. Moscow, Izdatel'stvo Akademii Nauk SSSR, 1958.

Gliantsev, 1962

Gliantsev, M., "Povysit' Rol' Rabotnikov po Normirovaniiu Truda na Predpriiatiiakh [Raise the Role of Normers at Enterprises], *Sots. Trud,* no. 5, 1962, pp. 83–87.

Gliksman, 1960

Gliksman, J. G., and collaborators, *The Control of Industrial Labor in the Soviet Union.* Research Memorandum RM–2494, Santa Monica, Calif., The Rand Corporation, 1960.

Goberman, 1970

Goberman, A., "Oplata Truda Stanochnikov" [Wages of Machine Tool Operators], *Sots. Trud,* no. 3, 1970, pp. 137–139.

Goldfinger, 1957

Goldfinger, Nathaniel, and Kassalow, Everett M., "Trade Union Behavior in Wage Bargaining" in *New Concepts in Wage Determination*, edited by George W. Taylor and Frank C. Pierson, pp. 51–82. New York, McGraw-Hill Book Company, Inc., 1957.

Goldman, 1967

Goldman, Marshall I., "Economic Revolution in the Soviet Union," *Foreign Affairs*, vol 45, January 1967, pp. 319–331.

Goldman, 1970

Goldman, Marshall I., "The Soviet Dual Economy," *Current History*, vol. 59, October 1970, pp. 232-237.

Golubia, 1962

Golubia, V., "Glavnoe v Sorevnovanii [The Main Thing in Competition], *Molodoi Kommunist*, no. 9, 1962, pp. 67–70.

Gomberg, 1964

Gomberg, Ia., "Kvalifitsirovannyi Trud—Odin iz Faktorov Differentsiatsii Zarabotnoi Platy" [The Qualification of Labor—One of the Factors in Wage Differentiation], *Voprosy Ekonomiki*, no. 7, 1964, pp. 21–30.

Gomberg, 1968

Gomberg, Ia., "Nekotorye Voprosy Teorii Zarabotnoi Platy pri Sotsializme" [Several Questions of Wage Theory under Socialism], *Voprosy Ekonomiki*, no. 12, 1968, pp. 56–66.

Granick, 1954

Granick, David, *Management of the Industrial Firm in the USSR*. New York, Columbia University Press, 1954.

Grigor'ev, 1959

Grigor'ev, A. E., *Ekonomika Truda* [Labor Economics]. Moscow, Gosplanizdat, 1959.

Gromov, 1957

Gromov, A., "Obespechit' Edinstvo v Regulirovanii Zarabotnoi Platy" [Provide Unity in Wage Regulation], *Sots. Trud*, no. 4, 1957, pp. 18–19.

Gruzinov, 1968

Gruzinov, V. P., *Material'noe Stimulirovanie Truda v Stranakh Sotsializma* [The Material Stimulation of Labor in Socialist Countries]. Moscow, Mysl', 1968.

Gurin, 1960

Gurin, L. E., *Novoe v Organizatsii Zarabotnoi Platy* [New Developments in the Organization of Wages]. Lenizdat, 1960.

Gur'ianov and Kostin, 1967

Gur'ianov, S. Kh., and Kostin, L. A. (eds.), *Trud i Zarabotnaia Plata na Predpriiatii, Spravochnoe Posobie* [Labor and Wages in the Enterprise, a Handbook]. Moscow, Ekonomika, 1967.

Harris, 1964

The citation refers to two unpublished works by Miss Mary Harris. One is a paper delivered to the Conference of Teachers and Research Workers on the USSR held at the University of London in March 1964. The other is her dissertation, which was subsequently revised and published. See McAuley, 1969.

Hicks, 1964

Hicks, J. R., *The Theory of Wages*, 2nd ed. London, England, Macmillan & Co., Ltd., 1964.

Hoeffding, 1959

Hoeffding, Oleg, "The Soviet Industrial Reorganization of 1957," *The American Economic Review (Proceedings)*, vol. S49, May 1959, pp. 65–77.

Holzman, 1955

Holzman, Franklyn D., *Soviet Taxation*. Cambridge, Mass., Harvard University Press, 1955.

Holzman, 1960

Holzman, Franklyn D., "Soviet Inflationary Pressures, 1928–1957: Causes and Cures," *The Quarterly Journal of Economics*, vol. 74, May 1960, pp. 167–188.

Iagodkin and Maslova, 1965

Iagodkin, V., and Maslova, I., "K Voprosu ob Ispol'vozanii Rabochei Sily, Vysvobozhdaiushcheisia v Sviazi s Tekhnicheskim Progressom" [On the Question of the Utilization of Labor Power Freed in Connection with Technical Progress],*Voprosy Ekonomiki*, no. 6, 1965, pp. 31–39.

I.A.M., 1954

What's Wrong With Job Evaluation, Washington, D.C., Research Department, International Association of Machinists, 1954.

ILO, 1960

International Labor Office, *The Trade Union Situation in the USSR*. Geneva, United Nations, 1960.

Incomes, 1967

Incomes in Postwar Europe: A Study of Policies Growth and Distribution. Geneva, United Nations, 1967.

Itogi Vsesoiuznoi Perepisi, 1962

Itogi Vsesoiuznoi Perepisi Naseleniia 1959 goda [Results of the All-Union Census of the Population in 1959]. Moscow, Gosstatizdat, 1962.

"I Vse-taki Tarif," 1965

"I Vse-taki Tarif" [And All the Same, Basic Wage Rates], *Ek. Gaz.*, March 3, 1965, pp. 11–12.

"Izmeneniia," 1966

"Izmeneniia i Dopolneniia v Polozheniiakh ob Oplate Truda i Premirovanii Rabochikh" [Changes and Additions in Regulations Concerning Workers' Wages and Premiums], *Ek. Gaz.*, no. 19, May 1966, p. 34.

"Job Evaluation Plans," 1957

"Job Evaluation Plans," *AFL-CIO Collective Bargaining Report*, June 1957, Washington, D. C., AFL-CIO, pp. 33–39.

"Kadry," 1965

"Kadry, Novaia Tekhnika, Upravlenie" [Cadres, New Technology, Management], *Ek. Gaz.*, Sept. 15, 1965, pp. 19–20.

Kalinovskii, 1966

Kalinovskii, N. P., *Raionnye Razlichiia Real'noi Zarabotnoi Platy Rabochikh i Sluzhashchikh* [Regional Difference in the Real Wages of Workers and Office Workers]. Moscow, Ekonomika, 1966.

Kaminer, 1964

Kaminer, L. "Edinyi Perechen' Professii Rabochikh" [Single Listing of Workers' Occupations], *Sots. Trud*, no. 12, 1964, pp. 50–55.

Kaplan, I., 1966

Kaplan, I., "Ucheba i Kvalifikatsiia" [Study and Qualification], *Trud*, November 4, 1966, p. 2.

Kaplan, N., 1970

Kaplan, Norman, *Earnings Distributions in the USSR*. Memorandum RM–6170, Santa Monica, Calif. The Rand Corporation, 1970.

Kapustin, 1957

Kapustin, E., "Raspredelenie po Trudu i Nekotorye Voprosy Uporia-docheniia Tarifnoi Sistemy Zarabotnoi Platy Rabochikh Promyshlennosti" [Distribution According to Labor and Several Questions of Reforming the System of Basic Wages for Industrial Workers], *Planovoe Khoziaistvo,* no. 7, 1957, pp. 25–36.

Kapustin, 1961a

Kapustin, E. I., "Uporiadochenie Zarabotnoi Platy i Neobkhodimost' Dal'neishego Sovershenstvovaniia ee Organizatsii" [The Wage Reform and the Necessity of the Further Improvement of Wage Administration], in *Zarabotnaia Plata v Promyshlennosti SSSR i ee Sovershenstvovanie,* edited by E. I. Kapustin, pp. 10–52. Moscow, Sotsekgiz, 1961.

Kapustin, 1961b

Kapustin, E. I., "Puti i Metody Sovershenstvovaniia Tarifnoi Sistemy", in *Zarabotnaia Plata v Promyshlennosti SSSR i ee Sovershenstvovanie,* edited by E. I. Kapustin, pp. 53–95. Moscow, Sotsekgiz, 1961.

Kapustin, 1961c

Kapustin, E., "Predislovie" [Introduction], in *Zarabotnaia Plata v Promyshlennosti SSSR i ee Sovershenstvovanie,* edited by E. Kapustin, pp. 3–9. Moscow, Sotsekgiz, 1961.

Kapustin, 1964

Kapustin, E. I., *Kachestvo Truda i Zarabotnaia Plata* [Wages and the Quality of Work]. Moscow, Mysl', 1964.

Kapustin, 1965

Kapustin, E. I., "Reduktsiia Truda" [The Reduction of Labor], *Ek. Gaz.,* May 19, 1965, pp. 5–6.

Kapustin, 1967

Kapustin, E. I., "Sovershenstvovanie Organizatsii Zarabotnoi Platy v SSSR" [Improving the Organization of Wages in the USSR], *Sots. Trud,* no. 11, 1967, pp. 63–72.

Kapustin, 1968a

Kapustin, E. I., "Ekonomika Sotsialisticheskogo Truda i ee Osnovnye Problemy" [The Economics of Socialist Labor and Its Basic Problems], *Sots. Trud,* no. 1, 1968, pp. 74–81.

Kapustin, 1968b

Kapustin, E. I., "Tarifnaia Sistema i ee Rol' v Organizatsii i Regulirovanii Zarabotnoi Platy" [The System of Basic Wages and Its Role in the Organization and Regulation of Wages], in *Trud i Zarabotnaia Plata v SSSR*, edited by A. P. Volkov, pp. 309–336. Moscow, Ekonomika, 1968.

Kapustin, 1969

Kapustin, E. I., "Raspredelenie po Trudu, Obshchestvennye Fondy Potrebleniia" [Distribution According to Labor and the Social Consumption Fund], *Ek. Gaz.*, January 1969, no. 2, pp. 21–28.

Kapustin, 1970

Kapustin, E. I., "O Reduktsii Truda v Sotsialisticheskom Obshchestve" [Concerning the Reduction of Labor in Socialist Society], *Ek. Gaz.*, no. 14, 1970, p. 14.

Kapustin and Mysev, 1961

Kapustin, E. I., and Mysev, N., "Opyt Sopostavleniia Slozhnosti Rabot Analiticheskim Metodom s Ekspertnoi Otsenkoi v Kuibyshevskom Sovnarkhoze" [The Experiment of Comparing the Complexity of Work According to the Analytic Method and Expert Evaluation in the Kuibyshev Economic Region], *Biulleten' Nauchnoi Informatsii*, no. 9, 1961, pp. 23–27.

Karapetian, 1958

Karapetian, A. Kh., "O Statisticheskikh Kharakteristikakh Raspredeleniia Zarabotnoi Platy" [Concerning the Statistical Characteristics of the Distribution of Wages], in *Voprosy Truda, Vypusk I*, pp. 142–152. Moscow, Profizdat, 1958.

Karinskii, 1963

Karinskii, S. S., *Pravovoe Regulirovanie Zarabotnoi Platy* [Legal Regulation of Wages]. Moscow, Gosiurizdat, 1963.

Karpenko, 1965

Karpenko, I., "Tarif ili Premiia?" [Basic Wage or Premium?], *Ek. Gaz.*, January 13, 1965, pp. 12–13.

Karpukhin, 1963

Karpukhin, D. N., *Sootnoshenie Rosta Proizvoditel'nosti Truda i Zarabotnoi Platy* [The Relationship between the Growth of Productivity and Wages]. Moscow, Izdatel'stvo Ekonomicheskoi Literatury, 1963.

Kerr, 1954

Kerr, Clark, "The Balkanization of Labor Markets," University of California, Reprint No. 59, Institute of Industrial Relations, 1964.

Kerr, 1957
Kerr, Clark, "Wage Relationships—The Comparative Impact of Market and Power Forces" (first pub. 1957), in *Wage Determination: Market or Power Forces,* edited by Richard Perlman. Boston, Mass., D. C. Heath and Company, 1964.

Khmirov, 1970
Khmirov, G., "Novyi Edinyi Tarifno-Kvalifikatsionnyi Spravochnik Rabot i Professii Rabochikh" [The New Unified Wage-Qualification Handbook of Workers' Jobs and Occupations], *Sots. Trud,* No. 7, 1970, pp. 89–92.

Khrushchev, 1959
Khrushchev, N. S., *Control Figures for the Economic Development of the USSR for 1959–1965.* Report delivered at the Twenty-First Extraordinary Congress of the Communist Party of the Soviet Union, January 27, 1959. Moscow, Foreign Languages Publishing House, 1959.

Kirsch, 1967
Kirsch, Leonard Joel, "A Study in Soviet Economics: Wage Administration and Structure in the USSR Since 1956." Ph.D. Thesis, Harvard University, April 1967.

Kishkin, 1965
Kishkin, S. M., "Putk Vysokoi Proizvoditel'nosti" [The Road to High Productivity], *Trud,* July 22, 1965, p. 1.

Knorring, 1962
Knorring, O., "Tul'skie Umel'tsy" [Tula Masters], *Ogonek,* no. 9, 1962, pp. 6–7.

Kostin, 1960
Kostin, Leonid, *Wages in the USSR.* Moscow, Foreign Languages Publishing House, 1960.

Kostin, 1963
Kostin, L., "Sovetskie Profsoiuzy v Bor'be za Povyshenie Proizvoditel'nosti Truda" [Soviet Trade Unions in the Struggle to Raise Labor Productivity], *Sots. Trud,* no. 10, 1963, pp. 3–12.

Kostin, 1967
Kostin, L., *Planirovanie Truda v Promyshlennosti* [Planning Labor in Industry]. Moscow, Ekonomika, 1967.

Kosygin, 1965

Kosygin, A. N., "Ob Uluchshenii Upravleniia Promyshlennost'iu, Sovershenstvovanii Planirovaniia i Usilenii Ekonomicheskogo Stimulirovaniia Promyshlennogo Proizvodstva" [Concerning the Improved Guidance of Industry, Improvement of Planning and Strengthening of Stimulation in Industrial Production]. *Trud*, September 28, 1965, pp. 1–3.

Kosygin, 1966

Kosygin, A. N., "Report on the Directives for the Five-Year Economic Development Plan of the USSR for 1966–1970," *Twenty-Third Congress of the CPSU*, pp. 165–174. Moscow, Novosti Press Agency Publishing House, 1966.

Kosygin, 1971

Kosygin, A. N., "Direktivy XXIV Sezda KPSS po Piatiletnemu Planu Razvitiia Narodnogo Khoziaistva SSSR na 1971–1975 gg." [Directives of the Twenty-Fourth Congress of the CPSU on the Five-Year Plan for the Development of the National Economy in 1971–1975], *Ek. Gaz.*, no. 15, April 1971, pp. 3–14.

Kotelkin, 1966

Kotelkin, V. I., *Sovershenstvovanie Normirovaniia Truda v Promyshlennosti* [The Improvement of Norming Work in Industry]. Izdatel'stvo Leningradskogo Universiteta, 1966.

Kozlovskii, 1962

Kozlovskii, S., "Koordinatsiia Nauchnykh Issledovanii v Oblasti Normirovaniia Truda" [Coordination of Scientific Research in the Sphere of Norming Work], *Sots. Trud*, no. 6, 1962, pp. 87–89.

Kuchenev, 1959

Kuchenev, N., "Edinyi Tarifno-Kvalifikatsionnyi Spravochnik Skvoznykh Professii Rabochikh" [The Single Wage-Qualification Handbook of General Occupations of Workers], *Sots. Trud*, no. 5, 1959, pp. 64–68.

Kudriavtsev, 1965

Kudriavtsev, A. S. (ed.), *Ekonomika Truda v SSSR* [Economics of Labor in the USSR], 3rd ed. Moscow, Profizdat, 1964.

Kukulevich, 1964

Kukulevich, I. L., *Zarabotnaia Plata v Voprosakh i Otvetakh* [Wages in Questions and Answers]. Moscow, Ekonomika, 1964.

Kukulevich and Machikhin, 1961

Kukulevich, I. L., and Machikhin, V. P., *Organizatsiia Zarabotnoi Platy na Predpriiatiiakh Mestnoi Promyshlennosti* [Organization of Wages at Enterprises of Local Industry]. Moscow, Gosplanizdat, 1961.

Kunel'skii, 1962

Kunel'skii, L., "Planirovanie Zarabotnoi Platy Rabochikh na Promyshlennykh Predpriiatiiakh" [Planning Wages of Workers in Industrial Enterprises], *Sots. Trud,* no. 5, 1962, pp. 47–52.

Kunel'skii, 1967

Kunel'skii, L., "Premirovanie Rabochikh v Novykh Usloviiakh" [Workers' Premiums under the New Conditions], *Ek. Gaz.,* no. 15, April 1967, pp. 12–13.

Kunel'skii, 1968a

Kunel'skii, L., "Glavnoe Napravlenie Rosta Dokhodov Trudiashchikhsia" [The Main Direction of the Growth of Income of Working People], *Sots. Trud,* no. 1, 1968, pp. 81–90.

Kunel'skii, 1968b

Kunel'skii, L., "Plius Shest' Milliardov v Semeinykh Biudzhetakh" [An Additional Six Billion in Family Budgets], *Ek. Gaz.,* no. 6, 1968, p. 15.

Kunel'skii, 1968c

Kunel'skii, L., "Sotsial'no-Ekonomicheskoe Znachenie Povysheniia Minimal'nykh Razmerov Zarabotnoi Platy" [Social Economic Significance of Raising the Minimum Wage], *Sots. Trud,* no. 12, 1968, pp. 14–22.

Kurskii and Slastenko, 1966

Kurskii, A., and Slastenko, E., "Nekotorye Itogi Perevoda Gruppy Predpriiatii na Novuiu Sistemu Planirovaniia i Ekonomicheskogo Stimulirovaniia" [Several Results of Converting a Group of Enterprises to the New System of Planning and Economic Stimulation], *Voprosy Ekonomiki,* no. 10, 1966, pp. 3–18.

Kuzminov, 1961a

Kuzminov, I. I., "Voprosy Politicheskoi Ekonomii Sotsializma" [Questions of the Political Economy of Socialism], in *Politicheskaia Ekonomiia Sotsializma,* edited by I. I. Kuzminov, pp. 3–84. Moscow, Izdatel'stvo V.P.Sh. i A.O.N. pri Ts. K. K.P.S.S., 1961.

Kuzminov, 1961b

Kuzminov, I. I., "Ekonomicheskaia Teoriia i ee Znachenie dlia Praktiki" [Economic Theory and Its Meaning for Practice], in *Politicheskaia Ekonomiia Sotsializma,* edited by I. I. Kuzminov. pp. 370–404. Moscow, Izdatel'stvo V.P.Sh. i A.O.N. pri Ts. K. K.P.S.S., 1961.

Kuznets, 1963

Kuznets, Simon, "A Comparative Appraisal," in *Economic Trends in the Soviet Union,* edited by Abram Bergson and Simon Kuznets, pp. 333–372. Cambridge, Mass. Harvard University Press, 1963.

Kuznetsova, 1956

Kuznetsova, A., *Organizatsiia Zarabotnoi Platy Rabochikh na Promy-shlennykh Predpriiatiiakh SSSR* [Organization of Workers' Wages in Industrial Enterprises of the USSR]. Moscow, Gospolitizdat, 1956.

Labkovskii, 1967

Labkovskii, B., "Pooshchrenie Otlichivshikhsia" [Stimulation of Outstanding Workers], *Ek. Gaz.*, no. 16, April 1967, p. 20.

Labok, 1962–1965

Labok, P. I., "Personal Promyshlennykh Predpriiatii [Personnel of Industrial Enterprises], *Ek. Entsik.*, vol. 2, pp. 368–370.

Labok, 1966

Labok, P. I., "Vyborochnoe Obsledovanie Zarabotnoi Platy Rabochikh, ITR i Sluzhashchikh v Promyshlennosti i Stroitel'stve" [Sample Investigation of Wages of Workers, Managerial-Technical Personnel, and Office Workers in Industry and Construction], in *Vyborochnoe Nabliu-denie v Statistike SSSR*, pp. 270–280. Moscow, NII TsSU SSSR, Statistika, 1966.

Labor Law, 1964

Labor Law and Practice in the USSR, Washington, D.C., United States Department of Labor, B.L.S. Report No. 270, 1964.

Lampman, 1960

Lampman, Robert J., "Comments 'On Choice in Labor Markets,' " in *Labor and Trade Unionism*, edited by Walter Galenson and Seymour Martin Lipset, pp. 56–71. New York, John Wiley & Sons, Inc., 1960. Originally published in 1956.

Lange, 1938

Lange, Oskar, "On the Economic Theory of Socialism," in *On the Economic Theory of Socialism*, edited by Benjamin E. Lippincott, pp. 55–142. Minneapolis, Minn., University of Minnesota Press, 1938.

Laptev, 1968

Laptev, V. V. (ed.), *Kommentarii k Polozheniiu o Sotsialisticheskom Gosudarstvennom Proizvodstvennom Predpriiatii* [Commentary on the Statute concerning the Socialist Governmental Productive Enterprise]. Moscow, Iuridicheskaia Literatura, 1968.

Lavruk, 1966

Lavruk, V., "Lichnaia Zainteresovannost" [Personal Self-interest], *Trud*, August 16, 1966, p. 2.

Lenin, 1918

Lenin, V. I., *The State and Revolution*, 2nd ed. of 1918. Moscow, Progress Publishers, 1965.

Lester, 1946

Lester, R. A., "Shortcomings of Marginal Analysis for Wage-Employment Problems," *American Economic Review,* vol. 36, March 1946, pp. 63–82.

Lester, 1947

Lester, R. A., "Marginalism, Minimum Wages, and Labor Markets," *American Economic Review,* vol. 37, March 1947, pp. 135–148.

Levcik, 1969

Levcik Bedrich, "Wages and Manpower Problems in the New System of Management in Czechoslovakia," in *Planning and Markets: Modern Trends in Various Economic Systems,* edited by John T. Dunlop and Nikolay P. Fedorenko, pp. 275–300. New York, McGraw-Hill Book Company, Inc., 1969.

Levin, 1967

Levin, Kh., and Rusinov, Ia., "Fondy i Stimuly" [Funds and Stimulation], *Planovoe Khoziaistvo,* no. 3, 1967, pp. 50–54.

Lewis, 1952

Lewis, W. Arthur, *The Principles of Economic Planning,* 2nd ed. London, Dennis Dobson Ltd., 1952.

Liapin, 1961

Liapin, A., "Real'naia Zarabotnaia Plata v SSSR" [Real Wages in the USSR], *Voprosy Ekonomiki,* no. 9, 1961, pp. 143–148.

Lifshits and Sofinskii, 1968

Lifshits, V., and Sofinskii, N., "Polozhenie o Poriadke Razrabotki Normativov po Trudu" [Statute on the Procedure for Elaborating Labor Norms], *Sots. Trud,* no. 9, 1968, pp. 109–116.

Livernash, 1957

Livernash, F. Robert, "The Internal Wage Structure," in *New Concepts in Wage Determination,* edited by George W. Taylor and Frank C. Pierson, pp. 140–172. New York, McGraw-Hill Book Company, Inc., 1957.

Loznevaia, 1968

Loznevaia, M., "Matematicheskie Metody v Planirovanii Zarabotnoi Platy" [Mathematical Methods in Planning Wages], *Sots. Trud,* no. 10, 198, pp. 126–135.

McAuley, 1969

McAuley, Mary, *Labour Disputes in Soviet Russia 1957–1965*. Oxford, Clarendon Press, 1969.

Machlup, 1946

Machlup, F., "Marginal Analysis and Empirical Research," *American Economic Review*, September 1946, vol. 36, pp. 519–554.

Machlup, 1947

Machlup, F., "Rejoinder to an Antimarginalist," *American Economic Review*, vol. 37, March 1947, pp. 148–154.

Madison, 1968

Madison, Bernice Q., *Social Welfare in the Soviet Union*, Stanford, Calif., Stanford University Press, 1968.

Maher, 1956

Maher, John E., "Union, Nonunion Wage Differentials," *American Economic Review*, vol. 46, June 1956, pp. 336-352. Reprinted in *Wage Determination: Market or Power Forces*, edited by Richard Perlman, pp. 127–146. Boston, Mass., D. C. Heath and Company, 1964.

Maier, 1960

Maier, V. F., "Povyshenie i Sovershenstvovanie Zarabotnoi Platy v Period Razvernutogo Stroitel'stva Kommunizma" [Increase and Improve Wages in the Period of the Further Construction in Communism], *Planovoe Khoziaistvo*, no. 10, 1961, pp. 33–42.

Maier, 1963

Maier, V. F., *Zarabotnaia Plata v Period Perekhoda k Kommunizmu* [Wages in the Period of Transition to Communism]. Moscow, Ekonomizdat, 1963.

Maier and Markov, 1958

Maier, V. F., and Markov, I., "Voprosy Mezhotraslevogo Regulirovaniia Zarabotnoi Platy v SSSR" [Questions of the Interindustrial Regulation of Wages in the USSR], *Sots. Trud*, no. 2, 1958, pp. 48–57.

Maitsen, 1964

Maitsen, P., "Bez Shablona" [Without Cliché], *Sovetskaia Litva*, May 17, 1964, p. 2.

Manevich, 1948

Manevich, E., "Novye Stimuly k Trudu i Zarabotnaia Plata pri Sotsializme" [New Stimulation of Labor and Wages under Socialism], *Voprosy Ekonomiki*, no. 10, 1948, pp. 18–34.

Manevich, 1961
Manevich, E. L., "Ekonomicheskoe Stimulirovanie Truda i Formy Perekhoda k Kommunisticheskomu Raspredeleniiu" [Economic Stimulation of Labor and the Forms of Transition to Communist Distribution],
Voprosy Ekonomiki, no. 5, 1941, pp. 76–85.

Manevich, 1966
Manevich, E. L., *Problemy Obshchestvennogo Truda v SSSR* [Problems
of Social Labor in the USSR]. Moscow, Ekonomika, 1966.

Mangum, 1962
Mangum, Garth L., "A Summary of Wage Incentive Practices in American Industry (Nonrailroad)," in *Studies Relating to Collective Bargaining Agreements and Practices outside the Railroad Industry*, appendix
volume 4 to the *Report of the Presidential Railroad Commission*,
pp. 231–261. Washington, D.C., U.S. Government Printing Office, 1962.

Markov, 1959
Markov, V. I., "Voprosy Differentsiatsii Zarabotnoi Platy v Zavisimosti
ot Uslovii Truda" [Questions of Wage Differentiation Dependent upon
Working Conditions], *Sots. Trud*, no. 5, 1959, pp. 57–63.

Marx, 1906–1909
Marx, Karl, *Capital*, vols. 1–3 .Chicago, Ill., Charles H. Kerr & Co.,
1906–1909.

Maslova, 1966a
Maslova, N. S., *Kollektivnye Formy Material'nogo Stimulirovaniia
Predpriiatii* [Collective Forms of Material Stimulation for the Enter-
prise]. Moscow, Nauka, 1966.

Maslova, 1966b
Maslova, N. S., "Kollektivnye Formy Oplaty Truda i Material'nogo
Stimulirovaniia" [Collective Forms of Wages and Material Stimula-
tion], *Voprosy Ekonomiki*, no. 7, 1966, pp. 14–21.

Maslova, 1967
Maslova, I. S., *Vysvobozhdenie Rabochei Sily v Promyshlennosti SSSR
i ee Ratsional'noe Ispol'zovanie* [Releasing Workers in USSR Industry
and their Rational Use]. Moscow, Izdatel'stvo Moskovskogo Universiteta, 1967.

Mathewson, 1931
Mathewson, Stanley B., *Restriction of Output among Unorganized
Workers*. New York, The Viking Press, 1931.

Mayo, 1933

Mayo, Elton, "What is Monotony," excerpt from *The Human Problems of an Industrial Civilization*, New York, Macmillan, 1933, in *Modern Technology and Civilization*, edited by Charles R. Walker, pp. 81–96. New York, McGraw-Hill Book Company, Inc., 1962.

Medvedev, 1967

Medvedev, M., "Vazhnyi Rychag Gosudarstvennogo Regulirovaniia Zarabotnoi Platy" [An Important Lever in Government Regulation of Wages], *Sots. Trud*, no. 3, 1967, pp. 51–56.

Melnikov, 1962

Melnikov, B., "Vazhnaia Oblast' Predpriiatiia" [An Important Sphere for the Enterprise], *Sots. Trud*, no. 8, 1962, pp. 152–154.

***Metodicheskie Ukazaniia*, 1969**

Metodicheskie Ukazaniia k Sostavleniiu Gosudarstvennogo Plana Razvitiia Narodnogo Khoziaistva SSSR [Methodological Instructions in the Construction of the Government Plan for the Development of the National Economy of the USSR], Gosplan SSSR, Moscow, Ekonomika, 1969, A translation is available under the title *Guidelines on Methods Pertaining to the Compilation of the State Plan for Development of the USSR National Economy*, Joint Publications Research Service, Department of Commerce, Washington, D.C. (JPRS 49344), December 3, 1969.

Mirgaleev, 1967

Mirgaleev, A., "S Uchetom Vlozhennogo Truda" [With Regard for Labor Invested], *Ek. Gaz.*, no. 49, December 1967, p. 13.

Mirgaleev and Peshkin, 1966

Mirgaleev, A., and Peshkin, P., "Bol'she Pribyl'—Bol'she Premiia" [High Profits, High Premiums], *Trud*, September 27, 1966, p. 2.

Mitin, 1962

Mitin, S. A. (ed.), *Spravochnik po Trudu i Zarabotnoi Plate v Stroitel'stve* [Handbook on Labor and Wages in Construction]. Moscow, Gosudarstvennoe Izdatel'stvo Literatury po Stroitel'stvu, Arkhitekture i Stroitel'nym Materialam, 1962.

Morgan, 1962

Morgan, Chester A., *Labor Economics*. Homewood, Ill., Dorsey Press, 1962.

Morozov, 1955

Morozov, P., *Tekhnicheskoe Normirovanie na Promyshlennykh Predpriiatiiakh* [Technical Norming at Industrial Enterprises]. Moscow, Moskovskii Rabochii, 1955.

Mozhina, 1961

Mozhina, M., "Izmeneniia v Raspredelenii Promyshlennykh Rabochikh SSSR po Razmeram Zarabotnoi Platy" [Changes in the Distribution of Industrial Workers in the USSR according to Amount of Wages], *Biulleten' Nauchnoi Informatsii,* no. 10, 1961, pp. 18–25.

Mutsinov, 1962–1965

Mutsinov, G. V., "Premirovanie" [Premiums], *Ek. Entsik.,* pp. 608–614.

Mysev and Obolenskaia, 1963

Mysev, N., and Obolenskaia, G., "Ob Otsenke Slozhnosti Rabot v Promyshlennosti" [Concerning the Calculation of the Complexity of Work in Industry], *Sots. Trud,* no. 3, 1963, pp. 67–72.

Nar. Khoz., 1959–1965, 1967, 1968

Narodnoe Khoziaistvo SSSR v 1959 (1960) (1961) (1962) (1963) (1964) (1965) (1967) (1968) *Godu* [The National Economy of the USSR in . . .]. Moscow, Gosstatizdat, respectively 1960, 1961, 1962, 1963, 1964, 1965, 1966, 1968, 1969.

"Nastoichivo," 1957

"Nastoichivo i Posledovatel'no Provodit' v Zhizn' Resheniia XX Sezda K.P.S.S." [Firmly and Consistently Put into Practice the Decisions of the Twentieth Congress of the CPSU], *Sots. Trud,* no. 7, 1957, pp. 3–8.

Nove, 1960

Nove, Alec, "Social Welfare in the USSR," *Problems of Communism,* no. 1, 1960, pp. 1–10.

Nove, 1961

Nove, Alec, *The Soviet Economy.* New York, Frederick A. Praeger, Inc., 1961.

Nove, 1966

Nove, Alec, "Wages in the Soviet Union: A Comment on Recently Published Statistics," *British Journal of Industrial Relations,* July 1966, pp. 212–221.

OECD, 1965

Organization for Economic Co-operation and Development, *Wages and Labor Mobility,* Paris, 1965.

Oblomskaia, 1968

Oblomskaia, I., "Nekotorye Voprosy Ispol'zovaniia Fonda Material'-nogo Pooshchreniia" [Several Questions about the Use of the Material Incentive Fund], *Voprosy Ekonomiki,* April 1968, pp. 131–137.

"Obshchee Polozhenie o Ministerstvakh," 1967

"Obshchee Polozhenie o Ministerstvakh SSSR" [General Statute about Ministries of the USSR], Decree (*Postanovlenie*) of the Council of Ministers of July 10, 1967, *Ek. Gaz.*, no. 34, August 1967.

"Oplata po Konechnym," 1965

"Oplata po Konechnym Rezul'tatam Proizvodstva" [Payment according to the Final Results of Production], *Ek. Gaz.*, May 19, 1965, pp. 21–28. Special supplement, pp. 1–8.

"O Podokhodnom," 1968

"O Podokhodnom Naloge s Rabochikh i Sluzhashchikh [Concerning the Income Tax for Employed Personnel], *Sots. Trud*, no. 3, 1968, pp. 139–141.

"Organization," 1963

"Organization of USSR Council of Ministers, June, 1963," *The ASTE Bulletin*, Spring 1963, p. 3.

Orlovskii, 1961a

Orlovskii, I. A., "Nekotorye Voprosy Sootnosheniia Rosta Proizvoditel' nosti Truda i Denezhnoi Zarabotnoi Platy" [Several Questions concerning the Relationship between the Growth of Labor Productivity and Money Wages], in *Voprosy Proizvoditel' nosti Truda v Period Stroitel'stva Kommunizma*, pp. 81–96. Moscow, Izdatel'stvo V.P.Sh. i A.O.N. pri Ts. K. K.P.S.S., 1961.

Orlovskii, 1961b

Orlovskii, I. A., "Dal'neishee Sovershenstvovanie Planirovaniia Zarabotnoi Platy" [Further Improvement in Planning of Wages], in *Zarabotnaia Plata v Promyshlennosti SSSR i ee Sovershenstvovanie*, edited by E. I. Kapustin, pp. 166–202. Moscow, Sotsekgiz, 1961.

Orlovskii, 1964

Orlovskii, I. A., *Planirovanie Zarabotnoi Platy v Promyshlennosti* [Planning Wages in Industry]. Moscow, Ekonomika, 1964.

Orlovskii, 1968

Orlovskii, I. A., "Proizvoditel'nost' Truda i Zarplata" [Labor Productivity and Wages], *Ek. Gaz.*, no. 16, April 1968, pp. 17–18.

Orlovskii and Sergeeva, 1961

Orlovskii, I. A., and Sergeeva, G. P., *Sootnoshenie Rosta Proizvoditel'nosti Truda i Zarabotnoi Platy v Promyshlennosti SSSR* [The Relationship between the Growth of Labor Productivity and Wages in USSR Industry]. Moscow, Izdatel'stvo Sotsial'no-Ekonomicheskoi Literatury, 1961.

Orlovskii, Iu., 1961

Orlovskii, Iu., "O Sverkhurochnykh Rabotakh" [Concerning Overtime Work], *Sots. Trud*, no. 5, 1961, pp. 137–141.

"Osnovy Zakonodatel'stva," 1970

"Osnovy Zakonodatel'stva Soiuza SSSR i Soiuznykh Respublik o Trude" [Basic Laws of the USSR and Union Republics about Labor], *Sotsialisticheskaia Industriia*, June 17, 1970, pp. 1–4.

"O Sostave," 1964

"O Sostave Fonda Zarabotnoi Platy Rabochikh i Sluzhashchikh" [Concerning the Composition of the Wage Fund for Employed Personnel], *Biulleten'*, no. 3, 1964, pp. 3–8.

"O Stabil'nykh Normativakh," 1969

"O Stabil'nykh Normativakh [Concerning Stable Norms], *Ek. Gaz.*, no. 16, April 1969, p. 11.

Pak, 1967

Pak, Iu., "Novoe Proiavlenie Zaboty Partii i Pravitel'stva o Blage Naroda" [New Manifestation of Concern of the Party and Government for the Well-being of the People], *Sots. Trud*, no. 11, 1967, pp. 12–17.

Palkin, 1962

Palkin, V., "Ob Osobennosti Sorevnovaniia" [Special Features of Competition], *Molodoi Kommunist*, no. 1, 1962, pp. 101–109.

Parfenov and Shor, 1968

Parfenov, P., and Shor, M., "Rabochie-Stanochniki: Organizatsiia Zarabotnoi Platy i Proizvoditel'nost' Truda" [The Worker-Machine Tool Operator: Organization of Wages and Labor Productivity], *Sots. Trud*, no. 2, 1968, pp. 26–32.

Parnes, 1960

Parnes, Herbert S., "The Labor Force and Labor Markets," in *Employment Relations Research*, edited by Herbert G. Heneman, Jr., pp. 1–42. New York, Harper & Brothers, 1960.

Pasherstnik, 1946

Pasherstnik, A. E., "Problems of Legal Wage Regulation in Wartime," *The American Review of the Soviet Union*, no. 3, 1946, pp. 61–76. Translated from *Izvestiia Akademii Nauk SSSR*, Section of Economics and Law, no. 2, 1945, pp. 13–23.

Pasherstnik, 1949

Pasherstnik, A. E., *Pravovye Voprosy Voznagrazhdeniia za Trud Rabo-chikh i Sluzhashchikh* [Legal Questions concerning Payment for Labor of Employed Personnel]. Moscow-Leningrad, Akademiia Nauka, Institute of Law, 1949.

Perlman, 1964

Perlman, Richard (ed.), *Wage Determination: Market or Power Forces.* Boston, Mass., D. C. Heath and Company, 1964.

Perlman, 1969

Perlman, Richard, *Labor Theory.* New York, John Wiley & Sons, Inc., 1969.

Perlo, 1961

Perlo, Victor, *How the Soviet Economy Works: An Interview with A. I. Mikoyan.* New York, International Publishers, 1961.

Peskin, 1959

Peskin, Z., *Oplata Truda na Predpriiatiiakh Ugol'noi i Slantsevoi Promyshlennosti.* [Wages at Enterprises of the Coal and Shale Industry]. Moscow, Profizdat, 1959.

Petrochenko, 1956

Petrochenko, P., "Puti Uluchsheniia Normirovaniia Truda na Pred-priiatiiakh" [The Roads to Improving Work Norms at Enterprises], *Planovoe Khoziaistvo,* no. 6, 1956, p. 3.

Petrochenko, 1962

Petrochenko, P., "Obespechit' Edinstvo pri Ustanovlenii Norm Truda" [To Gain Unity in the Construction of Work Norms], *Sots. Trud,* no. 1, 1962, pp. 60–70.

Petrochenko, 1963

Petrochenko, P. F., "Metodicheskie Osnovy Obespecheniia Edinstva Norm na Raboty Vypolniaemye v Odinakovykh ili Analogichnykh Organizatsionno-Tekhnicheskikh Usloviiakh" [Methodological Basis for Providing Identical Norms for Work Performed Under Identical or Analogous Organizational-Technical Conditions], in *Problemy Orga-nizatsii Proizvodstva i Truda,* pp. 222–230. Moscow, Izdatel'stvo Ekono-micheskoi Literatury, 1963.

Petrochenko, 1964

Petrochenko, P. F., *Normirovanie Truda v SSSR* [Norming of Work in the USSR]. Moscow, Mysl', 1964.

Petrochenko and Shkurko, 1958
Petrochenko, P., and Shkurko, S., "Usloviia Primeneniia Sdel'noi Oplaty Truda" [Conditions for the Application of Piece Rate], *Sots. Trud,* no. 6, 1958, pp. 45–53.

Pierson, 1957
Pierson, Frank C., "An Evaluation of Wage Theory" in *New Concepts in Wage Determination,* edited by George W. Taylor and Frank C. Pierson, pp. 31–32. New York, McGraw-Hill Book Company, Inc., 1957.

Pigou, 1932
Pigou, A. C., *The Economics of Welfare,* 4th edition (1932). London, Macmillan and Company, reprinted 1962.

Planirovanie, **1963**
Planirovanie Narodnogo Khoziaistva SSSR [Planning the National Economy of the USSR]. Moscow, Izdatel'stvo Economicheskoi Literatury, 1963.

Podolskii, 1962
Podolskii, Ia., "Rabotu Otdelov Truda—na Bolee Vysokuiu Stupen'" [The Work of the Labor Department—to a Higher Level], *Sots. Trud,* no. 8, 1962, pp. 93–100.

Pogostin, 1963
Pogostin, C., "Povysit' Rol' Tekhnicheskogo Normirovaniia v Khimicheskoi Promyshlennosti" [Raise the Role of Technical Norming in the Chemical Industry], *Sots. Trud,* no. 1, 1963, pp. 74–78.

Poletaev et al., 1969
Poletaev, V. E., Gaponenko, L. S., and Lel'chuk, V. S., *Rabochii Klass SSSR, 1951–1965* [The Working Class of the USSR, 1951–1965]. Moscow, Nauka, 1969.

Politicheskaia Ekonomiia, **1955**
Politicheskaia Ekonomiia, Uchebnik [Political Economy, a Textbook], 2nd ed. Moscow, Gospolitizdat, 1955.

Politicheskaia Ekonomiia Sotsializma, **1960**
Politicheskaia Ekonomiia Sotsializma [Political Economy of Socialism], "Vysshaia Shkola, Moscow, 1960.

"Polozhenie," 1965
"Polozhenie o Sotsialisticheskom Gosudarstvennom Proizvodstvennom Predpriiatii" [Statute on the Socialist Governmental Productive Enterprise], *Ek. Gaz.,* October 20, 1965, pp. 25–29.

Popov-Cherkasov, 1962

Popov-Cherkasov, I. N., *Voznagrazhdenie za Trud Rabochikh i Sluzha-shchikh v Lesnom Khoziaistve SSSR* [Wages for the Labor of Personnel in Forestry in the USSR]. Moscow, Goslesbumizdat, 1962.

Pravda

Pravda, daily organ of the Central Committee of the Communist Party of the Soviet Union.

Prigarin et al., 1968

Prigarin, A. A., Ryss, V. M., Sherman, E. I., and Kuznetsova, K. Kh., *Napriazhennost' Norm Truda* [The Tightness of Work Norms]. Moscow, Ekonomika, 1968.

Promyshlennost' SSSR, 1957

Promyshlennost' SSSR Statisticheskii Sbornik [Industry of the USSR, a Statistical Handbook]. Moscow, Gosstatizdat, 1957.

Proshko, 1963

Proshko, Ia., "Prava Predpriiatiia i Upravlenie Proizvodstvom" [The Rights of the Enterprise and Production Management], *Sots. Trud,* no. 3, 1963, pp. 103–105.

"Puti," 1962

"Puti Sovershenstvovaniia Form i Metodov Material'nogo Stimulirovaniia" [Roads to Improving the Forms and Methods of Material Stimulation], *Sots. Trud,* no. 5, 1962, pp. 35–46.

Rabkina and Rimashevskaia, 1966a

Rabkina, N., and Rimashevskaia, N., "Metod Perspektivnykh Raschetov Differentsiatsii Zarabotnoi Platy" [Method of Calculation of Perspective Differentiation of Wages], *Sots. Trud,* no. 7, 1966, pp. 124–133.

Rabkina and Rimashevskaia, 1966b

Rabkina, N., and Rimashevskaia, "Ekonomicheskie Osnovy Different-siatsii Zarabotnoi Platy" [Economic Basis for Wage Differentiation], *Voprosy Ekonomiki,* no. 12, 1966, pp. 79–89.

Rabochaia Gazeta

Rabochaia Gazeta [Workers' Gazette], daily organ of the Central Committee of the Communist Party of the Ukraine.

"Rabotnikam Predpriiatii," 1967

"Rabotnikam predpriiatii—o Praktike Perekhoda na Novuiu Sistemu Planirovaniia i Ekonomicheskogo Stimulirovaniia" [To Working People of Enterprises—On the Practice of Transition to the New System of Planning and Economic Stimulation], *Sots. Trud,* no. 2, 1967, pp. 49–55.

Raitsin, 1967

Raitsin, V. Ia., *Normativnye Metody Planirovaniia Urovnia Zhizni*, Moscow, Ekonomika, 1967. A translation is available under the title *Planning the Standard of Living According to Consumption Norms*, White Plains, N.Y., International Arts and Sciences, 1967.

Raschety, 1963

Raschety s Rabochimi i Sluzhashchimi, Sbornik Ofitsial'nykh Materialov [Calculations Concerning Employed Personnel, a Handbook of Official Material]. Moscow, Iuridicheskaia Literatura, 1963.

Raschety, 1965

Raschety s Rabochimi i Sluzhashchimi, Sbornik Ofitsial'nykh Materialov [as above], 3rd ed. Moscow, Iuridicheskaia Literatura, 1965.

Reder, 1955

Reder, Melvin, "The Theory of Occupational Wage Differentials," *American Economic Review*, vol. 45, December 1955, pp. 833–852.

Rees, 1962

Rees, Albert, *The Economics of Trade Unions*. Chicago, Ill., University of Chicago Press, 1962.

Reynolds, 1951

Reynolds, Lloyd G., *The Structure of Labor Markets*. New York, Harper & Brothers, 1951.

Reynolds and Taft, 1956

Reynolds, Lloyd G., and Taft, Cynthia H., *The Evolution of Wage Structure*. New Haven, Conn., Yale University Press, 1956.

Rimashevskaia, 1965

Rimashevskaia, N. M., *Ekonomicheskii Analiz Dokhodov Rabochikh i Sluzhashchikh* [Economic Analysis of the Income of Employed Personnel]. Moscow, Ekonomika, 1965.

Robertson, 1960

Robertson, D. J., *Factory Wage Structures and National Agreements*. London, Cambridge University Press, 1960.

Robertson, 1963

Robertson, D. J., *The Economics of Wages and the Distribution of Income*. London, Macmillan & Company, Ltd., 1963.

Ross and Rothbaum, 1954

Ross, H. G., and Rothbaum, M., "Intraoccupational Wage Diversity," *Industrial and Labor Relations Review*, vol. 8, April 1954, pp. 367–384.

Ross, A. M., 1957

Ross, Arthur M., "The External Wage Structure," in *New Concepts in Wage Determination*, edited by George W. Taylor and Frank C. Pierson, pp. 173–205. New York, McGraw-Hill Book Company, Inc., 1957.

Ross, D. F., 1966

Ross, David F., "Economic Criteria for Education and Training: A Comment," *The Review of Economics and Statistics*, vol. 48, February 1966, pp. 103–105.

Rothbaum, 1957

Rothbaum, Melvin, "National Wage-Structure Comparisons," in *New Concepts in Wage Determination*, edited by George W. Taylor and Frank C. Pierson, pp. 299–327. New York, McGraw-Hill Book Company, Inc., 1957.

Rottenberg, 1960

Rottenberg, Simon, "On Choice in Labor Markets," in *Labor and Trade Unionism*, edited by Walter Galenson and Seymour Martin Lipset, pp. 40–55. New York, John Wiley & Sons, 1960.

Routh, 1965

Routh, Guy, *Occupation and Pay in Great Britain*, 1906–1960. London, Cambridge University Press, 1965.

Rykov, 1966

Rykov, N., "Pooshchritel' nye Fondy Predpriiatii" [Enterprise Incentive Funds], *Trud*, December 9, 1966, p. 2.

Savich and Maksuri, 1963

Savich, D., and Maksuri, A., "Podniat' Rol' Otdelov Truda v Ispol'-zovanii Rezervov Proizvodstva" [To Increase the Role of the Labor Department in the Utilization of Production Reserves], *Sots. Trud*, no. 1, 1963, pp. 35–42.

Schroeder, 1966

Schroeder, Gertrude, "Industrial Wage Differentials in the USSR," *Soviet Studies*, January 1966, vol. 17, pp. 307–317.

Schultze, 1959

Schultze, Charles L., "Recent Inflation in the United States," in *Employment, Growth, and Price Levels*, Joint Economic Committee, Study Paper No. 1, pp. 4–16. Washington, D.C., U.S. Government Printing Office, 1959.

Schwarz, 1951
Schwarz, Solomon M., *Labor in the Soviet Union*. New York, Frederick
A. Praeger, Inc., 1951.

Schwartz, 1965
Schwartz, Harry, *The Soviet Economy Since Stalin*. Philadelphia and
New York, J. B. Lippincott Company, 1965.

Scitovsky, 1951
Scitovsky, Tiber, *Welfare and Competition*. Chicago, Ill., Richard D.
Irwin, Inc., 1951.

Scoville, 1966
Scoville, James G., "Education and Training Requirements for Occupations," *The Review of Economics and Statistics*, vol. 48 November 1966,
pp. 387–394.

Severianova, 1959
Severianova, A., "Novye Usloviia Oplaty Truda v Otrasliakh Tekstil'-
noi Promyshlennosti" [New Wage Conditions in the Textile Indus-
tries], *Sots. Trud*, no. 12, 1959, pp. 46–53.

Sezd, 1956
*XX Sezd Kommunisticheskoi Partii Sovetskogo Soiuza, Stenograﬁche-
skii Otchet* [Twentieth Congress of the Communist Party of the Soviet
Union, Stenographic Report], vols. 1 and 2. Moscow, Gosudarstvennoe
Izdatel'stvo Politicheskoi Literatury, 1956.

Shishkov and Kmets, 1957
Shishkov, I., and Kmets, A., "Nazrevshaia Perestroika" [Urgent Recon-
struction], *Sots. Trud*, no. 4, 1957, pp. 19–20.

Shkurko, 1956
Shkurko, S. I., "Voprosy Pravovogo Regulirovaniia Sdel'noprogres-
sivnoi Oplaty Truda v Promyshlennosti SSSR" [Questions of the Legal
Regulation of Piece-Rate Payment in USSR Industry], *Sovetskoe Gosudarstvo i Pravo*, no. 6, 1956, pp. 27–31.

Shkurko, 1961
Shkurko, S. I., "Razvitie Form i Sistem Zarabotnoi Platy" [Develop-
ment of Forms and Systems of Wages], in *Zarabotnaia Plata v Promyshlennosti SSSR i ee Sovershenstvovanie*, vol. 1, edited by E. Kapustin,
pp. 96–165. Moscow, Sotsekgiz, 1961.

Shkurko, 1964
Shkurko, S. I., "Mysliio Kollektivnoi Sdel'shchine" [Thoughts on Collective Piece Rate], *Ek. Gaz.*, August 15, 1964, p. 9.

Shkurko, 1965

Shkurko, S. I., *Formy i Sistemy Zarabotnoi Platy v Promyshlennosti SSSR* [Forms and Systems of Wages in Industry of the USSR]. Moscow, Ekonomika, 1965.

Shkurko, 1967

Shkurko, S. I., "Khoziaistvennaia Reforma v Otrasliakh Promyshlennosti i Material'noe Stimulirovanie" [Economic Reform in Branches of Industry and Material Stimulation], *Sots. Trud,* no. 2, 1967, pp. 18–30.

Shkurko, 1968

Shkurko, S. I., "Formy i Sistemy Zarabotnoi Platy" [Forms and Systems of Wages], in *Trud i Zarabotnaia Plata v SSSR,* edited by A. P. Volkov, pp. 337–360. Moscow, Ekonomika, 1968.

Shkurko, 1970

Shkurko, S. I., *Material'noe Stimulirovanie v Novykh Usloviiakh Khoziaistvovaniia* [Material Stimulation under New Economic Conditions]. Moscow, Mysl', 1970.

Shultz and Weber, 1960

Shultz, George P., and Weber, Arnold R., "Technological Change and Industrial Relations," in *Employment Relations Research,* edited by Herbert G. Heneman, pp. 190–221. New York, Harper & Brothers, 1960.

Sitnin, 1968

Sitnin, V., "Wholesale Prices: Results and Tasks," *Problems of Economics,* vol. 11, September 1968, pp. 26–31. Original in *Ek. Gaz.,* no. 6, 1968.

Slichter et al., 1960

Slichter, Sumner H., Healy, James J., and Livernash, E. Robert, *The Impact of Collective Bargaining On Management.* Washington, D.C., The Brookings Institution, 1960.

Smirnov, 1963

Smirnov, E., "O Merakh po Uluchsheniiu Sistemy Tarifikatsii Rabot i Rabochikh" [On Measures for the Improvement of the Basic Wage System for Jobs and Workers], *Sots. Trud,* no. 5, 1963, pp. 51–55.

Sonin, 1959

Sonin, M. Ia., *Vosproizvodstvo Rabochei Sily v SSSR i Balans Truda* [Reproduction of Labor Power in the USSR and the Balance of Labor]. Moscow, Gosplanizdat, 1959.

Sonin, 1965

Sonin, M. Ia., *Aktual'nye Problemy Ispol'zovaniia Rabochei Sily v SSSR* [Urgent Problems in the Utilization of Labor Power in the USSR]. Moscow, Mysl', 1965.

Sonin, 1966

Sonin, M., "Nekotorye Problemy Povysheniia Effektivnosti Ispol'zovaniia Trudovykh Resursov" [Several Problems Concerning the Raising of the Effectiveness of Utilized Labor Resources], *Voprosy Ekonomiki*, no. 8, 1966, pp. 28–40.

Sonin and Mechkovskii, 1958

Sonin, M., and Mechkovskii, G., "Sozdat' Polnotsennyi Uchebnik po Ekonomike Truda" [Create a Full-fledged Text on Labor Economics], *Voprosy Ekonomiki*, no. 10, 1958, pp. 125–132.

Sorochkin and Grishin, 1963

Sorochkin, I. M., and Grishin, L. I., *Organizatsiia Truda i Zarabotnoi Platy na Miasokombinatakh* [Organization of Labor and Wages in Meat Processing]. Moscow, Pishchepromizdat, 1963.

Sorokina, 1965

Sorokina, I., "Vosproizvodstvo Rabochei Sily" [Reproduction of Labor Power], *Ek. Gaz.*, July 30, 1965, pp. 6–7.

Sotsialisticheskaia Industriia

Sotsialisticheskaia Industriia [Socialist Industry], daily organ of the Central Committee of the CPSU.

Sots. Trud

Sotsialisticheskii Trud [Socialist Labor], monthly journal of the Government Labor Committee, Moscow.

Sovetskaia Moldavia

Sovetskaia Moldavia [Soviet Moldavia], daily newspaper of the Central Committee of the Communist Party of Moldavia and the Supreme Soviet of the Moldavian Republic.

Sovetskaia Rossia

Sovetskaia Rossia [Soviet Russia], daily newspaper of the Central Committee of the Communist Party of the Soviet Union.

Sovetskie Profsoiuzy

Sovetskie Profsoiuzy [Soviet Trade Unions], biweekly journal of the V.Ts.S.P.S.

Sovetskoe Gosudarstvo i Pravo

Sovetskoe Gosudarstvo i Pravo [Soviet Government and Law], monthly publication of the Institute of Government and Law of the Academy of Sciences of the USSR.

Stalin, 1952

Stalin, I., *Ekonomicheskie Problemy Sotsializma v SSSR* [Economic Problems of Socialism in the USSR]. Moscow, Gosudarstvennoe Izdatel'stvo Politicheskoi Literatury, 1952.

Stieber, 1959

Stieber, Jack, *The Steel Industry Wage Structure*. Cambridge, Mass., Harvard University Press, 1959.

"Stimulirovanie," 1970

"Stimulirovanie Rosta Proizvoditel'nosti Truda" [Stimulating the Growth of Labor Productivity], *Ek. Gaz.*, no. 46, November 1970, pp. 11–14.

Strumilin, 1963

Strumilin, S. G., *Izbrannye Proizvedeniia* [Selected Works], 5 vols. Moscow, Nauka, 1963–1965.

Strumilin, 1965

Strumilin, S. G., "Old Clothes Are Becoming Tight," *Soviet News*, January 18, 1965.

Sukharevskii, 1967

Sukharevskii, V. M., "Sila Ekonomicheskikh Stimulov" [The Power of Economic Stimulation], *Ek. Gaz.*, no. 41, October 1967, p. 15.

Sukharevskii, 1968a

Sukharevskii, B., "Material'noe Pooshchrenie v Usloviiakh Khoziaistvennoi Reformy" [Material Stimulation under Conditions of the Economic Reform], *Ek. Gaz.*, no. 29, July 1968, pp. 9–10.

Sukharevskii, 1968b

Sukharevskii, B. M., "Zarabotnaia Plata i Material'naia Zainteresovannost'" [Wages and Material Self-interest], in *Trud i Zarabotnaia Plata v SSSR*, edited by A. P. Volkov, pp. 267–308. Moscow, Ekonomika, 1968.

"Sverkhurochnaia," 1968

"Sverkhurochnaia Rabota i ee Oplata" [Overtime Work and Wages], *Sots. Trud,* no. 1, 1968, pp. 141–146.

Taylor and Pierson, 1957

Taylor, George W., and Pierson, Frank C., *New Concepts in Wage Determination*. New York, McGraw-Hill Book Company, Inc., 1957.

"Transition from School to Work," 1963

"The Transition from School to Work in the USSR," One-Day School at Birmingham University, Report on Papers and Discussion, May 25, 1963. Mimeographed, 35 pages.

Trud

Trud [Labor], daily organ of the All-Union Central Council of Trade Unions.

Trudovoe Pravo, 1959

Trudovoe Pravo: Entsiklopedicheskii Slovar' [Labor Law: An Encyclopedic Dictionary]. Moscow, Bol'shaia Sovetskaia Entsiklopediia, 1959.

Trud v SSSR, 1968

Trud v SSSR, Statisticheskiy Sbornik [Labor in the USSR, a Statistical Handbook]. Moscow, Statistika, 1968.

Trudenskii and Zanin, 1967

Trudenskii, G., and Zanin, V., "Biudzhet Rabochego Vremeni i Ekonomika" [Budget of Working Time and Economics], *Ek. Gaz.*, no. 11, March 1967, pp. 27–28.

Tsederbaum, 1963

Tsederbaum, Iu., "Rassmotrenie Trudovykh Sporov o Vyplate Premii" [Consideration of Labor Disputes about Premium Payments], *Sots. Trud*, no. 8, 1963, pp. 136–141.

Tulchinsky, 1965

Tulchinsky, L., "On Certain Problems of the Labor Reserves," *Komsomolskaia Pravda*, September 24, 1965, p. 2. Translated in *Current Digest of the Soviet Press*, November 17, 1965, pp. 18–19.

Unemployment in the Soviet Union, 1966

Unemployment in the Soviet Union, Fact or Fiction, Intelligence Report, CIA/ER 66–5, Washington, D.C., Directorate of Intelligence, March 1966.

Urzhinskii, 1962

Urzhinskii, K., "Poriadok Ustanovleniia Rabochim Tarifnykh Razriadov" [The Method for Establishing a Worker's Skill Group], *Sots. Trud*, no. 10, 1962, pp. 134–142.

Vardimiandi, 1966

Vardimiandi, I., "Sotrudnichestvo Stalo Pravilom" [Cooperation Has Become the Rule], *Trud*, November 18, 1966, p. 2.

Varga, 1957

Varga, E., "Nikakogo Krizisa Kommunizma Net" [There Is No Crisis of Communism], *Kommunist*, no. 10, 1957, p. 105.

Vasil'ev, 1967

Vasil'ev, E., "Resheniia Sentiabr'skogo Plenuma TsK KPSS—v Zhizn'" [The Decisions of the September Plenum of the CC CPSU—into Reality], *Sots. Trud*, no. 12, 1967, pp. 3–10.

Vechkanov, 1969

Vechkanov, G., "Povyshenie Effektivnosti Territorial'nogo Pereraspre-deleniia Trudovykh Resuŕsov" [On Raising the Effectiveness of the Territorial Redistribution of Labor Resources], *Ekonomicheskie Nauki*, no. 5, 1969, pp. 34–39.

Vedomosti

Vedomosti Verkhovnogo Soveta [The Supreme Soviet Gazette], Moscow, Verkhovnyi Sovet SSSR.

Vest. Stat.

Vestnik Statistiki [Statistical Herald], monthly organ of the Central Statistical Administration of the Soviet of Ministries of the USSR.

Viktorova, 1967

Viktorova, L., "K Voprosu o Klassifikatsii Rabotnikov Promyshlenno-Proizvodstvennogo Personala" [On the Question of the Classification of Industrial-Productive Personnel], *Vest. Stat.*, no. 9, 1967, pp. 26–32.

Vlasov, 1962

Vlasov, B. V., *Puti Ekonomii Truda na Vspomogatel'nykh Rabotakh v Promyshlennosti* [Roads to Economizing Labor at Subsidiary Work in Industry], 2nd ed. Moscow, Ekonomizdat, 1962.

Vlasov, 1961

Vlasov, M. A., *Kollektivnaia Oplata Truda za Produktsiiu* [Collective Wages for Production]. Moscow, Gospolitizdat, 1961.

Voilenko, 1966

Voilenko, E., "Prava i Obiazannosti Molodykh Spetsialistov" [The Rights and Responsibilities of Young Specialists], *Ek. Gaz.*, no. 41, October 1966, p. 37.

Volkov, 1957

Volkov, A. [P.], "Nashi Zadachi v Novom Godu" [Our Tasks in the New Year], *Sots. Trud,* no. 1, 1957, pp. 3–8.

Volkov, 1962

Volkov, A. [P.], "Posledovatel'no Osushchestvliat' Printsip Material'noi Zainteresovannosti" [Consistently Implement the Principle of Material Self-Interest], *Pravda,* April 4, 1962, pp. 2–3.

Volkov, 1964

Volkov, A. [P.], "Trud i Premii" [Labor and Premiums], *Trud,* December 1, 1964, p. 2.

Volkov, 1965

Volkov, A. [P.], "Moguchii Stimul Razvitiia Proizvodstva" [A Powerful Stimulus to the Development of Production], *Pravda,* November 14, 1965, p. 2.

Volkov, 1968

Volkov, A. P. (main editor), *Trud i Zarabotnaia Plata v SSSR* [Labor and Wages in the USSR]. Moscow, Ekonomika, 1968.

Volkov, 1970

Volkov, A. P., "Material'noe Stimulirovanie i Povyshenie Effektivnosti Proizvodstva" [Material Stimulation and Increasing the Effectiveness of Production], *Ek. Gaz.,* no. 27, July 1970, pp. 3–4.

Volkov and Grishin, 1966

Volkov, A. [P.], and Grishin, V., "Metodicheskie Ukazaniia" [Methodological Instructions], *Ek. Gaz.,* no. 7, Feb. 1966, pp. 31–32.

Voprosy Ekonomiki

Voprosy Ekonomiki [Problems of Economics], monthly journal of the Institute of Economics of the Academy of Sciences of the USSR.

Voprosy Filosofii

Voprosy Filosofii [Problems of Philosophy], monthly journal of the Institute of Philosophy of the Academy of Sciences of the USSR.

Voronikov, 1957

Voronikov, I., "Povysit' Rol' Organov po Trudu" [Raise the Role of Labor Organs], *Sots. Trud,* no. 4, 1957, pp. 15–18.

"Voznagrazhdenie," 1971

"Voznagrazhdenie po Itogam Raboty za God" [Bonus Payment for the Result of the Year's Work], *Ek. Gaz.,* no. 12, March 1971, p. 16.

Wages, 1964

Wages, A Workers' Education Manual. Geneva, International Labor Office, 1964.

Walker and Guest, 1952

Walker, Charles R., and Guest, Robert H., *The Man on the Assembly Line.* Cambridge, Mass., Harvard University Press, 1952.

Wootton, 1962

Wootton, Barbara, *The Social Foundations of Wage Policy,* 2nd ed. London, Unwin University Books, 1962.

Woytinsky, 1953

Woytinsky, W. S., and associates, *Employment and Wages in the United States.* New York, Twentieth Century Fund, 1953.

Yagodkin, 1967

Yagodkin, V., "Material'nye Stimuly i Vosproizvodstvo Rabochei Sily" [Material Stimulation and the Reproduction of Labor Power], *Ekonomicheskiye Nauki,* no. 12, 1967, pp. 20–27.

Yanowitch, 1960

Yanowitch, Murray, "Trends in Soviet Occupational Wage Differentials," *Industrial and Labor Relations Review,* vol. 14, no. 2, 1960, pp. 166–191.

Yanowitch, 1963

Yanowitch, Murray, "The Soviet Income Revolution," *Slavic Review,* vol. 22, December 1963, pp. 683–697.

"Zarabotnaia Plata," 1964

"Zarabotnaia Plata" [Wages], *Ek. Gaz.,* special supplement, January 25, 1964, 16 pages.

Zdravomyslov and Iadov, 1964

Zdravomyslov, A. G., and Iadov, V. A., "Opyt Konkretnogo Issledovaniia Otnosheniia k Trudu" [An Experiment in Concrete Investigation of Attitudes toward Labor], *Voprosy Filosofii,* no. 4, 1964, pp. 72–84.

Zelenko, 1962–1965

Zelenko, G. I., "Professional'no-Tekhnicheskoe Obrazovanie" [Professional-Technical Education], in *Ek. Entsik.* vol. 2, pp. 751–752.

Zenin, 1966

Zenin, I., "Otdely Kadrov i Problemy Kadrov" [The Department of Cadres and Cadre Problems], *Trud,* April 20, 1966, p. 2.

Zhamin and Egiazarian, 1968

Zhamin, V. A., and Egiazarian, G. A., *Effektivnost' Kvalifitsirovannogo Truda* [Effectiveness of Skilled Labor]. Moscow, Ekonomika, 1968.

Zingan, 1970

Zingan, Kh., "Novyi Zakon o Trude" [The New Labor Law], *Sovetskaia Moldavia,* August 7, 1970.

Index